Consumer Reports

Travel Well For Less 2002

THE EDITORS OF
CONSUMER REPORTS TRAVEL LETTER

Consumers Union • Yonkers, New York

Contents

PART 4   **HOTEL HOW-TO**

PART 5   **ROADS & RAILS**

PART 6   **TOURS & CRUISES**

REFERENCE SECTION

CONSUMER REPORTS:
The facts you need

Consumer Reports Travel Well for Less is just one of the many smart-shopping resources published by CONSUMER REPORTS. Here are other ways the CONSUMER REPORTS family of products provides the facts you need to make smart choices:

Consumer Reports Travel Letter. A monthly newsletter with solid money-saving information, last-minute deals, web-based travel tips, and more. To subscribe (12 issues, $39), write to P.O. Box 53629, Boulder, Colo. 80322-3629.

Consumer Reports. For more than 65 years, CONSUMER REPORTS magazine has provided impartial information on brand-name products, services, health, and personal finance. To subscribe (13 issues, including the annual Buying Guide, $26), write to P.O. Box 53029, Boulder, Colo. 80322-3029.

ConsumerReports.org. The CONSUMER REPORTS web site includes a wealth of recent information, useful listings, shopping guidance, and product recalls. Site subscribers pay $3.95 per month or $24 per year ($19 for magazine subscribers) for unlimited use of searchable Ratings, recommendations, and consumer advice.

Consumer Reports Special Publications. Specialty buying guides and newsstand special issues cover cars, computers, and products for the home. Books include titles on baby products, prescription drugs, and other issues of consumer concern. Consumer Reports

Special Publications are available on newsstands and in bookstores, or through our web store (*www.ConsumerReports.org*).

Consumer Reports on Health. A monthly newsletter, it covers fitness, nutrition, medications, and more. To subscribe (12 issues, $24), write to P.O. Box 56356, Boulder, Colo. 80322-6356.

Consumer Reports Auto Price Service. Comprehensive reports on new cars ($12 each) arm you with the information you need to get your best deal. Call 800 269-1139. Reports on used cars ($10 each) let you find market value and reliability data for many used cars and light trucks. Call 800 422-1079. Price services are available online at *www.ConsumerReports.org*.

Consumer Reports Television and other media. We produce a nationally syndicated consumer news service appearing in more than 100 markets nationwide. Information from CR is also available on radio stations around the country and in columns appearing in more than 50 newspapers.

The Changing Face of Travel

TRAVEL WELL FOR LESS. It's more than just a slogan. It's truly a way of thinking about travel that can help consumers reap the most from their vacation experiences. It's what keeps the staff of *Consumer Reports Travel Letter* busy throughout the year—and it's here for you in this book.

That mindset has never been more important than it is now. Few industries were more directly affected by the terrorist attacks on New York and Washington than the travel business. Overnight, the status quo changed, and outmoded thinking had to be discarded. Debates began raging about how security should be enhanced for airlines and all other sectors of travel, including rail lines, bus lines, car rentals, hotels, cruise lines, museums, theme parks, and national monuments. At every turn, *Consumer Reports Travel Letter* and Consumers Union took part in these national debates.

Simultaneously, the travel industry slumped, and failing companies created major disruptions for consumers. Airline passengers were faced with an unprecedented number of delayed, diverted, and canceled flights. Cruise lines rerouted dozens of ships. Hotel and car-rental reservations were in upheaval. And there was great uncertainty about policies purchased from travel insurance companies.

Advising travelers on the repercussions generated by unforeseen events has long been a part of this book. What to expect when your flight is delayed or canceled, your cruise ship changes course, your travel provider files for bankruptcy, or your travel insurance policy seems vague. This advice proved valuable for many travelers during the dark days following the terrorist attacks. You'll find the latest on all these topics in *Travel Well for Less.*

American travelers proved to be quite resilient in the months following Sept. 11. The sudden downturn in the travel industry spurred many unexpected bargains. All indications are that the year ahead will offer unprecedented discounts and incentives. You can turn to *Travel Well for Less* and to the *Consumer Reports Travel Letter* to help guide you through this new landscape.

On the other hand, there's no denying that travel is going to be much harder in 2002. You'll need to depart more promptly, pack more wisely, leave more items behind, exhibit more patience, exercise more discretion, and pay more money to help fund a more secure travel infrastructure for all Americans. In Chapter 11, "Avoiding Airline Hassles," you can find strategies to make the process a little easier.

In fact, Consumers Union, the nonprofit organization that publishes this book and the *Consumer Reports Travel Letter,* have taken a proactive role on the issue of airline security. In the days and weeks immediately following Sept. 11, we issued airline security proposals, offered practical advice for travelers, communicated those ideas to federal lawmakers and regulators, and counseled subscribers to *Consumer Reports Travel Letter.* We also think that security needs to be enhanced on our highways and roads, bridges and tunnels, rail lines and bus stations, waterways and ports, and museums, parks, and national monuments. We're going to continue to monitor progress on airline and travel security, and report our findings to the American public. You can find the latest in *Consumer Reports Travel Letter* or on our web site at *www.ConsumerReports.org/travel.*

Other factors have also altered the travel landscape. Purchasing travel is unlike buying any other product. The medium you choose to make the travel purchase influences price, selection, and the level of customer service you'll receive, a trend that has grown even stronger over the last year. The rapid growth of buying travel on Internet travel sites has remade the face of the travel industry. It's also brought distinct advantages and disadvantages for consumers. In recognition of the web's growing influence on travel, we have an entire section devoted to it. Turn to Part Two, "Travel and the Web," for help on researching, planning, and booking travel online. You'll also find our exclusive e-Ratings of travel web sites, including airlines, hotels, cruise lines, and more.

You'll also find results of two landmark studies conducted by *Consumer Reports Travel Letter* in late 2000 and early 2001. We found serious problems with both the major independent travel web sites and with travel agencies. We conducted real-time, side-by-side tests of four major sites—Cheap Tickets, Expedia, Lowestfare, and Travelocity—and found disturbing evidence of bias in how these sites listed airline flight options. We concluded that none of the four sites easily, fairly, and thoroughly delivered low fares and a full array of flight options. Subsequently, Consumers Union asked the U.S. Department of Transportation (DOT) to regulate online travel sites in the same way it regulates computer reservations systems used by travel agencies.

In another test, we surveyed 840 travel agencies throughout the United States. We asked for all the lowest-fare flights on specific routes and times, but received very disappointing results. You find details in Chapter 3, "Working with Travel Agents." Here's the gist: Only 51 percent provided all of the flights from all the airlines with the lowest fares upon first request. Only 63 percent of agencies provided them when the question was repeated; 12 percent didn't provide the lowest fares at all. We don't know why there was such a poor showing among travel agents, but we did note that airlines pay override commission bonuses to give travel agents incentives to book certain flights. After this investigation, Consumers Union asked the DOT to require travel agencies to disclose the existence of such override deals.

The most important lesson we learned from these investigations is that many consumers are more vulnerable than they realize. You can't just assume that an independent travel web site is truly independent. And you can't just assume that a travel agent is just that—*your agent,* and no one else's—even if you are paying an agency service fee. You can't even assume that a travel publication is working only in your best interests, rather than in the interests of its advertisers or marketing partners. Unless, of course, you're reading on of the CONSUMER REPORTS family of products, since CONSUMER REPORTS accepts no advertising, marketing deals, or free trips or gifts of any kind.

It's understandable if you're confused by the world of travel. Such confusion is intentional. The travel industry has its own language, its own rules and regulations, and its own hierarchy of customers. *Travel Well for Less* tries to deconstruct the industry for you by showing how to be the consumer whose needs are met quickly and completely.

You'll find detailed advice on how to select an airline seat, when to book a hotel room, whether or not to purchase optional car-rental insurance, how to choose a cruise ship cabin, when to buy airline tickets online, and where to buy travel insurance. We translate the travel industry's jargon and cut through its hype. And all the reporting in this book is supported by Consumers Union's research, fact-checking, survey, and statistics departments.

Having a guide to help you through travel's constantly changing maze is more important than ever. We hope that *Travel Well for Less,* will be that guide for you—the guide you buy *before* all those destination guides.

Consumer Reports Travel Letter

PART ONE

Planning Your Trip

CHAPTER 1

Finding Travel Information

Explore the wide world of advice and planning tools.

Many destination guides have Internet counterparts.

———————————————◼———————————————

Becoming well-acquainted with your destination before you leave can make travel easier and more enjoyable once you arrive. The Internet has become such a valuable travel source that Part Two is devoted to getting the best from this vehicle—and avoiding its pitfalls. Turn to those pages for how-tos, web-site Ratings, and more. Here, we cover other destination-oriented travel resources.

DESTINATION GUIDES

Guidebooks, typically costing $10 to $30, offer a wealth of information on locales worldwide, featuring travel intelligence on topics ranging from the expected (where to stay and what to see) to the more detailed, such as climate particulars, and visa and immunization requirements. (See "Guidebooks at a glance," this chapter.)

Travel publications are now available not only in bricks-and-mortar bookstores, but also on the Internet. And beyond traditional guidebook advice, these publisher web sites may also offer many helpful extras—up-to-the-minute tips and reviews, previews of your destination, and forums where you can ask questions of those who've been there and done that, or pass along your own experiences.

TOURISM BUREAUS

Almost every country and many cities have tourism bureaus to disseminate information on their particular region—scenery, attractions, lodging, dining—primarily through brochures and booklets.

Travel agents and ads in magazines and newspapers can direct you to tourism bureaus. But the Internet is the fastest way to track them down, since most are now online. Or simply check the Yellow Pages for "Tourist information." Materials usually take several weeks to arrive, unless you specify ASAP.

TELEVISION SHOWS

Millions of armchair tourists tune into television travel programs just for fun, but there's a wealth of information for the serious traveler, too. Check The Travel Channel for dozens of shows airing 24 hours a day. The Discovery Channel presents programs on exotic locales. PBS airs "Nature" and National Geographic specials, along with various travel-related documentaries.

PLANNING AHEAD

Security may be increased at locations nationwide. Expect metal detectors at national monuments. In national parks, coolers, backpacks, spare cameras, even diaper bags will be closely inspected or even banned.

Theme parks are also instituting visitor inspections. Hours may be reduced, show and event schedules could change, and some attractions may be periodically unavailable. Parking restrictions have also been tightened at many large venues.

Even art museums may inspect bags, or shut galleries without notice. And some destinations, such as government buildings in Washington, D.C., could simply be closed to tourists.

Before you go, call the location or check its web site to review conditions and special rules.

GUIDEBOOKS AT A GLANCE

GUIDE

IN DEPTH: The big picture plus details.

Fielding *(www.fieldingtravel.com)* Books on destinations worldwide, and on special interests like cruising or diving. Web site features "Dangerfinder" (least-traveled places on earth), "Buzzfinder"(critics' views), plus a forum and reviews for cruisers.

Fodor's *(www.fodors.com)* A wealth of guides, such as photo-filled Exploring Guides, upscale Gold Series, detailed CityGuides, and backpacker-geared UpClose books. Web site has a forum, plus travel tips, resources, and a create-your-own-guide feature.

Frommer's *(www.frommers.com)* Geared to deals and bargains, texts are also packed with useful information on lodgings, restaurants, attractions, and culture. Web site offers advice, vacation ideas, special deals, and a message board.

BACKPACKERS' BIBLES: Young at heart, and into travel's cheap thrills.

Let's Go *(www.letsgo.com)* A focus on budget-geared travel from the only guidebook company run and staffed by students. Web site provides travel links, tips, and articles, plus videos of on-the-road researchers.

Lonely Planet *(www.lonelyplanet.com)* Offbeat, irreverent guidebooks keyed to destinations or themes. Web site has "the scoop" (travel news), health info, a forum, videos, and free e-mail newsletter. The cable TV series is featured on The Travel Channel.

Moon *(www.moon.com)* Targets cities plus more remote destinations, with an accent on the outdoors and the nitty gritty of locations. Web site provides a (long) list of publications.

Rough Guide *(www.roughguides.com)* A multitude of destination guides under the slogan "Rough Guides Smooth Travel," plus subject-keyed reference books. Web site features coverage from guidebooks plus a quarterly online newsletter.

TRAVELER'S BASICS: The ABCs of your destination.

Berlitz *(www.berlitz.com.)* Destination guides focusing on culture, history, and language, all with color photos. Web site itemizes travel guides, phrase books, language courses, and CD-ROMs.

Michelin *(www.viamichelin.com)* Along with the venerable Red Guide (ratings) and Green Guide (local culture), publishes pocket guides for quick getaways plus the adventure-and-local-color-keyed Neos. Web site has publication lists, and planning help.

Open Road With the motto, "Be a traveler not a tourist," guides cover four continents (North/Central America, Europe, Africa, Asia) with an all-text format. E-mail Jopenroad@aol.com for a catalogue of titles.

Mobil Travel Guide *(www.exxonmobiltravel.com)* Guides for ten U.S./Canadian regions offers ratings, tours, and maps. Web site has tips, "notebook" feature.

Rick Steves *(www.ricksteves.com)* Budget roamings throughout Europe from the travel-expert creator of PBS series "Travels in Europe with Rick Steves." Web site has guidebook library, TV-show scripts, country info by destination, and a message board.

PERSONALITY	HELPFUL IF YOU . . .	BUT NOT IF YOU . . .
Thorough and detailed.	Want historical info and lots of rated lodging and dining options.	Prefer guides with lots of area-specific maps.
Serious, straightforward, practical.	Want hotel and dining choices in all price ranges (some reports may lack nitty-gritty facts).	Want a thorough history lesson and lots of cultural specifics–or if you're on a tight budget.
Reliable, time-tested, middle-of-the-road guides, with a recently updated format.	Are someone at any spending level, but especially if you're on a budget.	Seek a truly out-of-the-ordinary, off-road experience.
Irreverent, off the beaten path.	Are a student backpacker on a tight budget (or anyone who favors this travel style).	Want a bathroom in your room or a meal costing over $10.
Adventurous, intellectual, sometimes edgy.	Like to dive into a destination headfirst, taking a guidebook filled with background, history, and reliable recommendations.	Consider shopping your favorite pastime.
Earthy, eco-friendly.	Backpack on a budget.	Don't think of Days Inn or Quality Inn as "expensive."
Opinionated information for the independent traveler.	Value maps, historical facts, and destination particulars.	Want more than skimpy descriptions of hotels and restaurants.
Basic and no-nonsense.	Are interested in a sense of place.	Want hotel and restaurant ratings.
Red: Ratings, ratings, ratings. Green: Colorful, informative.	Have a tight schedule and want to know what's worth seeing.	Are put off by list-like format
Strives to put history and culture into perspective.	Like your background information written in an accessible way, and seek small, offbeat hotels.	Prefer guidebooks with maps, illustrations, or photos.
A detailed, informative survey.	Want lots of maps, "capsule summaries."	Are looking for more background and culture.
Practical, practical, practical.	Are budget-minded and don't want many surprises along the way.	Prefer to splurge.

(continued) |

15

GUIDEBOOKS AT A GLANCE CONTINUED

GUIDE

HISTORY LESSONS: Put art and culture into context.

Baedeker *(www.fodors.com)* Compact books that are a 170-year-old tradition. Each features a separate map and plastic cover.

Blue Guides *(www.wwnorton.com)* Straightforward, with sound historical facts, maps, and simple hotel and restaurant listings. Web site lists over 150 titles

Cadogan Guides to global destinations have help and up-front tips on organized tours and specific itineraries, plus solid historical background and hotel and restaurant listings.

COLOR COMMENTARY: When pictures are worth a thousand words.

Eyewitness *(www.dk.com)* Exuberantly colorful guides feature more photos than copy of locations, works of art, the populace, even specialty foods, like Viennese desserts. Web site has publications list.

Insight Guides *(www.insightguides.com)* History, culture, advice, and extensive photos. Insight Guides, Insight Pocket Guides, and Insight Compact Guides now co-branded by the Discovery Channel. Web site offers book lists, destination visuals, message board.

Knopf *(www.randomhouse.com)* Guides to places considered exotic, alluring, and steeped in art and history, along with City Guides. Web site has publications list.

EAT, DRINK, SLEEP, AND BE MERRY: Where to see and be seen

Access *(www.harpercollins.com)* Guides are arranged by city or neighborhood and color-coded (hotel descriptions are blue, restaurants are red). But historical and cultural facts may be limited. Publications listed on web site.

Time Out *(www.timeout.com)* City-based guides, by local writers, for U.S., European, and some Asian locales, plus Sydney and Johannesburg. Also has specialized books, such as "Book of London Walks." Chatty web site offers news, reviews, and shopping info.

SINGULAR APPROACHES: Different twists on travel.

Hidden Guides *(www.ulyssespress.com)* Goes off the beaten tourist track in search of one-of-a-kind places, local establishments, and outdoor adventures, but covers popular attractions, too. Web site lists publications.

Traveler's Companion *(www.globe-pequot.com)* Insider information on the "best adventure and romance a destination has to offer, in full, gorgeous color," plus practical trip-planning advice. Publications list on web site.

Unofficial Guide *(www.idgbooks.com)* Candid, critical (and exhaustive) studies of locations, with up-to-date advice on both planning and saving time and money. Web site lists publications.

PERSONALITY	HELPFUL IF YOU . . .	BUT NOT IF YOU . .
Steeped in antiquity.	Prefer art museums and ancient culture.	Are really looking for in-depth hotel and restaurant descriptions.
Cultured, traditional.	Are interested in serious, scholarly descriptions of art and history.	Want advice on nightlife.
Competent and efficient.	Have an eye for detail and an affinity for history.	Enjoy attractions more offbeat than castles, palaces, and art museums.
A highly polished cultural mosaic.	Have a short attention span for reading guidebooks.	Want background reading or want to carry with you (they're heavy).
Colorful and enticing.	Enjoy descriptive text on art and history.	Want money-saving tips and rec-ommendations.
A visual feast, plus some savvy guidance.	Are the sort who savors the finer things in life.	Tend to get lost and need practical contents like maps and directions.
Upscale, with snippets of information.	Want the best hotels, restaurants, and shopping.	Are nonplussed when categories are mixed together for aesthetic effect.
Hip.	Pursue the latest art exhibits and the trendiest neighborhoods and night spots.	Dislike trendy scenes–and ads in your guidebook.
Little-known spots in known locales; thrifty tips.	Want directions to low-cost, out-of-the-way settings.	Prefer cities, luxury, and glitzy nightlife.
Detailed tour of culture, sights, and people.	Are looking for a complete trip-planning tool.	Just want to find out where to stay and what to see.
In-depth, unbiased, authoritative, hefty.	Need to know every last thing about your destination.	Feel inundated by so much information.

CHAPTER 2

Timing and Travel Companions

Two keys to an enjoyable trip: Choose the right time to travel

and the right companion for your journey.

───────────────── ■ ─────────────────

Planning *when* to travel can have a huge impact on everything from cost, to weather, to crowds—even on *where* you decide to go. Likewise, the person or persons with whom you share the trip will play a major role in where you stay, what you see and do, and, ultimately, how enjoyable the whole experience will be. This chapter outlines some key things to keep in mind when you're planning these important elements of your vacation.

TIMING IS EVERYTHING

If you already know where you want to go, think carefully about when you will go. Investigate shoulder season and off-season, which can provide excellent savings. Also check out local conditions: Overcrowded events, inaccessible attractions, or intolerable weather are travel tribulations you can skip.

Aim for spring or fall. Your reward will be a combination of moderate savings and generally favorable weather. There are a few exceptions: the Caribbean in August, September, and October, when it becomes "Hurricane Alley," and certain European winter resorts, which often close from mid-April to mid-May before reopening for the summer. For the most agreeable weather, choose dates straddling summer—May/June and September/October are generally excellent times to travel, weatherwise.

Avoid summer crowds. Because summer is the time for family travel, popular destinations such as national parks (Yellowstone and Yosemite in particular), theme parks (Walt Disney World and Universal Studios), beach resorts (Cape Cod, Martha's Vineyard), and European capitals (Paris, Rome, and London) are almost always crowded. The U.S. Department of Transportation (DOT) estimates that one-third of all vacations by American households occur in July, August, or early September. The result? Scarce, expensive accommodations; oversold planes, trains, and buses; and long lines.

Ask about August. If you do decide to travel in summer, avoid aggravation with a little research. For example, major European cities may offer limited services during August, when locals take their vacations; the cities may be less crowded, but restaurants, theaters, and small shops may be closed. And Europeans often jam resorts along the Mediterranean and Aegean as well as in mountain regions.

Swap hemispheres. Winter in the Southern Hemisphere creates different weather in different places. Temperatures in Tahiti are 67°F to 84°, while Sydney, Australia, is a springlike 46° to 60°. Check with your travel agent or a guidebook; destinations closest to the equator will be hot, but you'll be able to ski during July and August in Chile and New Zealand.

Take advantage of 'shoulder' season. The shoulder is a very brief period, typically two to four weeks, just before and after peak season. Shoulder rates are listed in brochures for resorts, cruises, or condo rentals—you get moderate savings with generally good weather conditions. But these rates often sell out quickly. (See Chapter 6 for shoulder-season details.)

Don't expect a bargain during the holidays. Traveling during the Christmas or New Year's holidays can be fraught with frustration. Flights to places such as Florida, Mexico, and the Caribbean are often sold out far in advance and can cost double what they do just a few weeks earlier or later. You'll also run into holiday "blackout" periods, when you can't redeem frequent-flyer miles for free travel. Hotel rooms will also command top dollar.

There are bargains to be had. Some airlines and travel agents sometimes offer good deals to Europe during the holidays; check ads and call travel agents for quotes. But remember, it can be wet and cold, and some cities, like London, are "closed" on Christmas. Also keep in mind that Easter is a major holiday in the Catholic countries of Europe, when roadways, trains, and resorts will be crowded with locals.

See about conventions. You'll want to avoid major conventions that monopolize cabs and dinner reservations. Ask your travel agent or the hotel reservation clerk whether these crowds will be in town when you are. If so, you may prefer another date—or destination.

Be aware of local events. New Orleans during Mardi Gras (mid-February) is a vastly different experience than New Orleans at any other time of year. Ditto for Pamplona, Spain, during the running of the bulls (early July); Siena, Italy, during the Palio (July and August); London during Wimbledon (late June); or Auckland, New Zealand,

HOLIDAYS ABROAD

Just as in the U.S., other countries "shut down" during major holidays. Plan ahead to avoid transportation and service limitations.

WHEN	WHERE	WHAT
January 26	Australia	Australia Day
February 6	New Zealand	Waitangi Day
April 25	Australia and New Zealand	Anzac Day
May 5	Mexico	Cinco de Mayo
July 1	Canada	Canada Day
July 14	France	Bastille Day
August 15	Italy	Feast of the Assumption
October 1	China	National Day
November–December	Muslim countries	Ramadan

during the America's Cup (January). Some unsuspecting travelers who book accommodations months in advance arrive at what they expect to be an idyllic locale only to find it overrun.

Find 'off-season' pleasures. If a little rain won't ruin your parade, then check out the bargains of the off-season, when you can grab deals on airfare and lodging, such as savings of $350 per person on a winter weekend in London, a great rate available in early 2001. You'll also find discounted flights to Australia, New Zealand, and South America. Chapter 6 has off-season how-tos; Chapter 12 has tips on booking a low domestic airfare.)

TRAVELING COMPANIONS

Even if you think you know someone well, you'll discover new things about them on the road, away from familiar surroundings, language, and food.

The only reliable way to discover if you and another person have compatible—or at least mutually bearable—travel styles is to take a trip together. But advance trouble shooting can help iron out many wrinkles.

Traveling with a spouse or partner. Discuss prior travel experiences—both good and bad—to help plan a great trip.

Agree on the itinerary. If parts of it are unappealing to either of you, investigate other options. Or ask a travel agent, tour operator, or resort manager whether alternate activities are available.

Solve problems before you depart. Voice preferences. Then make sure those choices—whether shopping, bird-watching, or gambling —are doable at your destination.

Decide who is in charge of "travel business." A good rule is that whoever handles the bills at home will handle money, passports, vouchers, and such during the trip.

Compromise on different travel styles. One solution could be trading off every other trip on the destination (golf resort or European city), the time of year (warm weather or cool), the type of transport (cruise or fly-and-drive), and accommodations (hotel chain or country inn).

Do your own thing—alone or with others. If your travel styles are strikingly incompatible, agree that once at your destination, each can do his or her thing during the day, from museums or tours to tennis or fishing. Then you can both enjoy a special evening with a good meal or a moonlight walk.

Traveling with a friend. You'll face some of the same situations you might with a spouse. Keep the following in mind:

Pack similarly. Three pieces of luggage or one neat backpack? More formal clothing or casual wear? Agree in advance.

Ask about habits. Your adjustments to room-sharing may be easier if you know in advance that the other person snores, leaves a light on all night, or takes two hours to get ready in the morning. Armed with this knowledge, you can try to adjust to each other's idiosyncrasies and enjoy the trip.

Take time on your own. Traveling together needn't mean spending every minute as a team. Plan some separate activities, then meet back at the hotel or at a restaurant.

Pay separately. Keeping track of who paid for what can add stress to the trip. You can each pay separately with cash or traveler's checks. When using credit cards, ask hotels or restaurants if they'll divide the bill and charge each card.

Use a "kitty" for incidental expenses. This system can make sharing expenses in a foreign currency much easier. Take a small, zippered pouch to which you both contribute an equal amount. Use this kitty to pay admission fees, parking, and other small expenses.

Joining another couple or couples. Although many couples enjoy the group camaraderie, very often the multiple personalities and preferences involved in such trips can make them a challenge to plan and enjoy. What's the solution?

Start small. Your best bet is a long weekend, or a week at most, at an English-speaking destination with a variety of sights and activities so you can see whether your interests and travel styles are a good fit.

Plan time together and apart. Continual togetherness can be a strain. Stay at different hotels or villas, then meet for meals and more.

Be part of a bigger group. You and the other couples get to share the trip but also have plenty of other interesting people to meet.

Make it annual. If you find a compatible couple, you can return to the same place (a beach house or mountain resort, for instance) or try different cruises or tours.

Going it alone. You'll find myriad options for single, divorced, or widowed travelers in all age and price categories. You can set your own pace, choose your own sights, meet other travelers, and forge new friendships. Consider these suggestions:

Mix independent travel with short tours. Maintain your independent spirit but still join with group tours, either day tours of a city or attraction, or two- to four-day excursions through a specific region. Such a mix varies the pace, allows you to meet people, and often saves some money.

Look into "singles" tours, cruises, and resorts. But be certain of the point of the vacation. Is it to share the travel experience—or to hook up with a potential mate? Some singles resorts and cruises have wild reputations; ask before you book. Other trips may be geared to such activities as hiking, biking, diving, and skiing.

Decide whether you'll pay a single supplement. "Double occupancy" is the pricing guideline for much of the travel industry. If you want a hotel room or cruise cabin to yourself, you'll almost always be charged a "single supplement"—15 to 50 percent more than someone who shares a room. And during peak season, companies limit the number of rooms and cabins they'll sell at single rates. (Early bookers get them.)

Certain cruise lines and tour operators offer a guaranteed-share program; if a same-sex roommate isn't available, you get your own room or cabin. (With 12 women to every man on single-based trips, women are more likely to be matched up.) However, single travelers will typically get more consideration from smaller regional companies than from large tour operators and cruise lines.

Travel Companions Exchange publishes listings of (mostly 50-plus) individuals looking for like-minded travel partners of either sex. Call 800-392-1256 or go to *www.travelcompanions.com*. New members, $99 for six months, $159 for one year; subsequent rate, $298 annually. Travel-tips newsletter included with listings ($6 for a sample issue).

Go Solo Travel Club leads groups of singles (average age 45 and up) on private-accommodations trips. Call 800-354-4484 or 914 592-4316, or visit *www.gosolotravelclub.com*. The $35 initial membership fee is refundable upon booking your first trip.

Taking the children. Whether you decide to take the young ones with you or leave them with a sitter, kids add endless details to the travel picture.

Do you take them or leave them? There are "family" vacations; then there are "Mommy and Daddy" vacations. You might consider alternating one type of trip with the other. Most kids won't feel left out if you're already planning an upcoming trip that includes them. And many kids enjoy the change of pace when spending time with grandparents, aunts and uncles, or family friends.

Be ready for food fights. When planning a trip to a destination with exotic (as in spicy or unusual) cuisine, remember that kids can be reluctant to try unfamiliar fare. America is the land of convenience foods, but Europe, Asia, and other locales can be surprisingly bereft of the kind of snacks kids like.

Food is the No. 1 cause of illness for American travelers when abroad. And kids can be especially susceptible, not only because of their delicate systems, but because they're typically lax about hygiene. When traveling in areas known for potential gastrointestinal problems, pack plenty of antibacterial hand gels or wipes and don't let your kids eat unsupervised. (See "Health tips for travelers" in the Reference Section at the back of the book.)

Get discounts. Most transport—train, bus, cruise ships—offers children's fares at a discount, typically up to 50 percent.

CHAPTER 3

Working with a Travel Agent

Travel agents can save you time and money.

Be sure you get your money's worth for the fee.

Knowledgeable, experienced, and unbiased travel agents can offer service that no travel web site is likely to match. They can use technological tools quickly and efficiently to match travel options to your needs and your budget; track down discounts and bargains; set up complicated itineraries; and provide "insider information," such as reports from others who have taken your proposed vacation.

But some agents may be influenced by travel-supplier incentives. Now that most agencies charge fees, you may prefer to book uncomplicated items yourself. And with today's travel disruptions and uncertainties, you'll want a solid company that can weather the difficult conditions and provide expert 24-hour service if you experience problems or delays.

SHOPPING FOR AN AGENT

Start by choosing a reputable agency you're familiar with, or get references from your family and friends. Use an agency affiliated with the American Society of Travel Agents (ASTA), the Association of

Retail Travel Agents (ARTA), the International Airlines Travel Agent Network (IATAN), or the Institute of Certified Travel Agents (ICTA). These organizations can tell you if the agent is a member in good standing; ASTA has a consumer-affairs department set up to mediate disputes.

Then ask some questions. How long has the agency been in business? What experience and special expertise can agents offer? Can you get recent references? If the agency charges service fees, request a written description of the fee structure and an itemized list of fees. Many agencies, however, do not have a set fee structure. In that case, outline your proposed trip and ask about charges (see below).

See if the agency maintains preferred-supplier, override, or marketing agreements with travel providers, and get details. (See "The override issue," this chapter, for the impact of these travel-industry arrangements.) Ask what special assistance the agency provides—they may send e-mail alerts about special sales, keep track of frequent-traveler miles and points, or advocate for you in problems with a travel supplier.

THE PRICE OF SERVICE

In a 2000 survey by *Consumer Reports Travel Letter* of 45 agencies in 15 major metropolitan areas—large national chains, midsized regional agencies, and "mom and pop" outlets—we found that all the agencies charged for at least one service, but we uncovered no uniform fee structure. (See "What's being charged?" this chapter.)

• The most-common fee, in 42 of the 45 agencies, was for processing airline tickets. Fees for non-airline services, such as booking rail tickets or hotel rooms, are less common.

• The most complex services—for booking cruises and tours, and vacation planning—entail the most complex fee structures, ranging from flat prices to hourly rates to sliding scales.

• On the whole, larger agencies charge higher median fees than their midsized and smaller competitors, and are more consistent in pricing.

• Some agencies may charge only for time-consuming or unprofitable services, such as booking hotels that don't offer commissions.

AGENCY DISCLOSURE

AIRLINE ROUTE	AGENCIES CALLED	DISCLOSED LOWEST FARES?			
		ALL, IMMEDIATELY	ALL, AFTER 2ND REQUEST	SOME, AFTER 2ND REQUEST	NONE, AFTER 2ND REQUEST
Atlanta-New Orleans	69	58%	26%	13%	3%
Boston-Washington	55	51	0	7	42
Chicago-Santa Ana	100	54	23	23	0
Dallas-Fort Lauderdale	57	88	5	4	4
Denver-Los Angeles	70	30	4	61	4
Detroit-Tampa	97	80	4	1	16
Kansas City-Phoenix	34	77	2	0	21
Los Angeles-Las Vegas	79	17	13	70	0
Minneapolis-Orlando	57	58	10	28	4
New York-West Palm Beach	116	60	8	2	30
Raleigh/Durham-New York	59	32	27	37	3
Washington-Fort Lauderdale	47	0	0	72	28
RESULTS	840	51%	12%	25%	12%

Source: CRTL

THE OVERRIDE ISSUE

Overrides are basically incentive payments to agencies from airlines, cruise lines, hotels, tour operators, car-rental firms, and insurance companies in return for meeting specific sales quotas.

Such payment schemes can be quite complicated, but are usually tied to market share, not sheer volume. That is, an airline won't pay a bonus on a route with no competition. But let a competitor start flying that route, and travel agents are likely to receive incentives. Few small airlines pay overrides; most large carriers do, except for Southwest.

While overrides may provide some trickle-down benefits to you—say, preferred seating or a class upgrade on your next flight—their existence raises serious questions about the value of information a travel agent provides.

In mid-2001, *Consumer Reports Travel Letter* asked 840 travel

---

TROUBLE-SHOOTING TIPS

How to protect yourself

Before you book, check the agency's record with the Better Business Bureau (*www.bbb.org*). Should you detect signs of trouble once you've booked, bypass your travel agent and contact the supplier directly to verify your reservations and payments. Pay with a charge card, so you can dispute charges, if necessary.

If you think you've been scammed, file a police report, and contact your state's attorney general, the Federal Trade Commission (877-382-4357, *www.ftc.gov*), and the National Fraud Information Center (800-876-7060, *www.fraud.org*). Send copies of the complaints to the travel agency's professional association as well.

agents about airline fares for 12 of the most popular (and competitive) U.S. routes for leisure travelers, where two or more carriers typically offer the same low fare. (We knew all available flights and fares in advance.)

Only 51 percent of the agents disclosed all low-fare flights when we first asked; another 12 percent revealed all low-fare carriers when we repeated the question. Twenty-five percent of the agents never disclosed all the cheap flights. And 12 percent erroneously presented a higher-priced fare as the cheapest.

It's impossible to determine whether this poor showing resulted from lack of training, inadequate technology—or intentional bias. But you can defend yourself against misinformation (and missing information) by dealing with a trustworthy agency and being well-informed yourself.

GET THE BEST FROM YOUR AGENT

You're paying for good service. See that the agency delivers it.

Decide if you really need an agent. Airlines are prodding consumers to book directly via the Internet, with "web-only" sale fares and bonus frequent-flyer mileage. So you may be able to get a better deal yourself. For a ticket on a smaller carrier, the agent's fee may not be worth the service.

Be canny about fees. We found a wide range of fee structures even within a given market, so don't hesitate to play one agency off against another. If making joint bookings for a partner, family members, or a small group, ask the agent to waive the other travelers' fees in exchange for the volume. The more research you do yourself (the web has a wealth of information; see Part Two), the less you'll have to spend in hourly fees for trip-planning.

Be loyal. Once you've settled on an agency, stick with it, and try to use it for all travel services. Request that your agency maintain a file on the business provided by you and your family. And don't hesitate to ask for perks—fee waivers, plus the upgrades and preferred seating that agencies award to good customers.

Stay flexible. Providing a range of travel times may yield a better fare. For example, although your ideal departure day is Monday, maybe Sunday would work, too. Also ask about alternative flight types—connecting and direct (stopover)—as well as competing airlines, or a different airport. Any of these options may lower the price.

Ask twice. *Consumer Reports Travel Letter* has found that the second request often yields more information.

Be precise! You can never be too specific when booking travel. So if you'd rather not consider alternative options, clearly state your preferences for airlines, airports, and flight type.

Get all the costs. Make sure that the agent is precise as well. A DOT regulation requires travel agents to provide airfare information that includes all taxes, airport fees, and fuel surcharges. In addition, you should always inquire about a service fee, which may vary depending upon the airline. And do ask if you are getting the best fare the agent can find.

Defend your interests. "How to protect yourself," on the previous page, has tips on guarding your financial well-being when dealing with an agent.

CHAPTER 4

Facts About Travel Insurance

If an illness, accident, or emergency threatens your

vacation, travel insurance offers financial protection.

■

A vital part of trip-planning is securing insurance against the possibility that you may be forced to cancel your journey or cut it short. Although travel insurance can add up to an extra 5 or 10 percent to your travel bill, it can shield you against greater financial losses.

WHY YOU NEED INSURANCE

Travel insurance is, unfortunately, the most-overpriced of all travel services. But this investment can cover two travel perils.

Cancellation losses. Cruises, package tours, and airline tickets typically require 100 percent payment in advance—in the first two cases, often months before departure. If you're forced to cancel 60 days before the trip, the penalty may amount to pocket change. Closer to departure time, however, cruise and tour companies impose stiff penalties for cancellations. Worst case, you could lose your entire prepayment. Even after you start your trip, your own illness or a problem at home could force you to abandon your journey, meaning you would forfeit part of your expenditure.

Emergency medical transportation. If you suffer a severe accident or illness in a remote area, you might have to be evacuated to a medical facility—or even back home. Just rescheduling your ticket or paying for a conventional flight could be expensive; evacuation by helicopter or private jet—unlikely though that might be—could cost a small fortune. Depending on coverage limits, insurance can pay for all or part of the costs.

TYPES OF COVERAGE

Travel insurance offers two types of coverage, protecting you (or in some cases, not protecting you) from a number of potential risks.

Trip cancellation/trip interruption (TCI). Such policies reimburse you (or your heirs) for extra costs you might incur should you or a traveling companion fall sick, suffer an injury, or die, either before departure or during your trip. (They won't reimburse you for the companion's expenses unless the companion is insured.) The policies also provide reimbursement if illness, injury, or death of a close family member at home forces you to cancel or interrupt your trip.

TCI policies all have a "pre-existing condition exclusion," which states there will be no coverage for any loss if during a set period before travel commences (ranging from 60 to 180 days), there was medical care, advice, consultation, or treatment received for the condition, or if there was any adjustment of medication for the condition.

Typically, rules on pre-existing conditions apply to any person— you (the traveler), a traveling companion (insured or not), or a family member at home—whose medical condition causes a trip to be canceled or interrupted.

However, most TCI policies now waive the pre-existing-condition exemption, provided you insure the full value of your trip within seven days (or sometimes 10, or 14 days) of making your initial deposit or prepayment.

Emergency medical evacuation (EME). This coverage provides for emergency transportation in the event of serious illness or injury.

Operator failure. Supplier-default coverage has long been a major benefit of third-party insurance; if the cruise line, travel agency, or tour operator goes out of business, you're covered. But the slump in leisure travel has hurt many travel suppliers, even forcing some to shut down.

Fearing that other travel providers may be on shaky ground, several travel-insurance companies, including CSA Travel Protection, no longer provide default protection to consumers whose trips are cancelled or interrupted because of supplier bankruptcies. Two other leading firms, Access America and Travel Guard, still cover supplier default, but both companies added caveats and have lists of suppliers they will or will not cover. Be sure to check that your cruise line, tour operator, or other provider is covered by the insurance you purchase. Purchase your TCI directly from an insurance company—if you buy from a tour operator who subsequently fails, the coverage would be worthless.

To guard against losses caused by tour-operator failure, see that your cruise or package tour operator belongs to the U.S. Tour Operators Association (USTOA), or participates in an escrow program recommended by the American Society of Travel Agents (ASTA).

However, paying for your trip with a charge card offers protection against supplier failure. The federal Fair Credit Billing Act allows you to dispute a charge within 60 days of receiving a payment notice. The creditor must resolve the dispute within two billing cycles (but not more than 90 days) after receiving your letter.

Unforeseen emergencies. TCI covers a wide range of accidents and unpleasant surprises that might abort or interrupt a trip: a fire or flood in your home; a call to jury duty; an accident that makes you miss a flight or sailing; a natural disaster (fire, flood, earthquake, or epidemic); or a strike.

Recently, TCI policies have generally become more liberal on covered risks, many now including the term "unforeseen emergencies" rather than a long list of specifics. Still, even the most-liberal policies usually exclude personal financial circumstances, business or contractual obligations, or "change of plans," although some may then allow you to apply the premium to a future policy.

Exclusions. Standard travel insurance policies will not cover a number of "hazardous" activities, such as mountain- or rock-climbing (the criteria is typically the use of "picks, ropes, or other special equipment"), skydiving, hang gliding, bungee-cord jumping, and deep-sea diving. Less extreme outdoor endeavors, such as white-water rafting, bicycling, hiking, and trekking, are usually permissible. Always ask about excluded activities when you call. You may also find a list of exclusions in the company's brochure or on the web site.

Reputable adventure travel providers have their own insurance resources; however, these companies typically insure members of a tour for which the agenda is set in advance, and will probably not write a policy for an individual embarking on a potentially risky journey.

Another rule to note is that the typical maximum trip length is 180 days. If you're planning a longer getaway, you'll have to make special insurance arrangements.

INSURANCE PAYOFFS

When travel problems strike, TCI and EME offer relief for specific expenses. Here's what they cover:

Cancellation fees/penalties. In the event of a predeparture cancellation or postponement, TCI reimburses you for the fraction of your prepayments or deposits you can't recover from the supplier. You must first apply for whatever refund may be available from your tour operator, cruise line, or airline, under the terms of the ticket. TCI then pays the difference between your original price and that settlement.

Double/single adjustments. As a rule, you buy a tour or cruise at a per-person, double-occupancy rate. Should your traveling companion suddenly be unable to leave on a trip (for a covered reason, of course), TCI pays the single supplement so you can take the trip alone. Similarly, TCI covers adjustments required if your companion has to return home early.

Transportation reimbursement. Typical coverage stipulates a payoff in a variety of scenarios:

• When a covered reason forces you to postpone a trip, TCI pays the cost of switching your airline ticket to a later flight, or the extra cost of alternative transportation to join a trip in progress, say, air-fare to your cruise's first port of call. But there are coverage caps, so check what's offered.

• If a problem arising during your trip forces you to return home early, TCI covers the extra costs. But you must first find the best deal your airline will give you, then apply for TCI to pay for any additional fare or replacement ticket reissuing fee.

Emergency assistance. If you suffer an illness or accident, EME coverage may pay for a family member to travel from home to the location of your accident or hospital confinement.

Should your sickness or accident be severe enough, EME insurance typically will cover getting you to the nearest adequate medical facility—even a special evacuation—as well as your eventual transportation home. Generally, EME services are provided at the discretion of the insurance company's medical adviser. And most policies cap the benefit at $20,000 to $25,000—or $10,000 to $12,000 per person—although some may go as high as $50,000.

Worldwide help. Most TCI/EME policies include some form of worldwide assistance: a number to call for referral to a doctor, lawyer, or other person or service valuable in a pinch. But if you're looking for help with anything other than a covered medical emergency, although the insurance program will provide a referral, you must pay. And similar referral services are widely available as free benefits on some premium charge cards.

Special payments. Travel insurers have no single generic policy. Fine print in a typical policy exempts acts of war or, in some cases, terrorism. However, following the Sept. 11 attacks, and the suspension of flights nationwide, most travel insurers waived exclusions and agreed to pay otherwise valid claims for delays and cancellations.

POLICY OPTIONS

Travel insurance is sold in several versions.

Bundled policies. Most major travel insurance companies now sell only what is called a "bundled policy," which combines TCI, EME, and a number of other coverages, such as trip delay (your flight or cruise is late departing), baggage coverage (lost or delayed luggage), and even car-rental insurance. Costs are figured per person and vary with the length and price of the trip and, sometimes, the age of the travelers.

Custom policies. A few major insurance carriers also sell custom policies, allowing you to assemble your own travel-insurance package from a selection of options, each priced separately. Once popular, custom policies are losing ground to bundled options that often provide as much or more coverage. Investigate bundled policies first, unless you have very specific needs.

Wholesale policies. Many big cruise lines and tour operators sell wholesale policies under their own names (although the insurance is actually issued by an insurance company noted in the brochure's fine print). Wholesale policies are typically a bit cheaper than retail bundled policies, but not always; the cruise line or tour operator, not the insurance company, sets the selling price. But these policies don't cover some important risks, notably operator or cruise-line failure. Tour-operator failure has been a long-standing problem, and several cruise lines, such as Renaissance, have sunk as well.

FINDING THE INSURERS

Insurance prices vary for the same trip, so comparison shop. Insurer web sites have extensive information. Or you can call to get a brochure by mail or, from some carriers, by fax. (Allow enough time so that the pre-existing condition waiver doesn't expire.) These carriers all offer information and quotes by phone and on the web. You can purchase by phone (and, in some cases, on the web) with a credit card.

Access America: 800-284-8300, *www.accessamerica.com*

CSA: 800-348-9505, *www.csatravelprotection.com*

Travelex: 888-457-4602, *www.travelex-insurance.com*

Travel Guard: 800-826-1300, *www.travelguard.com*

Travel Insured: 800-243-3174, *www.travelinsured.com*

Universal Travel Protection: 800-211-8952, *www.utravelpro.com*

Some wholesale policies do have an offsetting advantage: If the underwriting insurance company rejects a claim for an aborted trip, the line usually offers partial compensation in the form of a substantial discount on a future cruise—but, of course, this extra is only good if the travel provider is still in business.

Cancellation waiver. Usually the cheapest form of trip-cancellation coverage, this is also the weakest. In fact, it's not really insurance. Instead, for a price, the issuing cruise line or tour operator agrees to waive its own cancellation penalties if you cancel your trip for a covered reason, typically only predeparture contingencies that occur more than 24 hours before departure. Waivers don't cover midtrip interruption at all, and compensation is nil if the tour operator or cruise line fails.

BUYING TRAVEL INSURANCE

The safest way to buy TCI is directly from an insurance company that offers supplier-default coverage. That way, you're protected even if your travel provider should fail, a credible risk in today's uncertain travel climate.

Be cautious if a travel agency pushes one company's policy. Agents usually get big commissions from policy sales. Most agencies are allied with the large, reputable insurers, so they're unlikely to steer you to a bum deal. But travel agents aren't insurance specialists, and consumers should consider what coverage they need—and which exclusions are unacceptable—before buying anything. (See "Finding the insurers," earlier in this chapter, for company names.)

Regardless of which supplier you choose, don't overbuy TCI. You can't recover more than your actual loss, so insuring for an amount beyond your total financial exposure is a waste. Cover only the risks you can't afford to absorb.

Always read all fine print carefully so you know exactly what you're getting—and what's excluded. The current travel situation and security issues can increase the chance of delays and cancellations. Shop around until you find the most liberal interpretation of conditions that would justify a decision to cancel. If you have questions about special circumstances, speak with a company representative.

CHAPTER 5

Money-Saving Strategies

Travel can be expensive—but maybe not as expensive

as you think. Here's a dollar-saving roundup.

■

Just because you want to save travel dollars doesn't mean you're willing to sacrifice comfort and enjoyment. Smart strategies can get you the best for less.

FOLLOW SOME KEY RULES

A good eye for deals plus some smart money-saving tactics will help you stretch your travel dollars. Consider these more-for-less tips.

Be an informed traveler. By subscribing to travel magazines and newsletters, reading your newspaper's weekly travel section, watching television travel shows, and surfing travel web sites, you'll be among the first to hear about deals.

Vet your travel operator. Don't gamble on any travel firm not familiar to you; the downturn in travel has put many concerns on shaky financial ground. Try to learn more about a company's economic status, and ask whether protection is provided either by a bond or by placing your advance payment into an escrow account.

Earn frequent-flyer miles without leaving the ground. With the many promotions and tie-ins offered by most major airlines, you can earn a ticket without being a "frequent" flyer (see Chapter 16 for other frequent flyer tactics).

Beat the airlines at their own game. The key to getting the best deal is to adhere to the airlines' 14-day-advance-purchase, Saturday-night-stay restrictions. And do your research. Becoming familiar with fare structures between your home city and a variety of places on your travel agenda will help you zero in on the best possible travel times and fares. (See Chapter 12 for money-saving airfare strategies.)

Book via the web. Booking an airline ticket, hotel room, or rental car is easy, and can bring you savings of 10 to 50 percent if you book directly on a travel-provider web site—and catch a deal.

Several top domestic airlines, including American and Continental, post bargain flights midweek for the coming weekend (and will e-mail news to you. In some cases, you need to register with the web site to access the information.) Many car-rental companies offer 10 to 20 percent discounts to anyone who books online. Leading hotel chains offer last-minute savings on many of their properties; book on or after Wednesday for the coming weekend at savings of up to 50 percent. Consolidators, cruise lines, and tour companies also use the web to post "deals" and "specials," mostly for last-minute travel. (Part Two has web strategies, Ratings, and cautions.)

Take advantage of currency fluctuations. American travelers are almost always able to find advantageous currency exchange rates somewhere in the world. By keeping track of exchange rates, then planning travel during times when the rate is favorable, you can reap substantial savings—especially if one of your favorite travel pastimes is shopping. For instance, in late-2001, the euro (the unified currency used by the European Monetary Union) still remained fairly low against the dollar, creating plentiful bargains for U.S. tourists.

Watch for hotel discounts. They'll yield considerable savings on a long trip. But even on a quick weekend getaway, savings of 30 to 50 percent "hands" you money. Savvy travel agents, the web, discount room brokers, and travel clubs are all viable savings channels. (Chapter 18 has hotel rate help.)

Make lunch your major meal. You may have noticed that prices at many restaurants are typically 20 to 30 percent lower at lunch than at dinner. If you make lunch your main meal of the day, you can sample the city's finer cuisine without blowing your budget. Have lighter fare for dinner—in a small café, for example.

Use ATMs when available. Savings sometimes equal 5 to 15 percent over the rate for exchanging traveler's checks or cash at foreign-exchange booths. Most major American banks, and some smaller ones as well, are connected to the Cirrus and Plus systems, which link thousands of ATM machines worldwide. You can withdraw money from your bank account at any machine with the Cirrus or Plus logos, following your familiar withdrawal procedure (you'll need a four-digit code outside the U.S.). Most international ATMs offer an "English" option. You'll be given the amount you request in local currency—usually at the best exchange rate without a transaction fee or, at the most, be charged a nominal amount. (See "Money Matters" in the Reference Section for more currency tips.)

CHECK OUT SPECIAL DISCOUNTS

If you're a senior or traveling with children, always ask about breaks. Corporate perks and travel club membership also confer deals.

Seniors. Discounts from organizations, travel providers, and even the government can save you travel dollars. Membership in the American Association of Retired Persons (AARP) yields savings on airlines; auto rentals; cruises; vacation packages; and hotels, motels, and resorts. Get specifics at *www. aarp.com/memberguide/privileges.*

Other seniors' organizations—Catholic Golden Age, Mature Outlook (a travel club), and National Association of Retired Federal Employees—also extend travel perks. Those over 62 get airfare bargains, too. Besides a standard 10 percent savings on most fares, they're eligible for senior coupons and membership in senior clubs. (See Chapter 15 for details.)

Most major hotel and motel chains offer a 10 to 15 percent discount off rack rate (the list price); always ask for a senior rate when you reserve.

The Golden Age Passport, allowing unlimited lifetime access to all U.S. national parks, is available to anyone age 62 or older for a one-time $10 fee. (Typical fees range from $2 to $20 per car per visit.) See the Nation Park Service web site, *www.nps.gov.*

Children's reductions. Airlines, trains, and buses all offer some fare markdowns for children. (See Chapters 15 and 25.) Some hotel and motel chains also offer a "kids stay free" deal for children under 12, plus special meals.

Employee discounts. Corporations may give employees special coupons, ranging from discounted theme park admissions to airfare price breaks. (Ask the human resources department.) You might also qualify for "corporate" rates at many leading hotels, even for nonbusiness travel. Inquire when you reserve; take your corporate ID to show at check-in.

Travel club discounts. Some clubs cover an entire family or household; others include just one individual. Full service clubs generally offer multiple benefits:

• Hotel deals are provided through either a half-price hotel program or the travel club's own discount. (See Chapter 18.)

• Airfare reductions are available with the club's own discount coupons (often heavily restricted) or through discounted consolidator tickets. (See Chapter 13 for consolidator information.)

• Dining discounts at participating restaurants are typically a mix of percent-off and two-for-one deals.

• Last-minute cruise and tour deals may be discounted through a travel club's program or an outside travel agency. But cruise discounting is so widespread, you can find a deal through almost any full-service or discount travel agency.

• Travel agency rebates (usually from the in-house travel agency run by most clubs) typically amount to 5 to 10 percent of the total price, issued as a refund check or a charge-card credit.

Special-interest clubs. Some clubs cater to narrower interests: those looking for expensive hotels and resorts, upscale rentals, or golf or tennis packages. The Automobile Club of America (AAA) also has many deals. Check the web site *(www.aaa.com)* for specifics.

CHAPTER 6

The Best Time to Book Bargains

Knowing where and when to go off-season

can save you as much as 50 percent.

■

Looking for bargains on everything from airfares to car rentals to hotels? Think "off-season." How much will you save? Plenty. Late in 2001, the off-season—plus the downturn in travel—yielded these bargains among many others for 2002:

• Free companion ticket on Lufthansa from 14 U.S. cities to 100 European cities, if flying from January 6 to March 24.

• Five-night/seven-day, air/hotel packages to Florence and Rome through March 15, starting at $599 (per person, double).

• A future free flight for booking a five-night Delta package to such places as Hawaii and Mexico through January 31.

A willingness to travel off-season can win you substantial savings on all aspects of travel. Here's what you can expect.

OFF-SEASON BENEFITS

Off-season is simply the time when most other tourists stay home —and when rates go down to lure in business. Available discounts will vary by region and season.

Lower airfares. These reduced fares can be the main perk. Time your trip to catch airfare "sales" and you can almost always save 30 to 50 percent—sometimes as much as 65 to 70 percent. Savings depend on the region and the route.

Intercontinental. These routes, linking the U.S. with Europe, Asia, South America, and the South Pacific, have at least two seasonal price levels, usually called high and low, which are limited only to Economy Excursion fares. Some routes have only one seasonal fluctuation each year; others may have several. In addition, several U.S.-to-Europe and U.S.-to-South Pacific fares have an intermediate "shoulder" level. Shoulder fares usually cover a period of several weeks between in-season and off-season. In most instances, your round-trip fare is determined by the day you start your trip. You may return at any time permitted by the ticket's length-of-stay restrictions, although in a few cases the round-trip price varies by your return date as well.

Domestic. Fares within North America are generally not called seasonal, but they often vary through seasonal promotions. (See Chapter 12.) Airlines also adjust the number of seats assigned to various price categories to change their yield without changing the advertised fare levels. And some low fares can be blacked out during periods of highest demand. On some routes, fares vary by week, day, or even hour.

Tactics. Most bargain airfares, available for a limited number of seats, are advertised for only a few weeks leading up to the earliest departure dates. Usually you must book by a certain date and travel by a certain date, typically within two months.

If you can, have a selection of several travel dates. When first choices are not available, ask the ticketing agent (or your travel agent) to search the days just before or after your preferred dates. You may also get a bargain by flying in the very early morning or late at night.

Rail deals. Amtrak, the private U.S. intercity rail passenger system, uses multiple rates for each route in its system and some vary seasonally. VIA Rail, Canada's passenger rail system, also offers off-peak rates on many routes. Eurailpasses are not priced seasonally, but savings are always available to two to five people traveling together. (See Chapter 25 for rail information.)

Cheaper car rentals. In some countries, several of the major car-

TRAVEL SEASONS

Peak season means top dollar and heavy crowds. Off-season nets the best deals along with uncrowded locales. Shoulder season is a great compromise—some savings and relatively few fellow tourists.

DESTINATION	PEAK SEASON	OFF-SEASON	SHOULDER
Western U.S.	June-Aug. Jan.-March (ski)	Nov.-Dec.	Sept.-Oct., April-May
Florida	Dec.-April	July-Oct.	Nov.-Dec., May-June
New York/Boston	June-Sept., Dec.	Nov.-March (except Dec.)	April-May, Oct.
Hawaii	Dec.-March	April-June	NA
Alaska	June-Aug.	NA	May, Sept.
Canada	June-Sept.	Nov.-March (except ski areas)	April, Oct.
Europe (cities)	May-Sept.	Nov.-March	April, Oct.
Europe (Riviera) and Greece	May-Aug, Dec.	Nov.-March	April, Sept., Oct.
Russia/Scandinavia	June-Aug.	Nov.-April	May, Sept., Oct.
The Caribbean/Mexico	Dec.-April	June-Oct.	Nov., May
South America	Varies greatly by destination; consult guidebooks.		
Asia (China/Japan)	June-Sept.	Dec.-March	April, May, Oct.
Southeast Asia	Varies greatly by destination; consult guidebooks.		
Australia/South Pacific	Dec.-Feb.	June-Aug.	Sept.-Oct., March-May
Africa	Varies greatly by destination; consult guidebooks.		
India	Oct.-March	April-Sept.	NA

rental companies adjust rates seasonally. They also offer special U.S. promotions during slow seasons.

Bargain hotel rooms. Seasonal price changes are common in the Caribbean, the main European beach destinations (French and Italian rivieras, Greek islands, Spanish coasts), Hong Kong (most big tourist hotels), the major South American vacation areas (Bariloche, Rio), the prime U.S. winter vacation areas (Arizona, Florida, and adjacent states, and Hawaii), and in many U.S. summer-vacation areas (lakes, mountains, coasts). Low-season rates may be less than half the peak rates. But note that special local festivals or conventions push up rates.

Reduced resorts. Seasonal adjustments in resort-hotel rates vary greatly according to destination. Some have only one high and low season per year, whereas others have several. Most resort brochures list prices for the various rates. Generally, rates will be highest in warm-weather locales—such as Florida and the Caribbean—when travelers wishing to escape their own winter weather generate the heaviest demand.

More affordable cities. Hotels in major cities don't peg their prices to the season, but some make seasonal adjustments by promoting special rates as part of airline packages. Tour operators offer reduced-rate promotions in major European cities during the colder winter months and during August, when locals leave for vacation and many businesses grind to a halt.

On the down side, half-price coupon and travel-club deals may be available only during the off-season. On the up side, you can bargain with certain hotels during low-occupancy seasons. Make an offer; many times the hotel will accept it rather than see the room go empty. (Chapter 18 has more tips on getting the best hotel rate.)

SHOULDER SEASON

In many places, spring and fall shoulder seasons deliver the best mix of weather and prices, along with uncrowded attractions. Those time periods can be relatively short, such as in Quebec, or quite long, as in the Greek islands. Australia's winter (our summer) offers a long season of good value and mild weather.

In the Caribbean, for example, the frigid winter months are always the busiest. Then demand lessens, and prices begin to drop— but the weather continues balmy and pleasant. Travelers looking for an early spring getaway, say, between early March and mid-April, when temperatures in Northern cities can still be quite chilly, can snag some good deals.

In early 2001, we found 35 percent savings on rooms in Bermuda; a "Sunshine on Sale" package for San Juan, Puerto Rico, offering the fifth night free; and savings of $75 per night on a balcony suite in Ocho Rios, Jamaica.

Tour-operator ads in your Sunday newspaper travel section will give you an idea of some shoulder-season values. And travel agents can usually quote current promotions offered by tour operators and individual hotels.

Before you book, however, check out your destination with a guidebook and/or travel agent. You'll want to know just what the weather might have in store. And ask about the availability of key attractions and tourist services. When fewer visitors are expected, they may be closed or operating on reduced hours.

WEATHERING THE SEASON

Know what weather you'll face when booking either a peak-season excursion or an off-season bargain—it can make the difference between a satisfying trip and a washout.

Rainy season. When traveling to specific tropical or subtropical regions—Southeast Asia, the South Pacific, Africa, and India in particular—pay careful attention to guidebook and travel-agent guidelines on "wet" and "dry" seasons. Although temperatures typically don't vary by all that much, "wet" season is definitely more humid than "dry" and characterized by heavy rains that can last several days. Monsoons are also a hazard. Translation: Your dream vacation could be ruined—or at the very least, soggy. If you want a bargain, consider visiting very early or very late in the dry season.

Hurricane season. Technically, hurricane season in the Caribbean,

WORLD WEATHER

Below are the average daily temperature ranges for 30 major tourist destinations around the world in each of the four seasons. The first number is the average daily high in degrees Fahrenheit, the second is the average daily low.

CITY	JANUARY	APRIL	JULY	OCTOBER
Acapulco	85°/70°	87°/71°	89°/75°	88°/74°
Amsterdam	40/34	52/43	69/59	56/48
Anchorage	22/5	48/22	65/50	48/22
Athens	54/42	67/52	90/72	74/60
Bangkok	89/68	95/77	90/76	88/75
Barcelona	56/42	64/51	81/69	71/58
Beijing	35/15	68/44	89/71	69/44
Bombay	83/67	89/76	85/77	89/76
Buenos Aires	85/63	72/53	57/42	69/50
Chicago	30/13	65/34	84/61	71/37
Denver	44/15	66/29	89/56	73/31
Hong Kong	64/56	75/67	87/78	81/73
Honolulu	80/65	84/68	88/73	88/71
Jerusalem	55/41	73/50	87/63	81/73
Lima	82/66	80/63	67/57	71/58
London	44/35	56/40	73/55	58/44
Los Angeles	65/47	68/51	76/61	76/55
Moscow	21/9	47/31	76/55	46/34
Munich	3/23	54/37	72/54	53/40
Nairobi	77/54	75/58	69/51	76/55
New Orleans	62/43	82/56	91/73	84/54
New York	38/26	65/40	84/67	70/46
Papeete	89/72	89/72	86/68	87/70
Paris	42/32	60/41	76/55	59/44
Rio de Janeiro	84/73	80/69	75/63	77/66
Rome	54/39	68/46	88/64	73/53
San Juan	80/70	82/72	85/75	85/75
Stockholm	31/23	45/32	70/55	48/39
Sydney	78/65	71/58	60/46	71/56
Tokyo	47/29	63/46	83/70	69/55

Florida, and along the East Coast begins June 1 and runs through November 30. But the greatest concentration of devastating storms occurs from August through October. Resorts and cruise lines will typically offer discounts during these months to lure bargain hunters.

Beware: Being caught in a major storm can be a frightening and potentially deadly experience. Should you decide to risk it, choose a date at either extreme—either July or November. Tropical storms also strike in the Pacific and Indian oceans, where they're known as typhoons and cyclones, respectively. Consult guidebooks for travel timetables to all tropical destinations.

Heat. Peak travel periods for many tourist destinations are the summer months. Unfortunately, summer brings very high temperatures (90° and above) in, for instance, Spain, Greece, Morocco, Egypt, India, Southeast Asia, the Middle East, Southern China, and parts of the Caribbean. In the U.S., the Southwest (particularly Arizona and Nevada) and the Southeast (Florida, Georgia, and Louisiana), can also have sweltering weather in July and August, as can Texas and Oklahoma. When you link heat with large crowds, the result can be extremely uncomfortable conditions, even becoming dangerous for travelers with medical conditions.

Cold. Freezing temperatures can be equally distressing, especially if you're unprepared. And certain regions are inaccessible during many of the coldest months, including Alaska, parts of Scandinavia and Russia, the Himalayas, and northern China and Japan. In the Southern Hemisphere, southern Chile and Argentina experience their freeze during July and August—their winter. Again, consult guidebooks to avoid the ultra-cold months of your destination. (See "Health tips for travelers" in the Reference Section for pointers on coping with the climate.)

PART TWO

Travel and
The Web

CHAPTER 7

The Lowdown on Online Travel

There's a world (wide web) of travel

information at your fingertips.

◆

The Internet is changing the way consumers research and buy travel. By going online, consumers now have access to the systems that were once exclusive to travel agents and airline reservationists. But if you're not a travel agent, you need to know how to sort the useful information from the not-so-useful.

Consumers are eager to check out this new venue. According to Internet analyst firm Jupiter Communications, U.S. consumers booked $18 billion in travel online in 2000, almost tripling what they booked in 1999. Jupiter expects consumers to book $63 billion in travel online by 2006.

Early on, the web travel attraction was cheap airline tickets. Forrester, another Internet research company, estimates that this year, consumers were on pace to spend $245 million online buying vacation packages—trips that integrate several travel components into one price.

To meet all that demand for online travel information and bookings, a huge number of travel sites have sprung up. Here's a rundown of the major sites, an assessment of when the web is a good tool (and when it's not), and tips for getting the most out of your time online.

For exclusive e-Ratings of travel web sites, see Chapter 9.

TRAVEL SUPERSITES

There are three major travel sites: Expedia, a Microsoft venture, Travelocity, a Sabre company, and Orbitz, which is jointly owned by several major airlines. They're good first stops for consumers new to researching and booking travel on the web. If you're a web-savvy consumer, these sites offer a host of advanced tools and features as well as rich content that you may find helpful, including articles, travel advice, and myriad links to other travel-related web sites.

Expedia and Travelocity, which are holding their reign as the top two travel sites on the web, both provide a sizable overview of transportation, lodging, vacation, cruise, and dining options for almost any trip. They also have helpful features, such as frequent-flyer mile trackers, flight trackers, and fare minders. They promote themselves as one-stop shopping and informational resources for travel online, allowing you to compare airfares, hotel room rates, and rental-car rates as well as research hundreds of destinations.

Although the supersites require you to perform your own searches and do most of your own legwork, improved customer service features have allowed these sites to emerge as full-service online agencies. After studying the offerings, however, *Consumer Reports Travel Letter* has concluded Expedia and Travelocity should not be used without cross-referencing information from other sources such as rival sites, airlines, or travel agents.

Here's a tour of the three sites:

Expedia. *www.expedia.com.* Microsoft has redesigned this site's home page and added new features to the site to make it easier to navigate. When you arrive at Expedia you can immediately book a flight, reserve a room, or rent a car. Simply click and follow the instructions and chances are you'll never get lost thanks to its new tool bar with clearly labeled tags.

Lodging. Thanks to Expedia's purchase of Travelscape.com and VacationSpot.com in early 2000, you can now use Expedia to book discounted hotel rates and independent lodging properties like private villas and condos.

Flight booking. Expedia has what could be considered one of the most flexible flight-booking systems on the web. You can instruct the system to shop fares by either best roundtrip fare or "build your own itinerary," which searches flights by time and lets you make your own combination of outbound and inbound flights. Expedia offers several tools to help find fares that suit you:

Price Matcher services. Similar to Priceline's reverse auction model. Tell Expedia your price, destination, and travel dates for air and hotel and enter your credit card number, and it will instantly let you know if it's made a match and book your flight or hotel stay. It will give you the lowest fare it finds, even if you bid higher.

Fare Calendar. Find out when airlines offer the best published fares to your favorite destination.

Fare Compare. The Fare Compare tool lets you see the best fares other Expedia users are finding on popular routes.

Destinations and activities. Expect information on such topics

---

DON'T GET SCAMMED

Online auction alert

According to the National Consumers League, auctions are the number-one category of Internet fraud—and that includes the auctioning of airline tickets and frequent-flyer miles. Look out for "sellers" claiming they have miles that are about to expire. Once they receive money from an eager bidder, they can claim the airline won't let them sell the miles. Other scenarios to avoid are people selling "nonrefundable but transferable" tickets or too-good-to-be-true travel packages.

You can protect yourself. Always ask for more details before sending money, and verify flight and/or sailing times with travel vendors to ensure the seller's on the up and up. Hold payment in an Internet escrow account until you get what you paid for (Tradenable, formerly I-Escrow.com, provides this service).

as business travel and family travel, as well as destination guides and articles with 360-degree virtual tours.

Other features. You can research golf courses, find available tee times, book online at some courses. A changing "deals" section lists last-minute and ever-evolving specials. There are profiles of cities and destinations, including Expedia's list of "best places." You can also get tips on travel planning, or send an e-card to a friend featuring one of several dozen locations.

Travelocity. *(www.travelocity.com)*. Clearly indicated links on the home page take you through the steps of finding and booking a flight, finding and renting a car, and finding and reserving a hotel room. It too has a fare-watching feature: Tell them your most traveled routes and they'll let you know the best fares each time you log in.

Destinations. Content is provided by Frommer's guides, geared to those who want history, background, and, perhaps, budget accommodations. There are also reviews, weather information, a currency converter, and multimedia presentations for some destinations.

Team Up to Travel. You and your travel companions can see all the same pages, at the same time, from your own computers using a built-in chat feature to instantly share thoughts about your travel options, and plan your trip.

Vacation Finder. Find and book a vacation package based on destination, month, and budget.

Tips and advice. Here you'll find expert advice on just about everything you need to know before you go, how to pack to airline food and what to do if you're bumped from a flight. Also offers practical advice for while you're on the ground, with accommodations and car travel as well as tips for successful business travel.

Other features include Dream Maps, which indicate where you can go depending on how much you want to spend, and seat maps, which let you choose where you want to sit on certain airlines.

Orbitz *(www.orbitz.com)*. Orbitz is a travel web site owned by five major airlines: American, Continental, Delta, Northeast, and United. In October 2001, it reported 6.3 million unique visitors. Low-fare carrier Southwest Airlines, however, refuses to allow Orbitz to publish its fares.

Other big sites. The next tier of travel web sites provide online pricing for airfare, hotel rates, and car-rental rates, but they have less informational content and provide fewer tools. You can find some good discounted rates through negotiated deals they have with travel providers. Cheaptickets.com, Lowestfare.com, Onetravel.com, and Trip.com are a few of the sites in this group:

Cheap Tickets *(www.cheaptickets.com).* Less content-oriented, this site has become one of the top four independent travel sites, not by having bells and whistles, but by offering great deals. Cheap Tickets offers 500,000 nonpublished discount airfares on over 35 airlines. It also offers deals on rental cars, hotel accommodations, and cruises.

OneTravel *(www.onetravel.com).* It's easy to find deals on this site. Its airline reservation system, Farebeater, lets you shop for published fares based on your criteria and then will offer a lower alternative fare. It also offers discounted White Label flights on domestic and international airlines but you don't know which airline or certain itinerary information until after you've booked. The HotelWiz feature searches more than 51,000 hotels. You can find discounted rates at many hotels. This site is also packed with news and tips from experts on destinations as well as advice on how to get the best travel deal to how to deal with the airlines.

Trip.com *(www.trip.com).* A bit hipper than others, Trip.com is not deep. The usual trip planner section allows you to research and book airfares and hotels. But destination guides, for example, fall short of the competition in content and range of covered locales. The "Traveler's Newsstand" and "Marketplace" are both helpful in theory but don't always deliver the information you want. Basically, this site still needs to fill in the blanks.

One effective feature, however, is the "Flight Tracker," which allows you to track any flight as it takes off, flies, and lands, using either a real-time onscreen map or regularly updated text—say, "153 miles SW of LaGuardia."

Provider sites. These sites from travel-service providers like airlines and hotels also let you scout prices, look for specials, and find information about specific travel providers. You just have to keep in mind that each site has a point of view. You can book online on many of them, and they can be a good starting point before shopping for rates and fares.

Airlines. All major airlines have web sites from which you can book flights directly, and most of these sites list online-only specials as well. Several, such as United Airlines and American Airlines have free e-mail newsletters to inform subscribers of sales and special offers—usually for last-minute travel. In addition, to counter the discount travel sites, six U.S. airlines (America West, American, Continental, Northwest, United, and US Airways) have joined together to create their own discount site.

Airlines are also linking with Internet service providers to offer rewards and discounts. American Airlines and AOL offer AOL AAdvantage, a miles-reward program that allows consumers to earn miles either by shopping online with AOL-affiliated merchants or through travel on American Airlines. Miles accumulated can then be used in exchange for travel or merchandise.

Hotels and resorts. All the large hotel chains have web sites that allow online booking. Most offer descriptions of the properties and their amenities as well as photos. More sites are beginning to add new multimedia features like video and 360-degree virtual tours.

Bed-and-breakfasts. There are thousands of individual property web sites that offer photos and descriptions. These often do not offer online booking. There are sites that allow you to search hundreds of listings with descriptions of the properties and the ability to book online.

Rental properties. You can pursue online listings to find the right villa, condo, or ski house.

Rental cars. These sites offer information about pricing and fleets as well and may sometimes offer discounts for booking online. See Chapter 9 for e-Ratings of several large rental companies.

Trains and buses. Check schedules and buy tickets and passes on Amtrak, Greyhound, Eurorail, and others.

Cruise lines. Explore itineraries, ship configurations, and ports-of-call. You're better off booking through an agency or a cruise broker, though. See Chapter 9 for e-Ratings of cruise-line sites.

Cruise brokers. Many are established cruise names, others are web-only outfits. While the search features are limited, the major cruise providers and cruise lines themselves all have sites with detailed itineraries information. Most do not offer online booking, but do provide e-mail reservation forms.

WEB PROS AND CONS

The Internet is an exciting new tool, putting a world of information at your fingertips and allowing you to browse at your leisure. But the idea that the web guarantees the best fare is not always true. In fact it's no more likely to garner you the best airfare than by picking up the phone and calling your travel agent or the airline. While "branded" sites obviously feature selected products, the notion that "integrated" sites should be free of all bias is strongly supported by Consumers Union, the nonprofit organization that publishes this book, *Consumer Reports Magazine* and the *Consumer Reports Travel Letter*.

The rapid growth of travel web sites has convinced many consumers that these online channels provide low fares and a full array of flight options. In reality, you really need to do your homework and look around before you book.

A recent readership survey by *Consumer Reports Travel Letter* revealed that 86 percent of *CRTL* subscribers have access to the Internet, and 47 percent have purchased travel over the web within the past year and that number is only expected to grow as travel providers and online agencies rush to sell more products via the Internet.

What's good. The web can be outstanding for convenience and the large number of choices. You can shop for and compare airfares, hotel rooms, car rentals online, and more anytime, day or night.

The Internet can make researching your dream vacation easier than ever before. With 360-degree tours and video, you can virtually visit destinations and properties before you really go there and you can share thoughts with other travelers in online forums.

While the web doesn't guarantee the best deal, it is virtual clearinghouse for specials with travel agents, airlines, hotels, car rental companies and cruise lines posting their current deals. There are even sites that just post deals from a variety of sources online and off.

> **WEB DISCOUNTS**
> Some hotel and car rental companies offer discounts of 10 to 20 percent for online bookings. Some airlines offer web-only discount airfares, either posted on the site or e-mailed to those customers who sign up for the special services.

The web also has put more power into the educated consumers' hands with online auctions that allow you to name your price for travel. This new breed of web site lets you tell sellers what you want and then they can come to you.

For those who don't feel comfortable booking online, new "click and mortar" web sites will match you with an agent who's an expert in a particular destination. These sites are packed with destination information and interactive forums that can help you decide where you'd like to go before you speak to an agent.

What's not. Buying travel online—especially airline tickets—can be convenient, but it also has its limitations. Travel agents can spend years learning how to get the best airfare, the best and worst airports, and how to get a direct flight or the best connection. This information is not always readily available online although some big sites offer tips on these and other similar issues.

When you're looking to buy an airline ticket online, you have to carefully look at your itinerary before clicking the button to book it. Some sites offer limited search functions. For example, many sites only offer the choice of a morning, afternoon, or evening flight, not specific times. And often if the site does offer search by a specific time, it will still return fares for other times than you requested. Lack of sensible itineraries also is a common problem, with multiple connecting flights, for example and even itineraries involving more than one airline.

Bias also is a concern not only because travel web sites may not be disclosing all flight and pricing information fairly (in other words, there's nothing to prevent an airline from paying to have its flights

Web traveler's toolbox

The following is a list of just some of the tools you can expect you can expect to find if you journey online:

Airfare comparisons. Travel supersites as well as some of the smaller sites will offer fare finders, which will deliver quotes of the lowest fares on all major airlines to most destinations worldwide.

Hotel finders. The rate comparisons are handy, but depending on the site, listings may skew toward budget and tourist hotels or those in the first-class and deluxe category—but rarely both.

Rental-car finders. Just plug in your destination, arrival/departure details, and car class and you'll get a breakdown of the best rates from the top rental-car competitors.

Last-minute deals. If you've got a flexible schedule, you can grab some great travel deals.

Loyalty-program tracking. Supersites as well as some airline sites let you track your miles in one place. You'll need to register for this service.

Fare minders. Just plug in a few cities to which you'd like a good airfare, and the site will notify you via e-mail when a low fare becomes available. This kind of service used to be offered by just the supersites, but smaller web sites are beginning to offer this service.

Flight tracking. If you've got a flight number and a date, you can check the arrival and departure status of flights on major carriers. Most large travel sites as well as airline web sites offer this function.

Destination guides. Most major sites have online destination guides that cover the major tourist cities. You may have to do some extra digging to find information on out-of-the-way locales.

Weather reports. Most major sites provide a link to one of the major web weather sites, where you can often get three- to five-day forecasts for most destinations worldwide.

listed first), but also because the methodology of the listings can be quite confusing. Placement is key, and should be consistent from airline to airline. In other words, if an airline offers a two-stop connection, such a flight should be listed below a one-stop connection. This is why Consumers Union recently requested that the U.S. Department of Transportation regulate Internet travel sites as it regulates computer reservations systems.

GETTING THE MOST FROM THE WEB

Here's a few tips for getting the most out of your Internet experience:

• Don't just log onto one site; compare results from different sites against each other, and against outside sources, such as travel agents or travel companies, airlines, hotels, and car-rental firms. Call a hotel directly to see how the price on the web compares with their direct quote.

• Don't confuse web-site ads with actual listings.

• The earlier you book, the better: Sites offer better options weeks in advance. You can also secure web-only discounts for busy travel periods from car-rental sites and others

• If you often book the same route, it helps to cross-reference timetables from the airlines serving it (available online, in ticket offices, or at the airport).

• Flexibility is key; try a range of times and alternative airports (airline timetables and web sites provide the airport codes).

• Try not to book electronic tickets on short notice; if you input a misspelled name, there may not be a record of your e-ticket, and you could be out of luck.

• Finally, note that airlines do not treat all passengers equally. For rebooking or canceling flights, compare the fees charged by web sites, travel agencies, and airlines.

• Write down (or print out) confirmation numbers when you book online. Take these with you to the rental-car counter, hotel, or airport.

CHAPTER 8

Finding Travel Information Online

More people than ever before are using the

Internet for travel planning. Here is how to find

what you want—fast.

■

While the Internet puts a world of travel planning at your fingertips, finding what you want can be daunting. With sites specializing in both the general and the obscure, it's difficult to know where to go first. But if you think of the sheer quantity of information as a plus rather than a minus, you're off to a great start.

Consumer Reports Travel Letter suggests that travel web sites work best as tools for searching out low fares and viable options because of possible conflicts of interest due to advertising or marketing partnerships not always disclosed to consumers. For best results, book through the web only after consulting with other sites; the airlines themselves (many offer exclusive deals on their own sites); or a travel agency.

SMART WEB TACTICS

Here are some steps to make the best of your web-surfing time.

Check supersites and guidebook sites. Just as you'd first read guidebooks or gather brochures, visiting similar reputable travel sites is a good first step on the web. Such sites are a vast repository of reliable—and generally up-to-date—information on hundreds of destinations. If you have a place picked out, you can determine specifics (where to stay and eat, what sights to see), then quickly and easily compare airfares and hotel-room rates. Large sites also generally have links to other travel sites (either affiliated or reviewed by experts). Once you have a general feel for your destination, you can print out any pertinent info to read later, then move on to the next step.

Conduct a search. Some of the best travel information on the web can be found by conducting a search. Using search engines, such as AltaVista, Excite, or Go/Infoseek, you can make your search as general or specific as you like. A search allows you to find sites all over the world containing information on a topic as broad as, say, "Scotland," or as narrow as "Glasgow bed-and-breakfast." Or if you'd like to research a specific city or hotel, simply type in the exact name, click, and see what pops up. If the hotel has its own web site, you might be able to see photos and even reserve online, saving yourself the cost of an overseas phone call or fax. (See "Finding what you're looking for," this chapter.)

Send out inquiries. Initial research done, it's time to begin the reservation process. Most hotel, rental car, and tour sites have either booking engines that allow you to make the reservation with a credit card or one-click e-mail links, which easily allow you to send a reservation inquiry. You type in the required data, click on "send," and wait to see if your request is accepted. With either option, you'll be notified by e-mail. Never send your credit-card number via e-mail on an insecure site.

Print out confirmation statements. Once you've received confirmation about a flight, hotel room, cruise, tour, or rental car, print out the e-mail and keep it until you receive your tickets or vouchers. Some travel web sites—including some airlines that issue e-tickets—consider the confirmation e-mail to be a valid voucher and will not send another one via regular mail. Confirm if this is the case. If you have

THE WEB

not received your tickets or vouchers in the promised amount of time, call the company's toll-free number with your confirmation e-mail in hand to investigate the delay. It's best to do business only with companies that list a customer-service number on their web sites.

If you feel at all uncomfortable booking on the web, you can still reap many online benefits. Simply do your research, then print out or write down details of the flights, fares, hotels, tours, or cruises. Take the details to a travel agent, who should then be able to book through traditional means. And because you've done the research, you'll know exactly what you're getting.

FINDING WHAT YOU'RE LOOKING FOR

Even if you already have your favorite travel web site, it's always good to look around before you book. Because travel is such a hot topic on the web, finding a travel web site isn't difficult. Internet portals

---

BROWSER BASICS

What you need to get around the web

To utilize the ever-expanding travel resources of the web, you'll need access to both a computer and a web browser. Most new PCs come fully equipped with a browser—either Microsoft Internet Explorer or Netscape Navigator. Both allow you to roam from site to site, viewing both text and photos as do Web TV and new "Internet Appliances." Some sites may require you to download an application known as a plug-in, which will allow you to view video or hear audio clips. Follow the link provided by the site and complete the downloading process.

Both also offer a way to save your favorite web sites. Internet Explorer has a "Favorites" folder where you can store your most-visited web pages and Netscape lets you "bookmark" pages.

To surf the web, you must also sign up with an Internet service provider. For a set monthly fee (typically about $20) you'll get an e-mail account and unlimited access to the Internet. Depending on where you live, you may have high-speed Internet access available through your local cable company or DSL (digital subscriber line) through a telecommunications provider.

and search engines can be a great place to start your search.

Search engine. A search engine consists of a searchable database of web pages that has been complied automatically by "spiders" or "robots," little pieces of software that a search site sends out to "crawl" across web pages to retrieve information about web sites.

In addition to being able to search by keyword, most Internet portals and some search engines have dedicated travel sections that you can link to from their home pages. These travel sections are travel portals from which you can link to hundreds of travel providers and informational sites.

AltaVista *(www.altavista.com).* One of the larger search engines with more than 350 million web pages indexed. Equally useful for novice users as well as web experts.

Excite *(www.excite.com).* You'll have access to to more than 250 million indexed web pages through Excite. Its "travel" link gets you information on airlines, rental cars, hotels, and vacation packages. You can also read about featured destinations, and find out about local events.

Google *(www.google.com).* Google's unique approach ranks search results according to how many sites link to it. It has 560 million indexed web sites.

Go *(www.go.com).* This site is affiliated with Disney, and uses the Infoseek search service. Its "travel" link has info on air travel, car rentals, hotels, vacations, currency conversion, and more. You can participate in a live chat, research destinations, and translate phrases that will be helpful if you're traveling overseas.

Overture *(www.overture.com).* This web site does not use any sly tactics getting its advertisers placed higher in search results. In fact it's quite blatant in its tactics. It lists sites based on how much money advertisers pay for placement and puts the highest paying advertiser at the top of the list. It has more than 15,000 advertisers.

Directories. Directories are also a popular way to find what you are looking for. A directory is an index of web pages that has been hand-complied by human editors and organized into categories and subcategories.

THE WEB

Ask Jeeves *(www.ask.com)*. This human-powered search engine, unlike other directories, lets you ask it a question and it tries to find the best web site to answer your question.

Lycos *(www.lycos.com)*. With links to more than 2 million sites, this is one of the largest portals on the web. Clicking "travel" will allow you to book airline tickets (through the supersite Travelocity), car rentals, hotels, B&Bs, vacations, and cruises. You can also search attractions by city or zip code, convert currency, research destinations, and find scenic drives and road trips.

MSN *(search.msn.com)*. This Microsoft portal offers an extensive directory of web sites. Expedia.com is a Microsoft-owned entity, so a fair number of search inquiries for "travel" will likely bring you to this supersite.

Yahoo! *(www.yahoo.com)*. Aside from listing links from 1.5 to 2 million unique sites, when you click on "travel" from the home page you access a fairly large travel center. You can book air travel (through supersite Travelocity), car rentals, hotels, cruises, and vacation packages online. There are also travel tips from experts, and daily travel news.

Meta-search engines. Meta-search engines "crawl" across various directories and search engines to return the closest match to your search criteria. Some of the popular ones are:

Dogpile *(www.dogpile.com)*

Inference find *(www.infind.com)*

MetaCrawler *(www.metacrawler.com)*

Mamma *(www.mamma.com)*

Online auctions. Reverse-auction web sites have become popular, with Priceline.com pioneering the "name your own price" model. Hotwire, which launched in 2000, is another major player. The idea of the reverse-auction web site is that you name a price for airline tickets, hotels, and rental cars and you will usually be notified immediately if the vendor has accepted the bid. The catch here is that you have to post your credit-card number before you find out if they can match your price. If they do, they use your credit-card number to make your reservation. If you absolutely need to be somewhere at a certain time, say, to attend a wedding or meet a cruise ship, you'd be better off finding a good deal using times and travel providers you determine.

Other sites have begun offering similar services. For instance, Expedia's Price Matcher lets you name your price for airline tickets or hotel stays. Expedia says it will give you the lowest price, even if your bid is higher.

Skyauction.com *(www.skyauction.com)*. This online auction service is run by an established tour operator in New York. It works more like a traditional auction and accepts bids on vacation packages and flights. The highest bidder wins. Bid4Vacations.com *(www.bid4vacations.com),* which has partnerships with some of the major online agency sites like Expedia and Trip.com, and BidTripper.com *(www.bidtripper.com)* also let you bid on air, car, hotel and vacation packages.

Before you enter a bid and offer your credit-card number, do your homework and check published fares to ensure you're getting a good deal. Make sure you're dealing with a reputable company. You may

---

CAST YOUR NET

Let sellers come to you

Don't want to do the legwork yourself? Let sellers come to you. A new breed of site has emerged over the last year or so that lets you post a request and then the sellers can come to you. You can determine how long you will accept requests. (Make your request as specialized as you like. For example, "I'm looking for a 10-day vacation in a villa in Tuscany that includes culinary tours.") Sellers will contact you once with a proposal and if you're interested, you may contact them.

Imandi.com and *Respond.com* offer their own brand of services and each works a little differently. See which one works best for you.

All of the sites have strict guidelines for sellers meant to protect your privacy. In some cases, the seller does not have access to your information at all. Since you have to provide personal information, you may want to carefully review the privacy policies and FAQ sections.

want to read the "about us" or "company info" sections for background and contact information.

NEWSGROUPS AND FORUMS

Want other travelers' opinions about the places they've been and the sights they've seen? The web offers literally thousands of travel newsgroups and forums to peruse, some general, others quite specific.

Newsgroups (also known as usenets) and forums are popular with travelers of all ages and backgrounds because they provide a platform for sharing ideas and thoughts and getting advice from people all over the world. These have become especially popular with adventure travelers planning extended jaunts through countries, across continents, or even around the world.

Both newsgroups (specific online areas where surfers voice and read opinions) and forums (generally, communities set up within an established travel or lifestyle web site) allow anyone with a web browser to post or read observations about any topic imaginable. You'll find some views quite useful—but much may be off-target for your interests.

In the travel area, newsgroup and forum users discuss a wide array of topics—where to stay, how to get the best airfares, the safety of a given locale, bad-weather repercussions, recommended restaurants or local guides, sights worth seeing (or skipping). Plenty of opinions are offered.

Remember, because many groups are open to the public, the views are not necessarily expert opinions or unbiased views. Keep in mind that what you'll find is real people relating their experiences. Seek a newsgroup or forum that matches your travel style and budget.

Newsgroups. Simply put, newsgroups are discussion groups that take place via e-mail or in online chat rooms, and you can find plenty online. To find a simpatico travel-oriented newsgroup, there are several sites that offer master lists: Deja.com, Topica, and Usenet.com all catalog a wide selection of groups by such categories as topic or destination, so you can more easily locate your areas of interest.

Deja.com *(www.deja.com)*. A subsidiary of Google, this site provides a specialized listing of newsgroup discussions (sort of a newsgroup with training wheels). Deja.com travel communities and forums are meant to help travelers make the best decision before booking their vacation. Here you can wade through posted opinions or post your own question or comment. Deja.com ranks products and service providers (cruise lines, airlines, travel agencies, etc.) by their "experts." Integrated shopping also allows users to book through links to suppliers' web sites.

Usenet. *(www.usenet.com).* To participate in the listed newsgroups, (and there are many) Usenet charges a monthly fee ranging from $9.95 to $19.95 per month. Type in a keyword, such as 'travel,' and

---

FELLOW-TRAVELER FEEDBACK

Online forums

FOR THE UPSCALE TRAVELER

    Concierge *(www.concierge.com/yourview/forums)*

    Fodor's *(www.fodors.com/discussion)*

FOR THE BUDGET TRAVELER

    Frommer's *(www.frommers.com)*

FOR THE INDEPENDENT OR ADVENTUROUS TRAVELER

    Lonely Planet *(thorntree.lonelyplanet.com)*

    Rough Guides *(travel.roughguides.atinfopop.com/talk)*

    Gorp.com *(www.gorp.com/gorp/interact)*

FOR CRUISERS

    Mytravelco.com *(www.mytravelco.com/community)*

    Cruise.com *(www.cruise.com)* Click on "discussion."

FOR EVERYBODY

    Expedia *(www.expedia.com/daily/community)* Sign up for a free MSN Passport. Post your pre-trip questions, your post-trip advice, and show off your best travel photos.

    Travelocity *(www.travelocity.com)*

Virtual counselor

If you're not sure where to go or what type of vacation will best fit your interests, you can go online to find a virtual travel counselor. VacationCoach.com *(www.vacationcoach.com)* is one such site. You'll be asked to answer a series of questions about what types of activities you enjoy. You can specify other criteria including region, budget, weather conditions, and type of environment. Based on your answers, you'll be provided a list of suggested vacations tailored to fit your personal interests. VacationCoach.com bills itself as an unbiased consumer-friendly site. Free of advertisers, it charges its members a $25 annual fee. Look for other similar sites to come online and for other online travel agencies and supersites to offer these "counselors" on their own web sites.

you'll get hundreds of ultraspecialized groups. You may also sign up for your own newsgroup server that carries only the newsgroup you are interested in.

Forums. You'll find forums on most major travel web sites and, based on the site sponsor, you should be able to match up with other people who share your interests and budgets. While most offer groups based on destination, some also offer forums for specialized groups that focus on specific issues for women travelers, senior travelers, and gay travelers, for example. Some also offer occasional live hosted forums with travel experts. Some require you register before taking part in the discussions. See "Forums" on page 67 for a few.

SECURITY AND PRIVACY

While major travel-related sites—airlines, hotel chains, car-rental firms, large travel agencies—all have secure servers that allow you to type in credit-card and personal information (name, address, phone number) without worry; other sites are not so vigilant about protecting credit data and privacy. Before offering any information, look for a privacy/security statement on the site. (See the e-Ratings in Chapter 9 to check the privacy and security policies of selected travel-provider web sites.)

Consider the source. Most well-known names in travel are on the web. But anyone can put up a site. So if the name is not familiar, use the site for information only until you check further.

Privacy. Your privacy online is just as important as your privacy offline, so you should be careful how you share your personal information online. If you want to avoid having your personal information sold on marketing lists, check the privacy policy carefully. Make sure it says it won't share or sell your personal information to third parties. Many companies will let you opt out of in-house e-mail programs

You should also be aware that web sites can track your usage on their site by placing "cookies" on your computer. A "cookie" is a unique identifier that tracks your every move on a web site.

STAYING SECURE

Protecting your charge-card data

Anytime you make a transaction on the web—be it financial or divulging personal information such as your address or phone number—make sure the site is reputable and secure. Look for these indicators:

Secure server. A security symbol should automatically appear whenever you are asked for sensitive information, such as a charge card number. You'll see an "s" in the site's URL (the http:// in the address changes to https://) and/or a small lock icon on the screen that changes from an unlocked to a locked position.

Customer service number and mailing address. Patronizing a site without a physical address—not a P.O. box—and a telephone number (preferably toll-free) can be risky. Also look for an entry on the site that details the company's background; it might be a link that says "About Us" or "Company History." Basically, know who you're dealing with.

Independent seals of approval. Some sites are approved by either the Better Business Bureau online *(www.bbonline.org)* or an independent web site monitoring organization called TRUSTe *(www.truste.org).*

Your own judgment. If a site makes promises that are just too good to be true—say a week-long vacation at a luxury resort for $199—be skeptical. Scam artists inhabit the web, just like anywhere else.

Netscape and Microsoft's Explorer, the two most popular browsers, support cookies. Some sites will give you the option to opt-out of their tracking program.

Be careful about divulging personal information online. Some travel sites will ask for extra information about your personal travel preferences that they will use to personalize offerings to you and enhance your shopping experience. For example, Travelocity offers a Fare Watcher feature that allows you to select your three favorite routes, and every time you log on, it will show you the best deals of the day.

Some sites will use such information to form marketing lists that they sell, or share with other providers. Most reputable sites will not sell or share any information with third parties (beyond travel providers solely for the purpose of booking your travel) unless you give explicit consent.

You should carefully read the site's privacy policy, so you know exactly how the site going to be using your information. Most reputable sites will offer an easy way to opt out of any type of in-house email or personalization programs. The best sites won't include you in such programs unless you sign up for them or "opt-in."

SOME TRAVEL SITES WORTH CHECKING OUT

The sites listed here are just a small slice of what's available on the web.

PRIVACY

Protecting your privacy online

You can learn more about Internet privacy issues and how to protect your own privacy from Junkbusters, a privacy advocacy firm. Its web site *(www.junk busters.com)* offers the latest privacy-related news and offers tips on how to protect your privacy online as well as offline. It also offers advice like how to reduce telemarketer calls and how to get your name taken off marketing lists.

The Electronic Privacy Information Center (EPIC), an independent non-profit corporation based in Washington, DC, is another helpful resource for privacy information. Its web site is *www.epic.org.*

See the Resource Guide at the back of the book for web addresses of airlines, car-rental agencies, hotels, cruise lines, and more.

Adventure/experiential. Packed with content, these sites can be your first step to adventure, whether you're looking to scale a mountain or take a gentle bike ride in the countryside.

Away.com *(www.away.com)*

Gorp.com *(www.gorp.com)*

iExplore.com *(www.iexplore.com)*

Family travel. Check out these sites when it comes time to plan your next family vacation.

Family Travel Files *(www.familytravelfiles.com)*

Family Travel Forum *(www.familytravelforum.com)*

Vacation Together *(www.vacationtogether.com)*

Gay and lesbian travel. Find special tours, cruises and more.

Gay Travel *(www.gaytravel.com)*

Planet Out *(www.planetout.com/travel)*

Out & About *(www.outandabout.com)*

Government web sites. Your tax dollars really are at work.

Bureau of Consular Affairs *(www.travel.state.gov)*. Travel warnings, plus important information about what you should do if you experience a crisis overseas.

Centers for Disease Control *(www.cdc.gov/travel/index.htm)*. All you need to know about health issues before you travel.

National Oceanic and Atmospheric Administration *(www.noaa .gov/wx.html)*. Great for weather buffs, this web site offers a range of informational tidbits, from weather warnings and climate charts to beach temperatures. Or go explore the Weather Channel's web site *(www.weather.com)* or Accuweather *(www.accuweather.com)* for national and international forecasts.

U.S. Customs *(www.customs.ustreas.gov/travel)*. Everything you need to know about import/export regulations.

Last minute/weekend travel. If you can travel on a moment's notice, you could score a great deal. From low-cost to lavish these sites cover all the bases.

Site59.com *(www.site59.com)*

THE WEB

Escapecity.com *(www.escapecity.com)*

LastMinuteTravel.com *(www.lastminutetravel.com)*

Reviews. Read what other people have to say about travel providers and share your own rants and raves.

Epinions *(www.epinions.com/trvl)*

Planet Feedback *(www.planetfeedback.com)*

Seniors. Options abound for the 55 and over set.

Senior.com *(www.senior.com/travel)*

ThirdAge *(www.thirdage.com/travel)*

Travel deals. Are you a bargain hunter? These sites offer a menagerie of travel deals from thousands of travel agents and providers.

Travelzoo.com *(www.travelzoo.com)*

TravelHub.com. *(www.travelhub.com)*

Women. These sites view travel from a woman's perspective.

Journey Woman *(www.journeywoman.com)*

Wild Women Adventures *(www.wildwomenadv.com)*

e-Ratings of Travel Web Sites

Consumer Reports judges usability and

content of 43 travel web sites

———————————■———————————

CONSUMER REPORTS regularly evaluates online shopping sites—including travel provider web sites. Sites are selected based on sales volume, site traffic, and popularity or relevance in a particular category. To rate each site, we follow a consistent online shopping scenario—browsing for products or services; booking a reservation, or looking for specific items and features. All site URLs have the "www." prefix.

We give an overall score that sums up the quality of a site's policies, usability, and content, and how well these elements combine to create an efficient and productive online shopping experience. The overall score is not necessarily an average of the site scores for policies, usability, and content. If one characteristic of the site is exceptional, the site may receive a higher overall rating, and if one of the components is far below standard, the site may receive a lower overall rating.

The policies judgment reflects our evaluation of the quality and clarity of a site's explanation of security, privacy, shipping, return, and customer-service policies. At minimum, all sites are expected to process customer information by using secure servers and to permit customers to easily keep their names off mailing lists. Companies receive higher scores if they: have relatively inexpensive shipping charges; promise to cover the first $50 of any fraudulent charge resulting from a site transaction; do not share customer information with third parties unless the customer agrees; offer a 100 percent satisfaction guarantee with a full refund.

The usability judgment evaluates how easily and efficiently a consumer can browse the site for products, search for certain items, and book a reservation. The content judgment evaluates the extent of product categories and choices within those categories; the quality and amount of product information given; and the availability of useful personalization/customization, special services, or unique features.

These evaluations were current as of December 2001. Consumer Reports Online revisits and re-evaluates such sites every three months. Site subscribers have full access to the e-Ratings.

DOMESTIC AIRLINE SITES

KEY NO	WEB SITE	OVERALL SCORE	POLICIES	USABILITY	CONTENT
1	**American Airlines** *aa.com*	○	○	◒	○
2	**Delta Airlines** *delta.com*	○	○	○	○
3	**Northwest Airlines** *nwa.com*	◒	◒	◒	◒
4	**Southwest Airlines** *southwest.com*	○	◒	○	○
5	**United Airlines** *united.com*	○	○	○	◒
6	**US Airways** *usairways.com*	○	○	◒	○

Overall Ratings — In alphabetical order — Excellent ⊖ Very good ⊖ Good ○ Fair ◔ Poor ●

THE WEB

1 **American Airlines** Searching for and booking flights at this site is a reasonably efficient process. But browsing can be tedious, and the site offers only a small number of helpful tools.

2 **Delta Airlines** The flight-search process at this site is reasonably efficient. Flight-status information is available for wireless-device customers too.

3 **Northwest Airlines** Searching for flights is especially effective here, and there are extensive opportunities for personalization, including the ability to track fares, monitor frequent-flyer miles for all airlines, and store itineraries. This site stands out compared with others in this category.

4 **Southwest Airlines** Searching for and booking flights at this site is an efficient process, but limited opportunities for personalization and

the lack of an e-mail address for communication with Southwest may leave customers feeling dissatisfied.

5 **United Airlines** Although easy to navigate, this site is a mixed bag when it comes to searching for flights. There are helpful options for selecting and sorting flights based on numerous criteria, but you won't find out the cost of a roundtrip flight until you piece together the legs of departing and return flights; that can be frustrating.

6 **US Airways** Although you can have a generally satisfying experience here, searching for flights is an inefficient process. You won't find out the cost of a roundtrip flight until you piece together the legs of departing and return flights; that can be frustrating.

FOREIGN AIRLINE SITES

	In alphabetical order				
		Excellent ⬒	Very good ⬓	Good ○	Fair ◖	Poor ●

KEY NO	WEB SITE	OVERALL SCORE	POLICIES	USABILITY	CONTENT
1	**AeroMexico** aeromexico.com	⬓	●	⬓	○
2	**Air Canada** aircanada.ca	○	●	○	⬓
3	**Air France** airfrance.com/us	○	⬓	⬓	○
4	**Air Jamaica** airjamaica.com	○	●	⬓	○
5	**British Airways** britishairways.com	○	○	○	○
6	**Japan Air** japanair.com	○	⬓	●	◖
7	**KLM** nwa.com	⬓	⬓	⬓	⬓
8	**Lufthansa** lufthansa-usa.com	○	○	○	○

1 **AeroMexico** There is no privacy policy information in the booking section. Booking is somewhat tedious for U.S. customers. Very little to recommend this site overall.

2 **Air Canada** The privacy policy is confusing and hard to find, and booking a flight is a somewhat lengthy process. The site offers detailed information on destinations, weather, travel tips, and more.

3 **Air France** Although policies are very good at this site, the flight-search process can be inefficient. You must register and enter a personal profile before you can book a flight.

4 **Air Jamaica** This site provides only brief traveler information and site destination guides. However, the flight searching and booking process takes place through Expedia.com, and is basically a smooth, hassle-free experience.

5 **British Airways** This site offers extensive information on booking online. But the flight-search process is limited, and browsing can be somewhat inefficient.

6 **Japan Air** Excellent security and privacy policies. Browsing the site can be confusing, and actual booking takes place through Travelocity.com. Few special features or helpful tools were found.

7 **KLM** KLM's partner in the United States is Northwest Airlines. All online activity for U.S.-based users of KLM's site is conducted via the Northwest site.

8 **Lufthansa** Policy information is very difficult to find, although the site does have a very good privacy policy. This site is easy to navigate, but you must register before you can book a flight.

LOW-FARE AIRLINE SITES

Overall Ratings	In alphabetical order	Excellent ⊖	Very good ⊖	Good ○	Fair ◔	Poor ●

KEY NO	WEB SITE	OVERALL SCORE	POLICIES	USABILITY	CONTENT
1	**AirTran Airways** *airtran.com*	⊖	○	⊖	⊖
2	**Frontier Airlines** *frontierairlines. com*	◔	◔	◔	○
3	**JetBlue Airways** *jetblue.com*	⊖	⊖	⊖	⊖
4	**Spirit Airlines** *spiritair.com*	○	◔	○	○

1 ▷ **AirTran Airways** Although some policy information is difficult to find, this site has a very good privacy policy. Browsing is easy, and booking a flight is a fairly straightforward process. The special deals and programs offered are a plus.

2 ▷ **Frontier Airlines** This site has a confusing privacy policy and a cluttered design. Also, there are few extras offered here compared with other sites in this category.

3 ▷ **JetBlue Airways** Easy-to-find policy information, a user-friendly design, and an easy-to-use booking process make this site stand out among others in this category. There are also many fun and useful extras, including virtual aircraft tours, in-depth destination information, and special discounts.

4 ▷ **Spirit Airlines** Policies are a mixed bag. In general, the site is fairly easy to use, but some category headings are unclear, and the lack of a Help or FAQ page can make navigating this site a frustrating experience.

THE WEB

HOTEL SITES

Overall Ratings	In alphabetical order	Excellent ⊖	Very good ⊖	Good ○	Fair ◐	Poor ●

KEY NO	WEB SITE	OVERALL SCORE	POLICIES	USABILITY	CONTENT
	MODERATE HOTELS				
1	**Choice Hotels** *choicehotels.com*	○	○	⊖	○
2	**Hilton** *hilton.com*	◐	◐	◐	◐
3	**Hyatt** *hyatt.com*	◐	○	◐	◐
4	**Marriott International** *marriott.com*	○	○	◐	○
	UPSCALE HOTELS				
5	**Four Seasons** *fourseasons.com*	○	○	◐	○
6	**Renaissance Hotels, Resorts and Suites** *renaissancehotels.com*	○	○	◐	⊖
7	**Ritz-Carlton** *ritzcarlton.com*	○	○	○	○
8	**Westin** *westin.com*	○	◐	⊖	⊖

MODERATE HOTELS

1> **Choice Hotels** Efficient browsing, searching, and booking, plus extensive hotel information and a discount for booking online, really make this site stand out.

2> **Hilton** Inefficient browsing, booking and limited helpful information makes for a frustrating experience.

3> **Hyatt** Inefficient browsing and booking and limited helpful information can make for a frustrating experience.

4> **Marriott International** The tedious navigation here can be frustrating, but a personal profile feature is helpful.

UPSCALE HOTELS

5> **Four Seasons** Browsing can be tedious here, but efficient booking and extensive information on golf courses and dining make this site worth the visit.

6> **Renaissance Hotels** Limited navigational menus can be annoying, but this site offers a very good privacy policy and useful, descriptive information for hotel properties.

7> **Ritz-Carlton** Although the privacy policy is less than satisfactory, this well-organized site is easy to browse via a constant main menu and a simple, neat design.

8> **Westin** The privacy policy is unsatisfactory, but a quick search feature and extensive hotel information are some good points.

CRUISE LINE SITES

| Overall Ratings | In alphabetical order | Excellent ⊖ | Very good ⊖ | Good ○ | Fair ◒ | Poor ● |

KEY NO.	WEB SITE	OVERALL SCORE	POLICIES	USABILITY	CONTENT
1	**Carnival** carnival.com	○	○	○	○
2	**Cruise411** cruise411.com	○	○	○	○
3	**i-cruise** i-cruise.com	⊖	○	⊖	⊖
4	**mytravelco.com** mytravelco.com/cruises	○	⊖	○	○
5	**Norwegian Cruise Line** ncl.com	⊖	○	⊖	⊖
6	**Princess Cruises** princesscruises. com	◒	◒	◒	○
7	**Royal Caribbean International** royalcaribbean.com	⊖	○	⊖	⊖

THE WEB

1 Carnival This site has a very good privacy policy, but an unclear cancellation policy. Although browsing and navigation are efficient, the booking process is limited in its usefulness.

2 Cruise411.com Browsing this site is fairly easy, and a "compare" tool lets you see cruise features side-by-side. However, the site lacks specific information on the destinations and ports of call.

3 i-cruise A very good privacy policy. Booking is available for most major cruise lines, but the search feature needs improvement and requesting information about cruises can make for a tedious experience.

4 mytravelco.com A very good privacy policy. Booking is available for most major cruise lines, but the search feature needs improvement and requesting information about cruises can make for a tedious online experience.

5 Norwegian Cruise Line This site has a very good privacy policy, easy browsing, and a thorough booking process. The wealth of detailed, useful, and well-linked information on ships, cruises, and destinations, along with some special interactive features, really make this site stand out.

6 Princess Cruises Navigation and browsing are easy, but the policy section is generally poor. You cannot book cruises on this site, but you can get ideas. There are some special text-based and interactive features that may make it worth a visit.

7 Royal Caribbean International Navigation and booking are fairly easy, and there is lots of useful information about ships, destinations and more on this site.

THEME PARKS SITES

| Overall Ratings | In alphabetical order | Excellent ⊜ | Very good ⊝ | Good ○ | Fair ◔ | Poor ● |

KEY NO	WEB SITE	OVERALL SCORE	POLICIES	USABILITY	CONTENT
1	**Anheuser-Busch Adventure Parks** 4adventure.com	○	◔	○	○
2	**Disney Vacations** disney.com/vacations	○	○	○	⊝
3	**Six Flags** sixflags.com	◔	NA*	◔	◔
4	**Universal Studios** universalstudios.com/themeparks	○	○	○	⊝

1> **Anheuser-Busch Adventure Parks** This site is easy to navigate via sensible browsing categories with information on parks, including ride specs and schedules. It's easy to order tickets and merchandise, but a more straight-forward privacy policy would be a welcome addition.

2> **Disney Vacations** Colorful and well organized, this site's stand-out features include live web cam shots, 360° virtual tours, and interactive travel planners. Buying park tickets through the site is easy, but the browsing categories are not always sensibly organized, making navigation a bit confusing at times.

3> **Six Flags** A constant menu makes browsing fairly easy, but navigating among park information can be tedious. Compared with other sites in this category, information is fairly limited.

4> **Universal Studios** A very good privacy policy. Browsing can be tedious, but this site provides almost all the information you need to plan a family vacation at Universal Studios.

No security or privacy polices at this site–site is informational only. No transactions take place at this time.

CAR RENTALS

KEY NO.	WEB SITE	OVERALL SCORE	POLICIES	USABILITY	CONTENT
1	**Alamo** *alamo.com*	Very good	Very good	Very good	Very good
2	**Avis** *avis.com*	Good	Good	Good	Very good
3	**Budget** *budget.com*	Good	Fair	Good	Very good
4	**Hertz** *hertz.com*	Good	Fair	Good	Very good
5	**National** *national.com*	Fair	Fair	Poor	Good

Overall Ratings — In alphabetical order

Legend: Excellent / Very good / Good / Fair / Poor

THE WEB

1 ⟩ **Alamo** This site has very good privacy and rental policies, easy navigation and booking, and many useful customer service features. There are thorough vehicle descriptions and detailed information on insurance options and rental contracts. This site really stands out among others in this category.

2 ⟩ **Avis** This site has a very good privacy policy and a thorough FAQ section, along with easy browsing and flexible booking. Useful customer service features include a mechanism for tracking awards and researching Avis travel partners.

3 ⟩ **Budget** Browsing and booking are easy here. There's an interesting Tips & Guidance section and online booking discounts are offered, but the privacy policy is poor.

4 ⟩ **Hertz** Browsing is efficient at this site, and there are some useful customer service features. But the booking process could use some improvement, the privacy and rental policies are poor, and "special offers" have numerous restrictions tied to them.

5 ⟩ **National** This site has a poor privacy policy and information on cancellations is buried. Inefficient browsing and booking can make for a frustrating experience.

PART THREE

Airlines & Airfare

CHAPTER 10

Coping with Air Travel Today

Advance planning and a cool head can help you deal with

increased delays and new procedures.

———————————◼———————————

The September 11 terrorist attacks led almost overnight to increased security measures and many new rules at airports in the U.S. and Canada. Since the procedures are designed to improve air traveler safety, it's in consumers' best interests to follow them—despite the often undeniable inconvenience.

However, policies vary from airport to airport, even carrier to carrier, depending on facilities and equipment. Curbside check-in may be available—or not. Security checkpoints may be numerous or few. Baggage may be searched at one time, not at another. While FAA regulations govern what you can (and can't) take aboard an aircraft, airlines may go beyond these rules.

Your best defenses are patience, planning, and accurate information. And do allow plenty of time to check in, clear security, and get to the gate—at least two or three hours, depending on the destination.

Here is a strategy for dealing with the new realities of air travel. All information was current as of press time. But things change, so always clarify any questions with your carrier before you leave for the airport.

ADVANCE ARRANGEMENTS

New regulations have created new hassles. Being ready to meet them can make your departure much smoother.

Leave home earlier. *Consumer Reports Travel Letter* and most airlines are suggesting that travelers arrive at least two hours before a scheduled domestic departure and three hours prior to an international flight. Call the airline to find out if you need more time (and ask if there are restrictions on how early you can check in your bags). Remember that at certain time these guidelines may appear to be overly cautious, but unexpected security checks could delay your departure.

Limit your carry-ons. Current FAA rules allow only one carry-on and one personal bag (a purse, briefcase, backpack, laptop, diaper bag, etc.) per person. Trying to carry on more than this allowance will only delay your passage—and others'—through security.

Be smart about packing. The FAA has announced that knives or cutting instruments of any length or material are now off-limits in carry-ons. Prohibited past the security checkpoints are metallic and nonmetallic knives, box cutters, straight razors, elongated scissors, corkscrews, metal nail files, and any device with a folding or retractable blade. In addition, such items as baseball bats, hockey sticks, and golf clubs are banned (canes are permitted). You may not carry on anything flammable or which might emit fumes, including cigarette lighters and matches. Hypodermic syringes and needles may be exempt with proper medical documentation; check with the airline.

Individual carriers are permitted to go beyond the FAA's list of banned objects, and officials have reportedly confiscated sewing and knitting needles, nail clippers, tweezers, and disposable razors. Don't pack questionable items; you can buy incidentals at your destination.

For more details on packing, see "Baggage notes" in the Reference Section. The FAA also posts an updated list on its web site; go to *www.faa.gov* and click on passenger information. If you have specific questions, contact your carrier.

Pack fewer items. You'll pass through security more quickly if you carry less. Can't do without something? Ship it ahead. Camera gear, radios, laptop computers, and cell phones are being closely scrutinized. Sealed packages will be opened, so leave gifts unwrapped for inspection.

Dress sensibly. For ease and safety of movement, wear comfortable, nonflowing clothing and flat shoes. Avoid metallic items. Belts and jewelry could slow you down at a checkpoint.

Choose paper tickets over e-tickets. Although some airlines offer nothing but electronic or "paperless" tickets, when you have a choice, ask for a traditional ticket. As of late 2001, there remained much confusion about standardization of proper e-ticket documentation. To clear security, you must have one of the following that shows that day's flight departure date: a receipt for an e-ticket, including ticket number; an itinerary generated by an airline or travel agency confirming an e-ticket, with the ticket number; a boarding pass; or a paper ticket. If you're uncertain about e-ticketing and documentation, talk to your carrier in advance. You may need to wait in line for a boarding pass prior to clearing security.

Another e-ticket down side: Such tickets are less easily endorsed by another airline if your flight is delayed, diverted, or canceled.

Carry proper identification. IDs are being closely scrutinized. You must present a photo ID (a driver's license is fine, but a current passport is the best), or two forms of ID without photo, one of which must be government-issued.

Book tickets in your exact name. "Exact" means the name on your driver's license or passport—the name on your ticket must match the name on your ID. This may pose a problem for recently married women who haven't yet changed documents, or for women who take their husband's name legally (and put it on documents) but do not use it professionally. However, you'll really need to have one name on everything.

AIRPORT PROCEDURES

Tightened security and expanding lines call for patience and cooperation. "Pack" plenty of both.

Don't plan to park near the terminal. All parking within 300 feet of airport terminals has been eliminated, which means that parking will be tighter than usual in some locations. Vehicles parked near a terminal will be closely monitored and may be towed away if left unattended. Take public transportation to the airport if you can.

Expect to check in at the ticket counter. Curbside or skycap check-in is available only on an airline-by-airline basis, depending on whether a carrier has special security procedures in place. (Call your airline for information.) If you don't have baggage to check, however, you can proceed directly to the departure gate, provided you have an approved proof of a flight reservation for that day. (See "Choose paper tickets," this chapter, for specifics.)

Limit your "guests." With long lines crowding airports and carriers permitting only ticketed passengers past security checkpoints, the days of group send-offs are behind us. Also ask friends or family not to meet you at the arrival gate when you return. Provision may be made for parents who need to meet unaccompanied minors (see

---

CHANGING POLICIES

Rules for unaccompanied minors

In light of new security restrictions, several airlines have changed their guidelines on unaccompanied minors. At press time, most airlines and airport authorities were allowing unticketed parents or guardians to escort unaccompanied minors past airport security checkpoints, but policies vary. (Adults planning to escort children to or from departure and arrival gates will need proper documentation from the airline before attempting to pass through airport security checkpoints.)

In some cases, unaccompanied minors can travel on nonstop flights only, and will not be accepted for travel to destinations requiring connecting or through flights.

To ensure there won't be a problem on the day of travel, contact your carrier for all rules, regulations, info on necessary documentation, and last-minute changes.

"Rules for unaccompanied minors" later this chapter), or for the safety of disabled or elderly persons.

Prepare for luggage searches. Expect additional questioning, inspections, and scanning. If you are detained, remain calm and answer any queries. Along with an increase in the number of uniformed law-enforcement and military personnel, you may also encounter aircraft and airport security sweeps.

Pay attention to your surroundings. Report suspicious behavior or packages. Security agents are authorized to search or remove unattended bags.

Have contact information. Keep a list of phone numbers for the airline, your travel agent, or both. If your flight is delayed or canceled, rebooking by phone might be quicker than waiting in a long line at the terminal. Also carry a copy of the airline's timetable, available online or at the airport.

Know your rights. Although airlines may provide assistance if your flight is delayed, canceled, or diverted, they really have only one responsibility: to give you a refund. And help may be less forthcoming when a problem is caused by a significant "force majeure" event outside their control. Force majeure events include weather, natural disaster, war or civil disturbance, or airline labor action.

However, when all planes were grounded on Sept. 11, 2001, airlines waived rebooking fees on nonrefundable tickets intended for that day and the period immediately after. (Rebooking fees are $100 for a domestic ticket and $150 for a ticket elsewhere. Travelers may also pay an additional fare if the new ticket is more expensive, and revised tickets generally must be used within six weeks to a year of the rebooking.) Carriers also offered refunds for nonrefundable tickets bought for trips in narrow time periods after Sept. 11.

For information on what you might expect in case of "everyday" delays, see "Flight delays," later in this chapter.

Keep a cool head. Airport security will not tolerate verbal abuse or other manifestations of "air rage." Harsh words or phony security threats—even in jest—could lead to an arrest. You must follow all instructions from airline and airport personnel.

IN-FLIGHT CHANGES

The atmosphere and amenities aboard the airliner may have changed since you last flew.

Meals may not be served. Certain carriers have (temporarily or perhaps permanently) stopped in-flight food service on shorter flights, aiming to expedite the boarding process and turn planes around more quickly. Security concerns may also play a part.

Ask your carrier about meal service when you book. You may want to bring your own provisions, or at least allow time to grab a snack at the airport. When you do get meal service, new security regulations ban the dispensing of all metal knives inflight, except for butter knives.

Security on board may be tighter. An undercover federal air marshal may be flying with you—although you won't know it. These individuals are armed and trained in the use of firearms onboard aircraft.

Flights schedules have been cut back. As of press time, service on some routes had been curtailed or dropped altogether. Don't assume that your usual carrier still flies to all its past destinations, or makes as many flights as in the past. Log on to the line's web site for up-to-date information.

SMART PRECAUTIONS

These strategies can help you minimize air-travel inconvenience.

Check flight-delay data before you book. After a long wait at the airport, you don't to wait out a flight delay, too. You can download the DOT's monthly airline on-time figures from the Air Travel Consumer Report at *www.dot.gov/airconsumer.* Zero in on your own proposed flight via the DOT's Bureau of Transportation Statistics database, available at *www.bts.gov.* Click on "Databases" to access specific information about airports, days, and times. (Details will reflect the previous year's performance.)

Schedule travel to avoid delays. *Consumer Reports Travel Letter* recently analyzed DOT data to determine when flights are most likely to be delayed.

The months. The holiday season (December through January) and the early- to mid-summer travel season (June through July) are also the delay seasons, due to increased demand and either winter snows or summer thunderstorms.

The days. Your flight is most likely to be delayed on Thursdays and Fridays, because Friday (and to a lesser extent Thursday) is getaway day. Saturdays, on the other hand, are particularly good for arriving on time.

The times. Our hour-by-hour breakdown showed that nearly all of the best on-time arrivals were clustered in the flights departing before 3 p.m. And nearly all of the worst delays were grouped around departures made between late afternoon and evening.

Watch the weather. If your summertime plans require a connection, for example, avoid connecting airports that are particularly prone to thunderstorms. Use the DOT reports or a trusted travel agent as a guide, or check current weather on the FAA web site.

Book a nonstop flight. Nonstops will get you there faster than connecting flights, which typically add an hour, even two. Changing planes also raises the risk of lost luggage. On a direct flight, you and your luggage don't change planes; you only make a stop. But your bags could be mistakenly taken off the plane at the stopover. Of course, nonstop flights often cost more than those involving a stopover or connection.

Don't schedule tight connections. If your connecting flight departs less than an hour after your scheduled arrival, a delay of 20 to 30 minutes on the first flight (or any unexpected security stipulations at your connecting airport) can turn a connection into a heart-pounding race. Should you miss your connection, the airline must get you on another flight, but when is another question. If you miss the day's last flight, you'll wait until morning.

Avoid code-share confusion. If you are traveling abroad, confirm when you book which airline will actually fly your plane. With all the airline alliances, your flight may be on Air France even though you may have booked through, say, Delta—and you certainly don't want to wait in the wrong line.

Write down your ticket number. If your ticket is lost or stolen, you have a reference when calling the airline.

Keep a copy of your passport. Copy the first page (on a black-and-white copier; it's illegal to make a color photocopy of your passport). Then put the copy in a separate bag from the passport. International air travel demands a passport. If yours is lost or stolen, a copy will expedite the replacement process, lessening the chance that you'll miss your flight home.

Reconfirm all foreign flights. Airlines in other countries don't assume your reservation is firm. Always confirm at least 72 hours in advance, especially in South America and Asia.

FLIGHT DELAYS

Airlines are not required to compensate passengers for a delay. Only those passengers who are bumped off flights due to overbooking are entitled to financial compensation under DOT rules.

Each airline has a "Contract of Carriage" (available at ticket offices, airport counters, and on most airline web sites), which states that the line does not guarantee its schedule and will provide little compensation if it cannot operate as intended. If your delay or cancellation is caused by weather or other force majeure, the airline's only legal obligation is to refund your ticket. Carriers often waive restrictions and offer to rebook at a later date—see "Know your rights," earlier in this chapter.

However, the airline will generally attempt to rebook you on the next available flight, when possible. You may receive hotel accommodations, meals, ground transportation, and phone cards at the airline's discretion. In some cases, the airline may place travelers on another carrier's flight—providing the carrier has "interline agreements." Smaller airlines may not have such agreements.

Unfortunately, passengers may be treated differently, even on the same flight. And airlines don't always volunteer their services. So arrive armed with the facts. The DOT's booklet, "Fly Rights: A Consumer's Guide to Air Travel" (available online at *www.dot.gov/airconsumer/flyrights.htm*), spells out what travelers are and are not entitled to get.

AIRLINES

ON-TIME PERFORMANCE

Overall percentage of reported flight operations arriving on time, ranked from best to worst.

AIRLINE	12 MONTHS ENDING SEPTEMBER 2001
1. Aloha	86.4%
2. Continental	80.1
3. Southwest	78.5
4. Northwest	78.1
5. US Airways	77.0
6. Delta	74.5
7. American	74.4
8. United	71.7
9. America West	70.2
10. Alaska	67.5

Ranking based on 2001 DOT statistics.

Also ask for assistance. And if you've endured lengthy delays and inconvenience (even for this era of ultra-inconvenience), see about extra perks beyond those listed above, such as discount certificates and frequent-flyer miles.

CHAPTER 11

Avoiding Airline Hassles

Long lines and complicated security checks

aren't the only challenges. Be ready to cope.

———————————— ■ ————————————

Many of the trials that air travelers have always faced are still with us—cramped seating, the chance you can be bumped from a flight, and conditions for the disabled that are sometimes difficult. What can help: Knowing how to manage potential complications.

BUMPING–A BUMMER OR A DEAL?

When an airline overbooks a flight, it must bump some passengers, who go voluntarily—or unwillingly. Here are DOT rules and tips on handling a potential bumping.

Voluntary bumping. When flights are overbooked, airlines always first ask for volunteers to give up their seats in exchange for a ticket on the next available flight, plus additional compensation. Before you take the airline's offer, the DOT has some advice.

Determine the next flight on which the airline can confirm your seat. Do not allow yourself to simply be put on a standby list; you could end up stranded. Find out if the airline will provide free meals, phone calls, ground transportation, and a hotel room if you have a long wait until the next flight. Quiz airline reps about any restrictions on a free ticket. When does it expire? Are there blackout dates? Is it good for international flights? Can you reserve the flight? "Free" may not be so free after all.

Airlines will try to get you to give up your seat as cheaply as possible. If you won't go for a rock-bottom deal, the staff will try to find someone who will. But if you happen to be the only volunteer, you've got bargaining clout.

Involuntary bumping. Generally, travelers with the latest reservations or those who check in last—or perhaps arrive too late to allow for long lines—are the ones who get bumped. In the case of involuntary bumping, the DOT requires airlines to give passengers a written statement describing their rights and explaining who gets bumped when flights are overbooked. And there are more requirements:

- Frequently, the airline must fork over an on-the-spot cash pay-

---

GOT A GRIPE?

Where to complain about air travel

Do you have a beef about air travel? The DOT Office of Inspector General, now conducting a review of airline customer service, wants to hear about it. To request complaint forms for the issues of overbooking, access to lowest fares, long on-aircraft delays, and accommodating air travelers with disabilities or special needs, log on to *www.oig.dot.gov* or call 800-884-9190 (automated menu only).

You may also call the DOT Aviation Consumer Protection Division 24 hours a day at 202-366-2220 to record complaints about any airline-service issue (calls cannot be returned) or write to Aviation Consumer Protection Division, U.S. Department of Transportation, 400 7th St., S.W., Room 4107, C-75, Washington, DC 20590. Or carp by e-mail: *airconsumer@ost.dot.gov*.

To report a safety violation, call the FAA Safety Hotline at 800-255-1111, 8 a.m. to 4 p.m., EST. (FAA personnel are on duty 24 hours a day for critical safety issues.)

Call the FAA Consumer Hotline, 800-322-7873, for information on airline safety; child-restraint systems; and service-related issues such as lost baggage, ticketing refunds, and on-time performance.

ment, with the amount depending on a passenger's ticket price and the length of the delay. There's no compensation if the airline can get you to your destination within one hour of your originally scheduled arrival time.

• With certain exceptions, if the airline can get you to your destination between one to two hours later (for domestic travel), it must refund you the cost of your one-way fare, up to $200.

• If it takes more than two hours to get you to your destination (more than four hours for international travel), the airline generally must pay you twice the value of your one-way ticket, up to $400.

• You get to keep your original ticket—for a flight, not for a refund.

To be eligible for compensation, travelers must have a confirmed reservation on the flight from which they're bumped, must have purchased a ticket within the required number of days after making the reservation, and must have arrived at the boarding lounge by the check-in cutoff time. Most domestic carriers have a deadline of 10 minutes before a flight, but some deadlines can be an hour or more ahead. Check-in deadlines on some international flights can be as long as three hours.

The DOT requires no compensation for charter flights, flights between foreign cities, international flights inbound to the U.S., or flights on planes that hold 60 or fewer passengers, nor if the airline substitutes a smaller plane.

AVOIDING BAD SEATS

Although airlines have been touting increased legroom—and the new (and pricey) premium economy service—a recent analysis of economy-class seating by *Consumer Reports Travel Letter* found that there are still seats to avoid.

Seating benchmarks. Comfort is measured by several criteria:

Pitch. This is the front-to-rear spacing of seat rows as measured in inches from seat to seat. Individual airlines, not aircraft manufacturers, determine seat pitch by deciding how many passengers to fit into each cabin. Economy-class pitch has currently settled on a tight 31 inches, though many long-haul planes have slightly more room.

Among the domestic carriers, American offered the most pitch, measuring up to 35 inches on A300s. The least pitch was on Northwest's DC10-40s. United's Economy Plus seating offered up to 36 inches on some planes. But the extra legroom comes at a stiff price—these tickets are much more expensive.

Width. The minimum standard is about 17 inches, measured across the cushion between armrests. The maximum we found is 18.5 (on American's 777s). A few seats were a cramped 16 inches, often in the last rows of the aircraft, where the cabin is narrower—an area to avoid.

Recline. A seat installed hard up against bulkheads has no room to drop back. When the seat in front of you is lowered, your upper-body space is reduced by as much as 20 percent. Seatback video, once found only in premium classes but increasingly common in economy, can add another four inches to the seat's thickness, gobbling even more space. There are three nonrecliner trouble zones: seats in the last row of the aircraft, those installed in front of bulkheads, and the seats in rows ahead of the exit doors.

Location. The worst economy-class seats are found near lavatories and galleys. Passengers nearby must contend with increased traffic, bathroom lines, noise, and even offensive odors.

Middle seats are the straightjacket of the skies, and the percentage depends more on the aircraft than the carrier. We found that 747-400s have about 37 percent of seats in this category, but a 767-200 has only 12 to 15 percent in the middle.

However, any location improves if the adjacent seat is empty—an adjoining empty equals a 4.25-inch wider seat for you, essentially a one-class upgrade. The odds of lucking into one are highest on planes with a 3-3 or 3-3-3 configuration. A movable armrest makes the deal even better, and seats with this armrest are typically available to all travelers who request them. Some may be reserved for travelers with disabilities, however, and released only on the day of departure.

How to seat yourself. Despite redesigned cabins, slimmer seat designs, and increased comfort features in economy-class cabins, there's little room to spare. Tight spaces aren't likely to loosen up either. Flights remain full, even packed on peak routes. So choose your seat carefully—in advance.

Ask precise questions. Airline web sites present detailed seating maps and sometimes even row-by-row particulars, so do your research. Always pin down the facts when booking by phone, because reservation agents or travel agents may not tell you that you're about to choose a nonrecliner, for example, or to stick yourself in the undesirable lavatory/galley areas.

Reserve seats when buying tickets. Don't wait. If you can't book seats, you may be on an oversold flight—always ask. Some airlines won't reserve seats for deeply discounted consolidator fares; those with such a ticket need to get to the airport early.

Fly reliable airlines and routes. Boeing researchers point to a "halo effect" of late flights. Passengers delayed more than 30 minutes report drastically lower comfort, regardless of actual seat differences. That is, even a good seat won't ease a bad flight, and a less-comfortable seat is more bearable if you arrive on time. (See Chapter 15 for an on-time flight booking strategy.)

Consider a less-booked flight. For domestic flights, midday and midweek travel may be less congested. Also consider red-eye flights. On international flights, try to avoid Friday and Saturday evenings.

Ask for front-end seats. Flights are often filled from rear to front, meaning you may be offered seats farther back than necessary. And the back of the cabin is often narrower, reducing seat width—and comfort.

Strategize seating requests. Consider an aisle seat in the center section. The seat next to you may be empty.

Remember seat downsides. Despite the increased knee room in bulkhead seats, you can't stretch your legs under the seats in front. They may not recline, and lack underseat storage. Viewing inflight videos may be difficult. And some airlines put bassinets on bulkhead walls.

Although you might snag an exit row seat at the airport (airline personnel must visually judge your ability to assist in an emergency before they will let you sit in an exit row), these seats may not recline either.

Make sure your seat reclines. Beware of the last row of any seating section, the location of most nonrecliners.

AIRLINES

Check in early. And make sure you get confirmed seat assignments all the way through your itinerary. Some more desirable seats are held until departure day, so showing up early is your best bet.

Beware of switching at the airport. Ask the agent to search for a more desirable seat—but don't cancel your reserved seat until you actually have a better one. You may end up in the rear of the plane, even if you booked months in advance.

YOUR CHILD'S IN-FLIGHT SAFETY

Each day, thousands of babies and toddlers fly cradled on the lap of a parent or grandparent. But when a plane is buffeted by turbulence, the effective weight of a 20-pound toddler can soar to more than 100 pounds in milliseconds, meaning that an adult's arms are by no means an adequate restraint. And federal weather researchers estimate that a commercial aircraft encounters significant turbulence somewhere in the U.S. every day.

FAA research has shown that a child safety restraint—the same safety seat that you use in your car—provides a youngster with the most protection. So the agency recommends, but does not require, that all children, regardless of age, use an approved child-restraint seat appropriate to the child's weight and size. (See "Car seats aren't just for cars," this chapter, for specifics.) If you book a seat on a plane for your child and you have an approved seat, the airline must allow you to use it. But do check with the airline in advance.

To avoid problems at check-in or on the plane, it's wise to bring a copy of the FAA regulations detailing your right to use a child-restraint seat on a plane. Call the FAA at 800-322-7873 to request a copy. Or print it from the FAA web site at *www.faa.gov*. Take particular care when flying on international carriers. Call ahead to request a written copy of the airline's policies.

PASSENGERS WITH DISABILITIES

The Air Carrier Access Act of 1986 requires all the country's airlines to accommodate the needs of passengers with disabilities, sweeping aside many restrictions that carriers once imposed. However, conditions are still far from perfect; numerous complaints are filed each year, and airlines have been fined for not complying with regulations.

Before you fly, know just what you can expect—even demand—from a carrier, and what recourse you have if an airline violates the provisions of the law. (See "Access for disabled travelers," in the Reference Section.)

Should you experience any accessibility problems while flying, you can complain to the DOT. Get complaint forms at *www.dot.gov/airconsumer/complaints1.htm* (this requires that Adobe Acrobat Reader be installed on your computer; you can download it for free from the Adobe web site). Also see the box earlier in this chapter for other DOT complaint channels.

CHILD SAFETY ALOFT

Car seats aren't just for cars

Acceptable safety seats. Look for a label that reads, "This restraint is certified for use in motor vehicles and aircraft." A safety seat no wider than 16 inches should fit in most coach seats. If wider than 16 inches, it's unlikely to fit properly, even with the airline-seat armrests lifted.

Unacceptable seats. Neither booster seats (backless platforms with no internal harness to restrain the child) nor seatless vest or harness systems are allowed. Although approved for autos, these don't work well in aircraft because airline seats, unlike automobile seats, tend to fold forward in a crash. In the U.S., supplemental lap restraints–"belly belts"–are banned from use in both cars and planes.

Seat placement. A child safety seat must be placed in a window seat so it won't block an escape path in the event of an emergency. (It may not be placed in an emergency exit row.) Firmly push the seat into the airplane seat cushions and fasten the aircraft seat belt around the safety seat as tightly as possible. Be sure that neither the plane seat belt nor the child-seat harness are twisted.

Who needs a safety seat? The FAA recommends that children weighing under 20 pounds be placed in a rear-facing child seat (facing the airplane's seat back) and that kids from 20 to 40 pounds use a forward-facing model. Children over 40 pounds may safely use the standard lap belt on all airline seats.

AIRLINES

CHAPTER 12

Good Deals on Airfare

Although air travel has become a little

less convenient, the upside is that

there are more good deals available.

■

Airfare can gobble a big chunk of your travel budget. So you need a strategy to get the most air miles for your dollar. We'll help you understand "airlinese," find flying bargains—and avoid ticket tactics not worth the risk.

DECODING AIRLINE LINGO

To find the best deal on the flight you want, know the terms.

Nonstop. The plane makes no stops between its departure city and its destination city: one takeoff, one landing.

Direct. Frequently mistaken for nonstop, "direct" just means you don't change planes. But you will make a stop or stops, which can add anywhere from 30 minutes to two hours to your travel time.

Connection. More common than a direct flight is a connecting flight, which means changing planes, usually at a "hub" city, where thousands of other travelers are also scurrying to make connections. Be wary of booking a flight with a very tight connection (less than one hour). Today's airport delays and complicated security procedures demand that you give yourself plenty of time to get from point A to point B—and get your luggage on the plane with you.

Layover. If the airline can't get you on a connecting flight in a certain amount of time (generally under two hours), you'll have a layover, meaning you sit in the terminal until the next scheduled departure to your destination. Or, if you arrive too late for your connecting flight, you may have an overnight layover—at your own expense.

Hub. As more airlines have turned to short-hop trips and connecting flights to fill planes and boost profits, hubs have grown in importance. Each airline has its own hub cities, where it concentrates its flight connections to maximize passenger capacity. (See "Whose hub is it anyway?" this chapter.)

Full fare. Also called an "unrestricted" fare, this is the top ticket price, the standard that airlines use to make discount claims. Leisure travelers rarely pay full fare, since they can book ahead to meet the advance purchase restrictions. Business travelers are often stuck with full fare, because of last-minute booking or not staying over a Saturday night.

Discount fare. Also called a "restricted" fare (because it entails numerous restrictions), the term discount fare covers any number of sale fares that the airline offers travelers who can book ahead and meet such requirements as length of stay and day of departure. These are the sale fares airlines advertise in newspapers and on TV.

Excursion. The lowest fares major airlines offer on a given domestic route, these are also known by the names Super Saver or Max Saver.

Apex. Sometimes called Super Apex, this is the cheapest economy excursion fare on an international flight.

Economy/coach class. This class, accounting for more than 75 percent of all seats on most scheduled flights, is the only one offering bargain airfares. For a good price, you sacrifice comfort (seats are smaller and more cramped than in luxury classes) as well as service (food and other amenities may be meager—even more meager now than in the past).

Business class. On airlines offering business class, you pay a premium (much more than coach, less than first class) for more comfortable seats and better service. As a member of a frequent-flyer program, you may be able to upgrade to business class on certain flights for a nominal number of miles—or even for free, if seats are available and you have "elite" status.

First class. Almost all regularly scheduled flights on U.S. airlines offer some first-class seating, from just four to eight seats (on some short-hop routes) to the entire front section of a 747 on transcontinental or international flights. Most first-class tickets are prohibitively expensive, but you can upgrade using frequent-flyer miles. Or you may occasionally be "bumped" to first class if economy/coach is overbooked—and you're in the right place at the right time.

Round-trip. The vast majority of airline tickets are round-trip, meaning the passenger flies from City A to City B and later returns from City B to City A. Virtually all discount tickets require round-trip travel.

One-way. One-way ticketing is possible, but it's usually very expensive, except on certain low-fare carriers. Those needing a one-way ticket (you're moving to a new city, say, or flying back home after having driven to a destination) often resort to a discount round-trip ticket, then discard the return portion.

Multileg. This itinerary involves three or more flight segments: from City A to City B, then from City B to City C, and finally from City C back to City A, all on different dates. Airfare depends both on the routes and the dates you fly.

Advance-purchase requirement. Discount fares generally entail an advance-purchase requirement—typically 14 or 21 days for domestic flights, 30 days for international flights. Many low-fare carriers do not require advance purchase.

Midweek departure. The lowest advertised discount fares often require a midweek departure: You must travel Tuesday (or sometimes Monday) through Thursday. Departing on Friday, Saturday, and Sunday (or, again, sometimes Monday) costs more.

Length of stay. All but the most costly unrestricted tickets have length-of-stay requirements. They vary by airline and route, but generally range from a minimum of three days to a maximum of 30 days—meaning you can't return sooner than three days or later than 30 days after your departure date.

Saturday-night stay. A stay-over in your destination of at least one Saturday night is almost standard on all discount fares. Business travelers, who prefer to depart and return during the work week, pay higher fares for that convenience.

Faced with a downturn in business travel, several major airlines have cut fares and eliminated the Saturday-night stayover on certain flights. United first abolished this restriction on some flights between Chicago and cities around the country. The move was matched by American, Continental, Delta, and Northwest. The requirement may be lifted on more routes; ask about the stayover when you book. Such tickets are round-trip only, nonrefundable, and require a seven-day advance purchase.

Nonrefundable. Read the fine print in airfare ads—most discount fares are nonrefundable. If you must cancel the trip, you won't get your money back. However, most discount tickets are *exchangeable*, so you can generally rebook at a later date. (You will pay a service fee; check the amount when you book the ticket.)

Code-share. With the recent alliances forged between the world's airlines, many more scheduled flights are, in airlinese, "code-share." Two (or occasionally three) airlines sell seats for the flight, but just one airline actually operates it. For example, a domestic airline may have code-share agreements with a variety of European partners. So if you book a trip from New York to Paris through the domestic line, it issues a ticket with its name and flight number. But you'll have to check in at the partner's terminal, because that carrier actually operates the flight and owns the plane. At check-in, you will see both the domestic and the European carriers' flight numbers posted on the departure board.

Code-share flights may not faze you—unless you fly a certain carrier based on its service and safety record. Always ask when booking an overseas flight whether it is a code-share flight and which partner operates the plane. If airlines do not volunteer this information,

AIRLINES

notify the DOT (see "Got a Gripe?," Chapter 11). Also check what each code-share partner is charging for the same flight; chances are that one of them is selling seats for less.

Under new DOT guidelines, U.S. carriers will now be required to show, at least every two years, that their international partners meet standards in such areas as plane maintenance, qualifications and training of the crew, and government oversight by the airline's country of origin. The FAA will review the audits for compliance.

Operator. The operator is the airline that runs the flight and, usually, issues the ticket. But in code-share situations or in some short-hop regional flights, the operator may be another airline altogether. For example, most major airlines have affiliate regional carriers that operate flights to secondary markets.

Interline ticketing. When one airline cannot get you where you want to go, your travel agent may book an interline ticket—one segment on one airline, another airline for the next segment. Quite common on overseas flights, an interline ticket may also be necessary on some domestic routes. Depending on the individual airline agreements, either your luggage will be transferred from one flight to the other or you'll need to claim and recheck your bags—allow enough time to clear airport security.

Equipment. Whenever you book a flight, whether through a travel agent, via the web, or directly with an airline, you should be able to identify the type of plane. Equipment may or may not matter to you. Some people prefer to avoid certain types of planes because of their crowded seat configurations. Or they may want to avoid smaller turbo-props (propeller- rather than jet-engine-driven planes) because of their safety records in certain weather conditions.

On-time performance. Depending on the airline and the route, on-time performance can range from 10 percent to 99 percent. A flight's on-time performance record should be available when you book. Some Internet low-fare finders and most airline web sites offer these stats. You can also check each airline's record for overall on-time arrival. DOT figures, updated monthly, are available at *www.dot.gov/airconsumer*. (Also see Chapter 10 for on-time flight tips.)

TIPS FOR GETTING THE BEST AIRFARE

Airlines use a complex pricing structure resulting in dozens of different ticket prices for seats on the same flight. Differences range from a few dollars to a few hundred. *Consumer Reports Travel Letter,* which regularly audits airfares, has these tips.

Act fast on sale fares. Advertised fares are extremely limited. An airline may offer no more than 10 percent of its coach/economy seats (or none on some flights) at the lowest advertised prices. Typically, the purchase window is quite small—some sales last just one day—although buyers usually have several months to complete travel at the sale prices.

Sale fares are usually advertised early in the week in major newspapers. You *can* get a head start by having a travel agent check the computer reservation system over the weekend, where all new fares, including some never advertised, show up first. A sale fare on a major airline, whatever type, is tough to beat. Here are some you're likely to see:

Straight-fare reductions. Domestic sale fares can run as much as 50 percent below regular coach-excursion fares (though 30 to 40 percent reductions are more common). Typical transcontinental sale fares hover around $350 to $400.

Free or low-cost companion tickets. Buy a ticket and a companion may travel with you for free, or at a discount of 30 to 50 percent.

A ticket to one destination yields a free ticket to another. In these more limited sales, you generally buy a long-haul ticket, such as one to Europe or Asia. The free ticket then covers a short-to-medium-haul domestic route.

Check another carrier. If you missed a good deal on one carrier, try another. They will almost always match sale fares, although the one that started the competition will probably have the most sale seats.

Travel at nonpeak times. Flights leaving very early in the morning, at midday, late at night, or during midweek will have far more sale seats available. If low fares are still sold out, try calling the reservation number after midnight or in the early morning, after the airlines reservation systems drop all nonconfirmed reservations. Airlines will also on occasion re-evaluate their pricing, then release some higher-priced seats at low prices.

Beat the clock. If you've missed an advertised sale's midnight deadline, get the airline's local reservation number (not the 800 number)in an earlier time zone. If it hasn't struck midnight in Los Angeles, for example, the sale's still on there.

Keep looking. Once you've paid, watch for even better fares. Nonrefundable tickets can almost always be reissued for a lower sale price. Despite the $50 or so per-ticket reissue charge, the price difference could still be worthwhile.

Get reductions for hubbing. On a few long-haul routes, some lines offer a lower fare if you connect through one of the line's hubs rather than taking a nonstop flight. However, hubbing can add considerable time to each one-way trip, and can pose the risk of a missed connection and lost baggage, and may mean more waiting in lines.

Mark your calendar. Leisure fares (as opposed to unrestricted fares) are highest from April through June, and are still fairly high from July through September.

The lowest fares are available between October and March. (This doesn't include so-called "Turkey Fares" that apply only on holidays.) If you're planning to travel in the winter or early spring, check prices in late October and early November—they often yield better prices than those heralded during the holiday season.

INTERNATIONAL FARE-SALE CALENDAR

Here are the times of year the airlines have more bargain seats available. If you can time your trip to match these travel windows, you're more apt to get a good deal.

DESTINATION	BARGAIN WINDOW
Europe	Late November through March
Caribbean	May through September
Asia	December through March
South America	Varies by destination
Australia	June through August

Track ticket prices. Enticed by ads for low fares? Make your own determinations about "sale" fares by tracking ticket prices for a few weeks in a selected market. You'll probably find that your results differ from the airline's ads.

Book before prices rise. When a fare for a given route drops by more than $50 in one week, the pendulum is probably about to swing back up, even by the following week. If fares and destinations fit long-term travel plans, consider booking multiple trips to lock in the low price.

Watch for hometown sales. Do you live near a major airline's hub city? Airlines may gear sales specifically to your hometown so they can fill seats, particularly for vacation destinations.

Monitor low-fare airlines. Keep abreast of low-fare airlines in the cities to and from which you travel. Frequently they will offer low fares as a way to entice new customers—or major airlines will reduce fares on competing routes to fend off the start-ups.

If your starting or destination city isn't served by a smaller airline, consider a nearby alternative airport. You may find welcome fare differences. (See Chapter 14 for more on smaller carriers.)

RISKIER TACTICS

Using loopholes in ticket-buying rules can cut costs, but does involve risks. And in a time of enhanced airport security, a questionable ticket could be a very big detriment.

Back-to-back tickets. Sometimes called a "nested" ticket, back-to-back ticketing lets travelers avoid the Saturday-night stay that the cheapest coach excursions normally require. (Back-to-back tickets still must comply with all the other restrictions.)

Here's how it works: Instead of buying one expensive round-trip ticket with no Saturday-night-stay requirement, travelers buy two cheap round-trip excursions, each of which does require a stay—one originating in their home city, the other originating in the destination city. They use the "going" portion of the first ticket to get to the destination and the "going" portion of the second ticket to return home. Since the two tickets are separate, the airline presumably can't tell how long the traveler stays at the destination.

Back-to-back tickets save money whenever the cheapest coach excursion is less than half the unrestricted round-trip fare. If airlines are vying for customers, the savings can be even larger.

Back-to-back tickets can save far more if used for two trips (both "return" coupons provide the second trip). The major limitation is that the traveler must typically take both trips within 30 days, the maximum stay allowed on many of the cheap excursions.

Airlines say that back-to-back tickets violate their rules, and have policed them through ticket audits. But passengers get around that barrier by buying the two tickets either on different airlines or from different travel agencies.

The best advice on this ploy is caution. Even if a traveler buys the two round-trip tickets on two different airlines, a violation is easy to spot. Not showing up for the return portion of a round-trip could be viewed as evidence of an intent to bypass airline ticket rules, and such no-shows would be easy to track. So rather than using the risky back-to-back maneuver, look for a flight on a smaller line that doesn't apply the onerous Saturday-night stay requirement.Or see if the requirement has been waived on some flights covering the route you want.

Hidden-city ploys. Some people have tried to save by overshooting their mark: A traveler headed from A to B buys a cheaper ticket

WHOSE HUB IS IT ANYWAY?

Making a connection with any of the major U.S. airlines? Here's where you'll probably change planes.

AIRLINE	HUBS
American	Dallas, Miami, St. Louis
America West	Columbus, Las Vegas, Phoenix
Continental	Cleveland, Houston, Newark (N.J.)
Delta	Atlanta, Cincinnati, Dallas
Northwest	Detroit, Memphis, Minneapolis/St. Paul
United	Chicago, Denver
US Airways	Charlotte, N.C., Pittsburgh

from A to C by way of B, then gets off the plane (or doesn't catch the connecting flight) at B, the real destination.

If hidden-city ticketing is detected, you or your travel agency may receive a bill for the difference between what you actually paid and the higher cost of the shorter flight. On round-trip tickets, your return space may also be canceled. And if you check in for the final destination of a through flight and get off at an intermediate stop, you could delay the flight several hours while the airline investigates the "loss" of one passenger. Basically, this tactic is too risky to be worthwhile—especially when passenger scrutiny is so intense and ticket violations may be taken very seriously. And you can't check luggage—your bags will automatically be directed to the ticket's final destination.

Frequent-flyer coupons. An entire underground industry has developed to broker frequent-flyer awards, which purchasers primarily use for upgrades. A broker buys the award from a frequent flyer to sell to someone else at a profit. If you see a discount agency's newspaper ad for "Business and First Class, up to 70 percent off," figure they're selling frequent-flyer awards.

Buying such an award isn't illegal, but it's dicey. Airlines are scrutinizing frequent-flyer awards more carefully; an award purchased from a broker may not be honored. Furthermore, airlines allot so few premium-class seats for frequent-flyer travel that you'll have a tough time using any coupon you buy. Our advice: Don't buy someone else's coupons unless you enjoy taking financial risks.

CHAPTER 13

Finding Discount Tickets

The web offers an increasing number of

airline deals. Consolidators—many with

web sites—are another source.

━━━━━━━━━━━━━━━━ ■ ━━━━━━━━━━━━━━━━

The best resource for low airfares today may be the web. But comparison shop, visiting individual airline sites as well as large travel sites, to get both the best fare and the most sensible route. (See Part Two for advice on using the web to the best advantage for airline tickets and other travel services.) In your surfing, you will probably come across sites for consolidators, another inexpensive fare outlet.

THE DISCOUNT TICKET MART

Sometimes even the lowest advertised fares don't fill planes, especially when air travel is down. But rather than offer discounts openly—and invite retaliatory cuts from competitors—many airlines choose to unload seats through other channels.

Consolidators. These specialized travel agencies have contracts with one or more airlines to distribute discount tickets. Some deal directly with the public, while others are strictly wholesalers, selling their airline tickets only through other travel agencies.

Discount agencies. These sell consolidator tickets (or other discounted travel services) to the public. Many have their own consolidation contracts with some airlines, but also buy other airlines' tickets from wholesalers. They may also specialize in a single type of travel service—air, cruises, or hotels. To find a discount agency, check newspaper travel sections for small, all-print ads with listings of discount airfares.

Full-service travel agencies. Besides selling a broad range of travel services to the public, these agencies also counsel clients and provide other customer services. Any full-service agency can obtain consolidator tickets for clients. However, some agents prefer not to—consolidator tickets aren't in the travel-agency computer-reservation systems, require extra work, and may pay a smaller commission than advertised-fare tickets.

WHAT'S THE FARE?

Consolidators handle discount tickets in two ways:

Net fares. Some consolidators contract with an airline to buy tickets at a specified net rate for each route. That price remains fixed even when the airline's advertised fares change. Consolidators add their markup, then sell to the public or other agencies. A net-fare ticket normally shows no dollar figure in the "fare" box. Such tickets may not earn frequent-flyer mileage credit, and can't be upgraded with a frequent-flyer award. And during airline price competitions, the airline's advertised fares may drop below net fares.

Overrides. Other consolidators negotiate an override—an agreement to sell only that airline's tickets on certain routes—in return for a larger commission. They can then sell these tickets for less. As fares change, prices for those tickets fluctuate. The airline's advertised fare usually appears in the "fare" box. Such tickets may earn frequent-flyer mileage and be eligible for a frequent-flyer-award upgrade.

Consolidators rarely mention airline names in ads or promotions. But when you call (or check the consolidator's web site) about specific fares and schedules, names are available.

AIRLINES

HOW MUCH DO YOU SAVE?

Savings depend on where you go, and when.

International. The biggest consolidator discounts arise on tickets to Asia, Europe, and Latin America—typically 20 to 30 percent off list, sometimes more.

Governments must still approve fares on many international routes, so airlines prefer to discount through consolidators instead of frequently changing their list prices.

In the summer, when the airlines' advertised fares to Europe are nearly double the winter ones, consolidators provide their best European deals—like 30 percent off. However, when carriers are vying for passengers, advertised fares may drop below typical consolidator prices. And in the off-season, even the best consolidator prices are no lower than the airline's regular fares.

Advertised fares to Asia and Latin America vary little by season, so discounts tend to be consistent year-round.

Domestic. With deregulation, U.S. airlines are free to adjust prices as often and as fast as they want. Those kinds of pricing adjustments have eliminated much of the need for back-door discounting through consolidators, meaning the best advertised fares—the big airlines' cheapest coach excursions and smaller airlines' regular rates—are almost always below the best consolidator prices, especially during a fare war.

FRONT-CABIN DISCOUNTS

Whereas the discount market focuses mainly on coach/economy tickets, some agencies handle business and first class. Even when you find a premium-seat discount, however, it's usually no more than 20 percent, and often less. That may represent a sizable dollar savings but seldom brings the premium-ticket cost even close to low coach/economy prices.

Beware: An agency advertising large business- and first-class discounts may actually be a coupon broker that resells frequent-flyer awards, very different from a discount ticket. This "deal" poses real risks—like not being able to use your ticket.

LIMITATIONS AND RISKS

Consolidator tickets do have certain drawbacks.

Limitations. Consolidator tickets have some restrictions—some acceptable, others that might ask too much of even the most bargain-hungry traveler.

They're inflexible. If your flight is canceled or delayed, the airline isn't obligated to transfer you to another airline (though occasionally they may do so). And you can get a refund only through the discount agency—if at all.

They often entail trade-offs. You may have to fly an airline you dislike, follow an inconvenient schedule, or take an indirect route with extra stops. You may not receive frequent-flyer mileage, be allowed to reserve a seat, or be eligible for special meals.

Choices may be limited. You might hear that only undesirable airlines sell tickets through consolidators, but many of the world's top airlines do it—at least some of the time. Bottom-dollar transatlantic tickets might be scheduled on minor airlines, but you can usually fly a major line for only a bit more. Specify which airlines you prefer—or refuse to fly—when you check prices.

Risks. Consolidator tickets have a reputation for being risky, but the risk is only in buying the ticket; too many discount agencies engage in sloppy or dishonest practices, such as:

Bait-and-switch tactics. Most common among discount agencies, these include not being able to deliver tickets for promised fares or highlighting fares based on a low figure that applies to only a tiny number of seats.

Deceptive advertising. Agencies sometimes advertise list-price charter fares as discounts, deceptive because while charter fares are usually lower than major-airline fares, they're certainly not discounted. Charters are cheaper for good reasons: They're usually jammed; they fly less frequently than scheduled-airline flights; check-in is much more difficult; and an equipment problem can cause long delays, or even a cancellation.

Ticket ownership. The biggest risk to consumers is the fact that consolidators don't own the tickets at the time of sale. The assumption is that consolidators buy seats cheaply in bulk for resale; in truth, they almost never actually buy and take title to a ticket until they have a customer's money in hand.

After receiving payment, a consolidator may find that the airline has no more seats at the promised fare. The consolidator must then ask the customer for more money (for a seat at a higher fare), switch airlines, or put the customer on a waitlist (perhaps without notification) rather than giving a firm reservation. Or a consolidator who's short on cash may keep the customer's money and wait until the last minute to buy the ticket—at best delaying delivery, at worst failing to provide the promised flight at the agreed-to price.

BUYING YOUR TICKET

The safest way to buy a consolidator ticket is through a regular full-service travel agency. If anything goes wrong, you can lean on the agency for a fix. Buying directly from a discount agency saves money by cutting the commission. But be careful.

Do your homework. Determine the major lines' lowest advertised fare to your destination for your specific travel dates. Check on the web and look into charter fares.

Comparison shop. Check prices among several discount agencies, making sure a fare covers your itinerary. For each quote, find out about any limitations, such as required stops or connections.

Weigh trade-offs. If a consolidator ticket yields no frequent-flyer credit, see if the discount is big enough to offset the value of that lost credit (figure about two cents per mile).

Think local. Deal with a discount agency in or near your home city. If anything goes wrong, you have convenient access to small-claims court for redress.

Charge it. Buy with a credit card. If you don't get your ticket in good time or if something's wrong with it, you can get your money back through a chargeback (bill-cancellation) claim.

CHAPTER 14

Smaller Airlines and Charters

Both these airfare options can offer savings,

but may also involve limitations and trade-offs.

———————————————— ■ ————————————————

Smaller airlines—often called low-fare airlines and charter carriers may offer lower prices and fewer restrictions than the major U.S. carriers. Although each also has its weak points, either one might work for travelers seeking a good bargain above all else.

GETTING THE BEST FROM SMALLER AIRLINES

A *Consumer Reports Travel Letter* analysis of smaller carriers around the country showed that these airlines can offer lower fares and more personalized service. (However, lower fares are not an absolute given.) But you might have to make some trade-offs, due to limited flight frequency and the line's inability to cope with delays and cancellations. Here's a small-carrier strategy:

Research the fare. When a small carrier starts serving an airport or flying a specific route, larger carriers will match their fares to keep customers from defecting. So you don't actually have to fly a smaller line to benefit; the competitive presence alone can drive down costs. (The reverse is also true: Where no small carriers fly, prices remain high.)

But majors are often selective in duplicating lower prices. For example, if the small carrier has a 10 a.m. departure, the larger carrier may drop its price at that time—but keep it high on an afternoon flight when the smaller line may not be competing. So check a number of flight prices before booking.

Evaluate the location. Many smaller airlines operate into and out of less-congested secondary airports, frequently a plus. But be sure the airport is really convenient for you. You will probably face delays at any airport due to new safety precautions; you don't want to face a long trip to the airport as well.

See about booking (and rebooking) ease. Most small airlines we surveyed offer electronic tickets (either optional or mandatory), and accept bookings via their own web site. However, with current airport security conditions, we do not recommend electronic tickets, since they can cause questions and delays at check-in (see Chapter 10). Many, but not all, can also be booked through the large independent travel web sites, such as Expedia and Travelocity. And several are in the major computer reservations systems used by travel agents.

A majority also provide toll-free 24-hour service lines. But if your chosen line doesn't, and you need to change a ticket—particularly on the road—you may not be able to reach anyone. Ask in advance to head off any problems.

Consider the delay potential. Many smaller carriers lack the crew and aircraft resources to address, for example, mid-schedule repairs to an aircraft. (In the past, this very situation has caused some dramatic delays.) If the disadvantage of a possible delay outweighs the smaller carrier advantages of a potentially lower fare or a less-congested airport, you might prefer a major carrier.

But do some research before you decide. Ask about interline agreements, which mean other airlines will honor your ticket if there's a long delay. And check a small airline's timetable (available at airport ticket counters, ticket offices, or online) for the number of daily flights offered on your selected route. No interline agreements and/or fewer than three flights per day on your route? That adds up to a bigger chance of being unable to get another flight if yours is delayed or canceled.

Assess extras and service. Ask about food service when you book. Even major airlines are cutting back on in-flight meals, and edibles on a smaller line may be no more than drinks and chips. If the menu sounds sparse, you may want to brownbag it—but be prepared to have your homemade in-flight meal examined by airport security.

Many lines offer some version of business class or first class, and most also have assigned seats (rather than that boarding scramble). Seat pitch—the front-to-rear spacing of seats—ranges from a fairly roomy 37 inches to tight 29 inches.

Frequent-flyer programs vary with smaller carriers. While some offer low earning thresholds, redemption opportunities are limited by the airline's own size and scope. Several smaller airlines have signed agreements with larger programs run by major and foreign airlines.

Deal with the safety question. The number of years in business and the average age of the fleet are two criteria that consumers use when choosing a small carrier. Unfortunately, these two may be in opposition: An older line may also have an older fleet. However, while a newer fleet may appeal, industry experts advise that fleet age is less important than sound maintenances procedures.

And although some small airlines have run afoul of government regulators, this doesn't mean that flying a smaller carrier is unsafe. All U.S. airlines must remain certified by the FAA, which says the same standards apply to all carriers regardless of size.

Protect yourself. A number of small carriers have gone belly-up. So charge your tickets; refunds can be easier.

FLYING A CHARTER

Charter airlines operate on select routes and schedules that are "chartered" by tour operators, and most don't sell their tickets directly to the public. The travel industry terms "charter" as the opposite of "scheduled." But charter airlines, just like the conventional ones, must operate on a schedule as best they can. "Wholesale" is a more-accurate term for charter lines, while those operators that sell directly to the public are "retail" lines.

Some small airlines also operate what amounts to scheduled ser-vice under charter rules—starting up a charter line requires less red tape than launching a scheduled line. And a few former charter lines (such as Germany's LTU) still operate like charters, although they now hold scheduled-line certificates.

The main distinction between a charter flight and a flight on a scheduled airline is a legal one. With a charter, the customer's con-tract is with a tour operator, not an airline—and the operator is financially responsible for getting passengers to the destination and back. The tour operator charters planes and crews from one or more airlines that actually operate the flights.

When things go well, you seldom notice the distinction between the two types of flights. But when a problem arises with a charter, the tour operator must solve it—finding a substitute airline, for example. When travelers are left stranded, it's usually because a tour operator went bust and couldn't pay an airline for the return trips.

SMALL AIRLINES THAT FLY INTERNATIONALLY

AIRLINE	HOME BASE	DAILY FLIGHTS	ROUTES
Aeropostal	Caracas, Venezuela	64	South America, Caribbean, Florida
buzz	London	64	Western European cities
easyJet	London	115	U.K., Switzerland, Spain, France, Greece
Freedom Air International	Auckland	8	New Zealand, Australia
Go	London	226*	Western Europe
LAPA	Buenos Aires	300	Argentina, Uruguay
Ryanair	Dublin	235	Western European cities
Skymark Airlines	Tokyo	12	Major Japanese cities
Virgin Express	Brussels	70*	Western European cities

Source: CRTL, May 2000   * Weekly

SMALL AIRLINES THAT FLY IN THE U.S.

AIRLINE	HOME BASE	DAILY FLIGHTS	ROUTES
AirTran Airways	Orlando	324	East Coast, Fla., some Midwest cities
American Trans Air	Indianapolis	140	East Coast, Ireland, L.A., S.F., Hawaii
Delta Express	Orlando	190	East Coast, Fla., some Midwest cities
Frontier	Denver	111	Midwest, West Coast, N.Y., Orlando
JetBlue	Kew Gardens, N.Y.	94	N.Y., Fla., D.C., Denver, Salt Lake City, California, Seattle
National	Las Vegas	54	N.Y., Miami, Dallas, Chicago, Phila., L.A., S.F., Las Vegas, D.C., Newark
Southwest	Dallas	2,700	Nationwide
Spirit	Miramar, Fla.	80	N.Y., N.J., Detroit, Fla., San Juan, L.A., Oakland, Chicago, Myrtle Beach, S.C.
Sun Country	Mendota Hts, Minn.	20	Major U.S. cities, Mexico, Caribbean
Vanguard	Kansas City, Mo.	60	Major U.S. cities

Source: CRTL

AIRLINES

Charter pluses. Here are the good things about charters.

The right price. A charter is usually cheaper than a scheduled line for any given trip. Even when a scheduled line seems to have a price advantage, it may offer just a few seats at the advertised fare, whereas most charters sell all their seats at the same low price.

Fewer restrictions. Charter tickets have fewer restrictions than the cheapest tickets on the major airlines. The minimum advance-purchase period usually depends on how long it takes to complete the paperwork, and the minimum stay depends on how often the charter line flies a particular route. A few charter operators do, however, offer restricted fares (advance-purchase or minimum-stay) at slightly lower prices than their walk-up fares. And some impose a maximum-stay limit on their lowest fares.

A better route. Because charters may operate where regularly scheduled airlines don't, a charter flight may be the only way to fly between certain cities without making either a stop or a plane change at a hub airport.

A possible premium option. A few charter lines offer optional seats (and often food service) equal to what you'd find in business class. While a charter's premium seat is more expensive than one of its economy seats, it is still much less expensive (about 60 percent less) than a business- or first-class seat on a scheduled line.

Charter minuses. But be aware of the disadvantages, too.

Not always cheaper. Within the U.S., smaller scheduled airlines increasingly match or beat charter prices. Even major scheduled lines may offer lower prices during fare wars. And the major lines' advertised winter fares to Europe are usually low enough to discourage charter competition in that season. Discount tickets bought on the web or from consolidators often undercut charter fares as well. Compare before you book.

Less-frequent flights. Many charter programs operate only one weekly "back-to-back" trip: The plane loads up with vacationers, ferries them to their destination, and picks up the previous week's group for the trip home. Unless the flight days correspond with the beginning and end of your vacation, a charter could cut away several days at your destination. Some programs, however, offer more frequent service. Even on weekly programs, you can usually stay additional weeks (sometimes for an additional charge).

Odd schedules and potential delays. Charter carriers own fewer planes, so schedules are tight and flights may arrive or depart at odd hours. Any significant delay of a single flight can throw a charter line's schedule out of whack for days.

Difficulty rescheduling. If your flight is canceled or significantly delayed, the tour operator is the only one who can reschedule. Charter airlines don't have "interline" agreements with each other or with scheduled lines, so a charter line can't sign your ticket over to another line. Nor will you be able to switch flights.

Extreme crowding. Unless you book a premium seat, a charter virtually guarantees a cramped trip. Seating on charter flights isn't necessarily worse than on a scheduled flight, but it's hardly ever better.

Most charter flights operate close to full; one reason charters are relatively cheap is that each flight is nearly 100 percent booked, rather than the 70 percent or so on scheduled airlines.

Long check-in lines. Charter lines normally use other airlines or independent airport-service organizations to handle check-in, boarding, and baggage claim. Many apparently skimp on those services, judging by the three-hour check-in lines often seen for charter flights. Under today's travel conditions, you'd be well advised to get arrive at the airport very early. Confirm with your charter operator how much time you will need.

No computer listings. Charters are not listed in the computer reservation system used by agents. So some travel agents dislike booking charters because of the extra work required.

Tough refunds. If you must cancel a flight, you may have a hard time getting a refund, and your ticket may not be as easily "exchangeable" (rebookable for a fee) as a coach/economy excursion ticket on a scheduled line. Ask about refunds and exchanges any time you consider a charter. If a ticket isn't exchangeable, you can protect yourself with trip-interruption insurance. But factor in the cost of that insurance when you compare ticket prices (see Chapter 4 for insurance details).

AIRLINES

CHAPTER 15

Cashing in on Special Fares

Special reduced fares are available for seniors,

children, or someone headed to a relative's funeral.

————————————————— ■ —————————————————

Reduced fares are sometimes granted to people because of their status—their age or a bereavement. Some of these fares cut a percentage off a fare available to anybody. Others are priced independently, and may or may not be good deals, depending on other alternatives.

Be prepared to prove your eligibility when you buy your ticket and again when you travel: You'll need proof of age for senior, child, and youth fares, an official school ID to get a student fare, and a funeral or death notice or some equivalent documentation to qualify for a "compassionate" fare. Since status fares are "published," you can buy tickets from an airline or through a travel agency.

DEALS FOR SENIORS

Airlines offer older travelers a variety of discounts. In most cases, the minimum age for eligibility is 62, although some programs set it at 65.

Senior coupons. A qualifying senior can buy a round-trip to anywhere in the lower 48 states (some lines include adjacent points in Canada and the Caribbean) for no more than $338. (For a long-haul flight, that can be less than even the best sale fares.) You can fly to Alaska or Hawaii for two coupons each way (one coupon to Alaska on United). However, there are no senior coupons for travel to Europe, Asia, or other overseas destinations. Coupons are sold in groups of four.

The "Special Fares Roundup" on the following page shows the seven major U.S. airlines that sell senior coupons and their prices (as of late 2001 and subject to change). Each coupon is good for a one-way trip. Connecting flights are permitted on a single coupon, as long as you don't stop over at a connection point. Each traveler must have a separate coupon book—a couple can't use one four-coupon book to take a single round-trip together.

The pros. For a confirmed seat, you must book at least 14 days in advance, but you can also travel standby. Since round-trip travel isn't required, there's no minimum-stay requirement. Senior coupons also earn frequent-flier miles.

The cons. Senior coupons are valid for only a year after they're issued. So if you can't take at least two round-trips a year, coupons are not a good deal. As with most promotional fares, seats are limited.

The payoff. Coupons are a good deal whenever the cheapest alternative round-trip airfare exceeds the coupon cost ($298 to $338, depending on the airline), almost always the case on long-haul routes and often true for shorter trips. But always check the low-fare competition before buying coupons.

Senior clubs. One major airline still runs a senior club—United has Silver Wings Plus. Open to travelers age 55 and over, this club offers a variety of deals rather than a standard schedule of benefits. Their zoned fares generally beat even good sale fares and, for all but the longest trips, win out over senior coupons, too. Membership costs $75 for two years or $225 for lifetime. Members must also pay an extra fee ($25 to $50) to take advantage of some promotions. Call 800 720-1765 for more information, or check the web site at *www.silverwingsplus.com.*

Senior discount. All the lines listed in the special fares table except Southwest (and many carriers not listed) give a 10 percent senior discount on virtually any published fare for travel in North America, from the cheapest coach/economy excursions (including some short-term sale fares) up to first class. All except Midwest Express and

SPECIAL FARES ROUNDUP

Special fares on North American airlines, as of late 2001.

AIRLINE	SENIOR	YOUTH/ STUDENT	CHILD	COMPASSIONATE DISCOUNT
Alaska	10% off some fares	–	–	50%
America West	10% off/selected routes; $596 for 4 coupons	–	Reductions from full fare only	50%
American	10% off; $676 for 4 coupons	Selected routes	Selected routes	Varies
American Trans Air	10% off	–	–	–
Canadian	10% off/selected routes	–	–	50%
Continental	10% off; $596 for 4 coupons	Published discount on some routes	–	50%; sometimes lower
Delta	10% off; $676 for 4 coupons	Discount coupons on selected routes	–	50%; sometimes lower
Midwest Express	10% off	Discounted youth fares	–	Varies
Northwest	10% off; $676 for 4 coupons	–	–	Varies
Southwest	Published discount on some routes	Under 21 discount fare	Under 21 discount fare	–
United	10% off; $628 for 4 coupons	–	–	Varies
US Airways	10% off; some published senior fares $676 for 4 coupons	–	–	Varies

Senior discount rates for minimum age 62, on most airlines also apply to companion of any age. Most airlines figure compassionate rates from walk-up coach/economy fares, often required to be round-trip; others waive advance-purchase restriction for 7-day excursion fare or make ad hoc adjustments. Percentage can vary slightly with the route.

Child rates for children under two with a government-approved safety seat and accompanied by an adult are 50% of full adult fare. Always ask when booking.

Southwest give the same reduction to a companion of any age following the same itinerary as that of the qualified senior.

The 10 percent discount is a fall-back deal when you can't find anything better. On short-haul coach excursion tickets and sale-priced tickets, it doesn't amount to much. And coupons are usually a better deal for a long-haul trip.

Frequent-flyer rules are generally the same as those for the any-age fare from which the senior discount is to be deducted.

Southwest publishes separate fares for seniors age 65 or over, usually with reductions based on the line's unrestricted coach fares. Seniors traveling on Southwest are often better off buying a 21-day advance-purchase ticket at the any-age fare and forgetting about the discount.

Fares to Europe. Seniors (minimum age 62) headed to Europe generally get the same 10 percent reduction they get within North America. Some airlines are more generous, but others offer no senior discounts at all—so shop around before booking. And although the reduction applies to most fares, it may not apply to all sale deals; check with individual airlines for particulars.

DEALS FOR KIDS AND TEENS

Infants. Those under age two may occupy a half-fare reserved seat on most airlines, if seated in a government-approved child safety seat provided by the adult traveling companion. Alternatively, an infant can travel free and can occupy an empty seat, if available. (On a full plane, an accompanying adult would be required to hold the child throughout the flight.) As a third option, an adult without a safety seat can reserve a seat for the infant, but only at an adult fare. (For safe flight information for children, see Chapter 11.)

The half-price infant reduction applies to most published adult fares, including the cheapest 21-day advance-purchase excursions. However, the exclusions include senior-discount trips, military fares, and tour-package fares. Each traveling adult may purchase up to two half-price infant tickets, but seats are limited and may not be available on all flights. Airline ticket agents don't always mention the half-price option—so be sure to ask.

On most international flights, children under age two without a reservation pay 10 percent of the accompanying adult's fare. Travelers who want a confirmed seat for an infant must buy a child's ticket, typically 50 to 75 percent of the adult fare.

Children. Deals for children over the age of two are sparse. Some airlines publish children's fares on a few routes, though these fares are often based on reductions from full-fare coach or premium class and frequently cost more than an any-age coach excursion ticket. Otherwise, you're pretty much stuck with buying adult tickets for children age two and older. Of course, they can take advantage of other deals—the 10 percent companion discount when accompanying a qualifying senior or the free-companion promotions that airlines often run. On most international flights, children ages two to 11 pay 50 to 75 percent of the adult fare (including economy excursion fares).

Youth/students. There aren't many deals around for this group. Certain airlines, such as American, offer web bargains for students. Check the carrier's home page for a "Specials" listing. And some U.S. and European airlines publish separate youth fares to Europe for travelers age 12 to 24. Typically, travelers can make reservations only within 72 hours of departure; the return portion of the round-trip is left open, with the same 72-hour reservation limit, but with a maximum stay of up to a year. Seats are restricted and may have blackout dates. These fares may be no cheaper than discount (consolidator) tickets available to people of any age—compare before you buy.

COMPASSIONATE FARES

Air tickets booked at the last minute are normally very expensive. But most major airlines offer compassionate (or bereavement) fares. The most-common formula is 50 percent off the lowest last-minute fare (usually that means unrestricted coach), which can still be quite a bit higher than the lowest restricted round-trip coach fare. A few airlines depart from that policy, and a few treat compassionate fares as individual cases.

On international routes, several overseas airlines may waive the advance-purchase restriction on an economy excursion ticket.

Each airline has its own rules about the qualifying circumstances for compassionate fares. All airlines typically grant the fare for attendance at a relative's funeral. Only some allow it for severe illness or imminent death. Airlines differ in how distant a family connection can qualify. If the first airline you try turns you down, try another. All lines require proof of the relative's death—either a photocopy of a death certificate or the phone number of the funeral home.

CHAPTER 16

Guidelines for Frequent Flyers

Even if you fly just once or twice a year, joining an

airline frequent-flyer program can pay off. But terms

and conditions have become more complicated.

■

The frequent-flyer program, which began over 20 years ago as the brainchild of American Airlines, has evolved into an entire industry, with some 67 million members. And these days you have more ways than ever to redeem miles—for travel, upgrades, and merchandise.

But airline partnerships are shifting. In 2001, American acquired bankrupt TWA, and United's proposed merger with US Airways was rejected by the U.S. Department of Justice. And award terms are changing. You need a clear strategy to get the most mileage from your miles.

EARNING (AND BUYING) OPPORTUNITIES

When the program first began, the only way to rack up miles was to take a flight. All that has changed.

On-the-ground earning. Consumers can now acquire miles through everything from purchasing groceries to refinancing a home. Overall, at least 40 percent of frequent-flyer miles are obtained without consumers leaving the ground. Mileage-linked credit cards, telephone service, car rentals, and hotel stays account for most of these nonflight miles.

Mile marts. Shopping, particularly via the Internet, is also creating new opportunities. Some carriers currently have links to mileage-earning online shopping malls. Retail web sites such as Clickrewards.com bestow miles on shoppers for buying merchandise. (Other Internet benefits are a mileage bonus for booking an airline ticket online or for getting your account updates by e-mail.)

Mileage for sale. Travelers now can also buy miles for awards on Air Canada, Alaska, Continental, Delta, and United. Carriers typically limit how many miles travelers can purchase, and they may also restrict where the miles can be applied. For example, Delta will let flyers buy up to 20,000 miles (at $25 per 1,000-mile increment, the upper end of what you should pay) for award travel only within the U.S. and Canada. Other airlines limit mileage purchases to a percentage (typically 10 percent) of the award mileage cost; United limits purchases to 15,000 miles per year.

America West, Continental, Delta, and Northwest also put miles up for sale through Miles4sale.com. But this mileage-selling scheme is a bad value for consumers. Purchased miles are routed into a buyer's (or gift recipient's) frequent-flyer account, and so are subject to the same restrictions and blackout dates. And Miles4sale.com charges from 0.036 to 0.04 cents per mile, depending on the quantity purchased—almost double *Consumer Reports Travel Letter's* recommended 2-cents-per-mile valuation. With a price of $719.80 for 20,000 miles, this tactic becomes an expensive way to amass enough miles for a "free" frequent-flyer award.

American's popular Plan AAhead Awards can be bought with earned miles plus a cash copayment. Domestic coach awards cost 20,000 miles plus $125; 15,000 miles plus $225; or 10,000 miles plus $295, with other combinations available for Hawaii, the Caribbean, and Europe. With these transactions, the going rate for the miles is 0.019 cents to 0.025 cents a mile.

Prefer not to buy your miles? Be on the lookout for reduced-mileage award promotions, featured by some airlines on some routes. You may get a circular in your monthly program update. With the declines in air travel, more of these opportunities have become available. Call your carrier to check.

Southwest has a different program structure: Travelers earn one free round-trip ticket for every eight round-trip flights taken within one year. Members can earn double credit by booking online—which amounts to a free ticket after just four round trips.

THE GLOBAL ALLIANCES

Big global alliances are still going strong, and may offer extra mileage-earning opportunities—as long as you research the restrictions.

Who belongs to what. The oneworld alliance, with American as its U.S. representative, also knits together British Airways, Cathay Pacific, Aer Lingus, Qantas, Finnair, Iberia, and Lanchile, as well as smaller affiliates.

Star Alliance, anchored in the U.S. by United, also claims Air Canada, Air New Zealand, Austrian Airlines, Lufthansa, Mexicana, SAS, and Singapore Airlines, among others.

Now a new alliance has been created: SkyTeam, with Delta as its U.S. carrier, counts Aero Mexico, Air France, Korean Air and Czech Airlines as members.

Star is the strongest global alliance because it has the most members (15 carriers), while oneworld comes in second with eight. SkyTeam is weaker with five members, but is expanding.

Alliance terms. The big alliances operate similarly. Mileage earned on any member flight can be credited to the frequent-flyer account you choose, and those miles count toward elite status. Elite flyers are recognized by all member airlines, with perks like preferential boarding, mileage bonuses, and access to airport lounges. But even for elite flyers, security and boarding is still time-consuming, and some airport lounges have been closed.

Each alliance has its restrictions, however, and it's important to know what will be imposed. For example, oneworld flyers can't earn

AAdvantage miles on transatlantic flights operated by British Airways. Star travelers may not earn mileage on some deeply discounted or consolidator tickets. And only the highest-level SkyTeam flyers (those with Elite Plus ranking, equivalent to Delta's platinum status) will enjoy reciprocal lounge benefits.

GETTING WHAT'S DUE

Take steps to secure the correct credits and preserve your miles.

Give your number when reserving. Be sure the agent gets your account number when you book the flight. Check-in can be so hectic, you might forget. If you use a travel agent, make sure all your numbers are coded into the computer when making reservations.

Look over your statement. Your account should be credited for a flight in the next statement or two, although sometimes it takes longer. (If you flew a partner airline, be extra vigilant.) Always keep your boarding passes and, if miles don't show up on your statement after two or three months, call customer service.

Confirm expiration policies. Be sure you'll be able to rack up enough mileage to claim an award before some miles expire. ("Earning miles," this chapter, lists expiration policies.)

COMPARING MILEAGE PLANS

AIRLINE	MIN. MILES PER TRIP	EXPIRES (if no acct. activity)	BUSINESS-CLASS BONUS	FIRST-CLASS BONUS
Alaska	500	3 years	25%	50%
America West	500	3 years	–	50
American	500	3 years	25	50
Continental	500	None.	50	50
Delta	500	3 years	25	50
Northwest	500	3 years	50	50
Southwest	1 credit	1 year (renew for fee)	–	–
United	500	3 years	25	50
US Airways	500	3 years	50	50

CLAIMING YOUR REWARDS

Once you've accrued all those miles by flying and/or buying, you have more ways than ever to redeem them, such as cashing them in for the increasingly available merchandise and nontravel awards. But most travelers aim for a free flight or upgrade.

Be flexible. When booking award travel, have several dates and times. Be aware of blackout dates—days you cannot fly on an award ticket—typically around major holidays and on summer flights to Europe.

Determine restrictions. For example, US Airways has added a Saturday-night stay requirement to all standard domestic awards.

Investigate mileage add-ons. You may be able to put together a better package by adding some purchased miles or paying part of your fare in cash.

Look at premium awards. Typically costing twice as much as standard benefits, these awards carry no blackout dates or other restrictions, so they do minimize hassles. Still, since they cost so many miles, they may not always be the best value. (However, some airlines, such as American, offer a miles-plus-cash deal for premium seats, too.)

Scout around. A few airlines are making it easier to book award seats. American, Continental, and Delta have begun listing routes with better availability on their web sites, arranged by departure city. Delta flyers can also access this information through a dedicated toll-free award line (888-750-6699), which is updated weekly.

Book ahead. Travelers can typically claim award seats almost a year before they plan to fly. Seat inventory, both seats for sale and award seats, becomes available 331 days in advance on most airlines. So call as far ahead as possible to redeem award seats, particularly on high-demand routes and during peak travel times.

However, remember that award inventory is constantly changing, and more free seats may become available in the weeks before departure. And some popular destinations may not be available far in advance as a matter of policy: Continental won't book award travel to Hawaii more than 30 days in advance.

That said, call as early as you can anyway. If you're a flexible traveler, you may also have good luck landing free tickets close to departure day. The possibility is worth a follow-up call—or two.

MOVING UP WITH UPGRADES

Hate to fly coach? An upgrade can be the solution. But with all the upgrade awards, elite perks, and partnership agreements, business-class and first-class can face a seating crunch. Airlines typically give first dibs on upgrades to their own best customers, especially full-fare and very frequent flyers.

Calling far in advance may—or may not—help you get an upgrade. Unless you are fairly far up the elite ladder, you usually can't secure a "positive space" upgrade—space reserved at the time of booking. Ask anyway, of course, but usually 24 hours in advance of the flight is the closest you can get. Your best strategy is to choose a midday, midweek flight, which is apt to be less crowded.

PREMIUM-TRIP AWARDS

On all the big U.S. airlines, you can exchange frequent-flier miles for free business- or first-class tickets to most parts of the world. But before you cash in, look at what the big lines require for an off-peak, round-trip ticket on a premium class.

Domestic flights. For trips within the lower 48 states (usually also to nearby cities in Canada and the Caribbean), you typically trade in 40,000 to 60,000 miles. Figuring credit at 2 cents a mile, a premium domestic trip "costs" about $800 to $1,200.

Hawaiian trips. For a trip to Hawaii, you usually surrender 60,000 to 80,000 miles. But 60,000 miles of credit is worth $1,200; using miles that way makes sense mainly for travelers from the East Coast, Midwest, or South. West Coast travelers can buy first-class seats for about the same money.

Europe and Asia. Going to Europe, the bite ranges from 100,000 to 125,000 miles; to Asia, it's 100,000 to 125,000 miles. At about $2,000 in credit, a premium round-trip to Europe effectively costs many travelers over twice as much as a cheap economy excursion.

Miles/money-saver. In addition to straight miles-for-tickets awards, some programs, such as American's, allow you to combine miles with a cash payment for a premium seat.

ELITE FREQUENT-FLYER CLASS

Contrary to popular belief, you don't have to be a 100,000-miler to qualify for the very-frequent-flyer class, known as elite.

The major airlines have been quietly loosening restrictions on the kinds of miles that count toward membership in their top-tier programs. Flights on partner airlines, as well as miles from a credit-card provider and bonus promotions, can speed your journey there.

But there's a catch. Although the airlines have made it easier to qualify for elite status, they've also made it harder to upgrade, particularly when flying on discounted coach tickets.

Even so, it's worth working toward entry-level elite status. Carriers generally offer a set of 15 or so core privileges to first-tier elite members. However, most travelers care about only two: front-cabin upgrades and preferred coach seating.

GETTING TO ELITE

Elite status is an easy target for strategy-minded leisure travelers. The key to success is concentrating all your flights on one airline. Just two trips to Europe plus one domestic flight per year may be all you need to break into the first tier.

In the past, there were only one or two levels of elite. Today there may be up to three. The net effect has been a downgrading of the first-level programs, once the only option for elite flyers. And as this "class" has devolved, so have the requirements for entry.

Elite perks kick in as soon as you earn them. Once you're a member, your status remains valid for a full calendar year or through February of the next year, depending on the airline.

Mileage thresholds. To qualify for elite status, you must log lots of miles—at least 25,000 annually, which generally includes miles earned on short-haul trips of between 500 and 1,000 miles minimum. If you're a frequent shuttle flier, the biggest airlines will credit flight segments rather than miles. On Delta, for example, either 30 segments or 25,000 miles will earn elite status. So if you travel frequently to visit a nearby city, you may reach elite status faster than if you take several long-haul trips. The airlines are also bending a bit on another restriction—that only actual flown miles qualify toward elite status.

Code-shares and partners. Some airlines allow miles earned on code-share and alliance-partner airlines to count toward elite status. But beware: Code-share partners will often reduce credit for flights taken with members of an affiliated frequent-flier program. When making reservations, it pays to verify the amount of credit you'll receive.

ELITE PERKS

For first-level elite members, the benefits outweigh those of standard-class frequent-flyer status, but still aren't as rich as those afforded the higher tiers.

Flight benefits. Members earn 25 to 50 percent more on each flight than the average frequent flyer—in addition to bonuses earned for purchasing or upgrading to front-cabin seating or for limited-time promotions. Many airlines also offer bonus mileage for passing certain milestones. A handful give elite members the advantage on getting free seats. And some of those also allow their elite members to bypass blackout dates, a perk usually reserved for higher-level flyers.

Upgrades. Behold the brass ring. But for first-level elites with discounted coach tickets (just as for regular frequent-flyers), this step up can be difficult. Timing is critical. That's because the farther up you go on the elite ladder, the earlier you can call in for an upgrade. Occasionally, the highest elite programs allow flyers to confirm upgrades when they book. For most elite flyers on cheap tickets, 24 hours before the flight is the closest they'll get. Call anyway: Reservation agents will sometimes confirm a low-level elite upgrade when the front cabin is less full.

When you qualify for an elite program, the airlines will generally

AIRLINES

send you a starter kit of upgrades that might get you through one or two trips, depending on how far you're traveling. The airline will reward your continued patronage with free coupons for every 10,000 miles you fly. Of course, you can always buy upgrade coupons before your flight (through city ticket offices, by mail, or online). But be careful. At anywhere from $12.50 to $45 per 500-mile coupon, those upgrades can sometimes cost more than the flight itself.

Other benefits. Besides upgrades, most major carriers offer a host of benefits for their lowest-level elite members: Aisle and window seats toward the front of the coach cabin are typically blocked off for elite members of all levels; every carrier now lets you waitlist for sold-out flights as well as front-cabin upgrades; most airlines offer elite reservations phone numbers, plus a special check-in line at larger airports. Also, low-level elite members may receive priority baggage handling and the opportunity to upgrade a travel companion.

CHAPTER 17

Strategies for Flying Overseas

Planning a smooth, efficient, and

economical international travel itinerary is possible,

thanks to deals all over the globe.

∎

Flying to Asia, South America, or the South Pacific? Once you get there, air travel is not only the fastest way to get around, it can also be surprisingly economical. In Europe, you may want to combine flight segments with car or train travel.

AIR PASSES ARE GREAT BARGAINS

Many countries and airlines offer tourist air passes. Visitors buy either an all-inclusive pass for air travel in a particular country for a set period, or coupons (usually sold in sets of two or four) for individual travel segments. Both options are priced far below prices charged to local travelers. Deals vary by region.

Europe. Compared with train fares, airfares in Europe are relatively high. But you can find bargains. Several European airlines and airline partnerships offer special—and affordable—visitor fares.

The basics. The general formula is the same as most visitor airfares: You buy a specified number of flight coupons at a set price per coupon. Although coupon prices don't always beat the lowest economy excursion fares, they're usually significantly lower than unrestricted economy fares. And coupons carry far fewer of the restrictions that can make an ordinary excursion fare impractical.

However, you must usually buy the visitor pass or coupons before you leave the U.S. Some fares also require that you buy an international air ticket from the U.S. to the area where the visitor program will be used (a "conjunction" ticket, in airlinese). Some conjunction tickets must be on the same airline that sponsors the visitor airfare. And in most cases, frequent-flier-award tickets do not qualify.

Most visitor fares do limit you to one stop in each destination city. You can usually travel through the sponsoring line's hub (or hubs) more than once, however, if just changing planes there. As their most-serious limitation, most visitor airfares make you use a coupon for each flight segment. So a trip that entails a connecting flight requires two coupons, doubling the cost.

Most passes and coupons also require you to specify your full itinerary when you buy them; rerouting could be extra.

EUROPEAN AIR-PASS PROGRAMS

Passes are an affordable way to see Europe.

AIRLINE	AVAILABLE PASSES
Air France	EuroFlyer Pass
Alitalia	Europlus Air Pass
Austrian	Visit Europe
British Airways	Europe Air Pass
British Midland	Discover Europe Air Pass
Iberia	Europass
KLM	Passport to Europe (with Northwest)
Lufthansa	Discover Europe Pass
Malev	Hungarian Pass to Europe
SAS	SAS Visit Europe Air Pass

Which airlines offer them? Almost all European carriers have some sort of pass or coupon program. North American visitors will find the best bets among programs covering most or all of Europe. See "European air-pass programs," this chapter, for a list of lines and passes.

National and regional tickets. About a half dozen single-country or regional air passes (mostly for Scandinavia) are available. Most people traveling within a single European country or a small multi-country region will probably do better with a rail pass or a rented car. But flying may still pay.

The low-fare option. A number of smaller carriers in Europe also offer unrestricted bargain fares between, say, Amsterdam and London or London and Dublin. Even if you travel mainly by car or train, you may want to include a flight segment to save time along the way or to get back quickly to your departure city.

Australia/New Zealand. Expect to cover a lot of ground when visiting these two South Pacific nations—Australia is the size of the United States, New Zealand the size of California. Air travel is not only practical but economical.

Single-country passes. Qantas, Ansett, and Air New Zealand all have air-pass/coupon programs that allow city-to-city travel in either country; coupons cost about $140 to $200 per segment, depending on distance. You must reserve and pay for these tickets before you leave the U.S., but you can schedule your flights once you've arrived. In most cases, you will need to have an international air ticket—but not necessarily with the airline that issues the coupons.

Both countries. Ansett and Qantas offer a two-country coupon program, which allows travel within both countries and between Australia and New Zealand (the flight from Sydney to Auckland takes about three hours).

Other South Pacific destinations. Air New Zealand has a very appealing South Pacific air pass allowing a predetermined number of stops not only in Australia and New Zealand, but in such South Pacific locales as Fiji, the Cook Islands, Tahiti, and Hawaii. You must fly round-trip from Los Angeles, schedule an itinerary before departure, and travel in one direction only, say, from Auckland to Sydney to Fiji to the Cook Islands to Tahiti, with no backtracking. Other airlines serving the region also offer air passes, so check with your travel agent.

South America. The major airlines serving South America, including Aerolineas Argentinas (Argentina), Varig (Brazil), and LanChile (Chile), offer several air-pass options.

Mercosur Air Pass. An alliance of South American carriers provides this air pass, good for travel to Argentina, Brazil, Chile, Paraguay, and Uruguay.

LanChile South America Air Pass. Chile's carrier has a coupon-based air pass to most of the airline's destinations in South America.

One-country passes. Three South American airlines offer passes good only in their home countries: the Visit Argentina Air Pass from Aerolineas Argentinas; the Visit Chile Air Pass from LanChile; and the Varig Air Pass Brazil.

Asia. An outstanding bargain during the economic downturn of the late 90s, Asia can still be affordable if you book a package tour, combining airfare, a hotel booking, and some sightseeing. (Most will also allow free time for exploring on your own.) Airline web sites—those of Cathay Pacific, Singapore Airlines, and Japan Airlines, as well as domestic and European carriers—are a good starting point. Or ask your travel agent for package info.

ONE-WAY TICKET TACTICS

Buying from a consolidator overseas can save on a number of one-way tickets: a short-haul trip to close the gap in an open-jaw flight (a round-trip arriving and departing from different cities, say going to Athens and returning from Madrid); a local side trip; a one-way long-haul; or a one-way ticket back to the U.S. (though generally only when the dollar is strong).

When shopping for airfare discounts abroad, deal with a consolidator that has an office in the country where you plan to buy. However, long term, you'll probably do better with a good local overseas travel agency, rather than working directly with consolidators. A retail travel agency can get discount tickets wholesale, then charge you about the same price you'd end up paying the consolidator.

Before you collect quotes from discounters, check the cheapest airline list prices. If the airlines are offering low fares to entice passengers, (and you can abide by the cheap ticket's restrictions), the airline's advertised price may be your best bet.

No matter what a consolidator's price list says, get a specific quote for an individual ticket. And be prepared to buy a full-fare ticket should the consolidator deal fall through.

HOW TO BOOK OVERSEAS FLIGHTS

Booking international tickets, either before you leave or while you're traveling, is fairly straightforward.

Booking before you leave. Practically all visitor air passes require you to reserve and buy in the U.S. Almost any travel agency will arrange them. Or call the sponsoring airline's North American office.

Using a foreign travel agent once you're there. Most foreign travel agents offer bargain package deals to nearby countries—for example, a three-night trip to Sydney from Auckland, New Zealand. And if the exchange rate is favorable to Americans, the deal is even sweeter.

REMEMBER TO RECONFIRM

When flying in a foreign country—especially in Asia and South America—a phone call to the airline 72 hours in advance of departure saves headaches. Some airlines simply do not consider you a "reserved" passenger unless you reconfirm. Neglect to call and they may give away your seat to another passenger who checks in earlier than you. Show up about three hours in advance for any foreign flight, too, since language, airport security, and customs questions could delay your arrival at the gate.

SAFETY AND SECURITY

How safe are foreign air carriers? Some, mainly those in Europe, Australia, and New Zealand, have safety records on a par with or better than those of U.S. airlines. But a number of African and Central American carriers have had some problematic safety records.

The FAA maintains a report on the adherence to international safety standards by different countries at *www.faa.gov/avr/iasa*. The site provides a look at an individual country's ability to license and oversee air carriers in accordance with aviation safety standards; it does not rate individual airlines. For your protection, keep these factors in mind when flying overseas:

The reputation of the carrier. When booking a flight on a carrier you don't know, ask your travel agent about its safety record. Have there been any crashes or recent safety violations?

The equipment. Many of the world's airlines use modern jets from Boeing and Airbus; others fly older planes, including some with questionable safety records. In general, try to book flights on airlines with modern fleets of American- or European-made jets.

The conditions. Consider local weather conditions and terrain. Navigation equipment is often less sophisticated in some parts of the world than in the U.S. Radar may be old and wind-shear detection nonexistent. So you may not want to fly into a mountainous region in fog, snow, or other perilous weather conditions.

Airport safety. In October 2001, the FAA issued a list of noncertified air carrier stations at foreign airports. The agency specifically prohibits flights to the U.S. from certain airports such as Punta Cana International Airport (Dominican Republic) and Freeport

---

WEATHER DELAYS

Check FAA web site for weather

Is a storm about to intrude on your air-travel plans? Visit the FAA web site at *www.fly.faa.gov* to find out. You can click on weather data for 40 U.S. airports, to see if such conditions as high winds or a low ceiling may cause delays or cancellations. (Weather accounts for nearly 70 percent of flight delays.)

Reports are updated every five minutes. However, you'll still have to contact your airline for specific flight information. Even if your plane is delayed, you'd be wise to get to the airport early anyway. Otherwise, you might lose a good seat, risk getting bumped—or even miss a plane that was able to take off after all.

International Airport (Bahamas) by several airlines, both domestic and foreign. Not all airlines are prohibited at those airports, and not all airlines mentioned by the FAA are prohibited. The stations themselves are the problem.

As of December 2001, the list included 26 airports in 16 countries, and several U.S. carriers operating scheduled and charter flights. The updated list can be found at *www.faa.gov/ats/ata/airport_cert/for eignairport.html.*

PART FOUR

Hotel How-To

CHAPTER 18

Getting the Best Rates

Why pay full price for a hotel room?

Strategies and perseverance can save you money.

━━━━━━━━━━━━━ ■ ━━━━━━━━━━━━━

Night after night, more than one-third of the nation's estimated 4 million hotel rooms are without "heads in beds," and therefore worthless to hoteliers. Like airlines, hotels have intricate formulas for selling their particular commodity (a room with a bed instead of a seat on a plane) at vastly different prices, a practice known in the industry as "yield management." With hotels, the mix of room rates may change with the season, room location, and past and projected demand. Prices may also differ not just room to room, but day to day.

Some strategies to make the hotels' pricing practices work for you.

16 PRICE-LOWERING TECHNIQUES

These tactics can knock a substantial sum off a hotel's "rack rate"—the (usually very high) price posted behind the door of each room. Persistence also pays off—if your first tactic doesn't work, try another approach.

Check out web offerings. Consumers booked $6 billion worth of hotel stays online in 2000, mostly through web-based travel sites.

Although 90 percent of hotel companies have a web site, according to the American Hotel & Lodging Association, reserving a room is possible on fewer than half these sites; many simply feature descriptions, maps, and photographs. However, certain sites do offer bargains, such as a 10 percent web-reservation discount or last-minute packages, and let you book online with a credit card. Some airlines may also air-and-hotel packages, either last-minute or as a seasonal deal, with a lodgings price break.

Online discount brokers are also worth a shot. According to our findings, they don't always offer the sweetest deals (see "Hotel brokers," this chapter), but they have negotiated special rates with some chains that are at least lower than the rack rate.

Or try Priceline *(www.priceline.com)*—but be aware of the drawbacks. You can't choose a particular hotel, only specify the luxury level and the neighborhood. And once your bid is accepted, you can't renege.

Call the hotel directly. We've found this tactic usually yields the best deals overall, and gives you more bargaining opportunities. Don't stop with the national reservations lines; although these central operators can provide rates and information, you'll usually get a lower rate by calling the specific property. The local staff has a better grasp of supply and demand, and more discretion in setting rates. And do phone more than once; our second calls often yielded a better rate.

Seek a group discount. You can usually save at least 10 percent off the rack rate by using an auto club (AAA) discount, a senior discount (those from AARP start at age 50, although some chains set the threshold as high as 65), or a discount for members of the military, government employees, or convention attendees. Even with a group discount, don't hesitate to bargain; that combo often nets an even bigger savings.

A number of chains also run senior-traveler membership programs (minimum age, 50 to 60). Discounts are typically modest, although they can run as high as 50 percent in a few chains. Some require AARP membership to qualify. You may join as you register and get an on-the-spot price break.

HOTELS

Investigate special offers. Ask about promotions or packages, which may vary with the time of the year. Off-season and shoulder season can also offer outstanding values—provided the weather remains agreeable. (See Chapter 6 for off-season information.)

Ask about corporate rates. Many hotels serving business travelers offer these to any traveler who can produce even vague evidence of corporate or professional employment at check-in (a business card will usually do). However, you usually get no more than 20 percent off the rack rate, maybe less. And sometimes these rates are higher than the lowest rack rate, to cover some extra amenity, such as a "superior" room or an "executive" floor. So don't accept this discount at face value.

Be flexible. Shifting your travel dates can lower the room price. Since upscale and luxury hotels often cater to a business crowd, rates

---

BUDGET HOTELS

Weigh the pros and cons

Readers who answered a recent CONSUMER REPORTS hotel survey weren't always pleased with budget hotels, despite lower rates. These facilities may be older properties, with smallish (250- to-300-square-foot) rooms, and may also lack an onsite restaurant, and such luxuries such as a health club. But they do offer some benefits:

Car-convenient locations. Generally situated outside city centers –along major highways, in suburban areas, and near airports–they're handy for road-weary motorists.

Space for kids. All but a few chains allow one or two kids (usually with an age limit in the teens) to stay "free."

Swimming pool. Pools are increasingly common; if such a facility is important to you, check when you reserve.

Certain amenities and perks. You'll be offered a smoking or nonsmoking room, have individually controlled heat and air conditioning, and nearby ice and vending machines. Many chains also provide a complimentary morning meal (if only rolls and coffee or tea); offer business conveniences, such as modems and incoming fax service; waive any charge for local and toll-free calls; and include premium cable access and in-room VCRs.

are usually higher on weekdays, then drop on weekends. At many less-expensive hotels, the tourist trade peaks on weekends, meaning better deals are available during the week.

Book early—or late. This one's complicated. Reserving at least three weeks ahead may save money, because hoteliers prefer a sure reservation to an empty room. (You must generally pay for your first night's stay within a week of reserving.) On the other hand, waiting until the last minute may save more. But of course, the hotel may be fully booked by then.

Our advice: Book early and call back a few days before you arrive. If the rate has dropped, cancel and rebook, or request credit for the price difference. When you make your original reservation, ascertain how late you can cancel without paying a fee or losing your deposit (usually between 24 and 72 hours, but rules vary).

Bargain. Don't be afraid to say, "That's beyond my budget" or "Is that the best you can do?" And be willing to walk away. Suggesting that you have an alternative hotel—one offering you a warmer welcome—may produce a more attractive counteroffer.

Enroll in a frequent-guest program. Programs like Hilton HHonors or Marriott Rewards cost nothing to join and offer repeat guests such benefits as free nights, future discounts, frequent-flyer miles, and room upgrades. (See "Frequent-stay programs," this chapter.)

Buy a half-price program directory. They can save you money—provided that the hotel has a room available, not always the case during busy seasons. ("Half-price hotel programs," this chapter, has details.)

Pick up a discount guide. Free brochures at visitor centers and gas stations along highways have coupons for hotels in every price range, with discounts of 30 to 50 percent off rack rates. You can download coupons at *www.roomsavers.com*.

Review tour-operator offerings. Tour operators book blocks of rooms at a special price—and may sell you just the lodging at a 20 to 40 percent discount, without the transportation or sightseeing that normally completes a tour package. You can find these bargains by checking a range of tour brochures.

Contact local reservations services. In some cities, local services

HOTELS

can get reduced rates. These services are listed in tourist-board brochures from specific regions or cities, or on the web.

Explore overbuilt destinations. When too many hotels are built in a region, the resulting oversupply strongly affects rates. If the hotel you're trying to book now is located in such an area, you may have an advantage. As a long-term strategy, ask your travel agent about such destinations to see if any appeal to you.

HOTEL OVERBOOKING

When a 'guaranteed reservation' isn't

Like airlines, hotels overbook–often in popular destinations and at peak travel times. So even a guaranteed reservation paid for with a charge card may not protect you against being turned away (or "walked"). However, hotels have contractual obligations to find you alternative lodging. You might expect:

• One free night at a nearby hotel of the same or better quality or the price difference between the original room and the new room.

• A free phone call to notify friends or family of your hotel change, plus having all phone calls, messages, and packages routed to your new hotel.

• A free room or upgrade on a future visit.

Take these steps to protect against being walked:

• Arrive as early as possible. If you expect to be late, say so when you reserve. In case of unexpected travel delays, call the hotel.

• Pay with a charge card; the charge-card company will then go to bat for you. Cash customers are legally entitled to the same protections, but it may be hard to collect. If you cannot get satisfaction, consider small-claims court.

• Report problems to the Federal Trade Commission, Consumer Response Center, 600 Pennsylvania Avenue NW, Washington, D.C. 20580 (877-382-4357; *www.ftc.gov*).

No-shows who "guarantee" a reservation with a charge card, then fail to cancel within the specified time limit, are usually out one night's room rate. And some chains have tightened cancellation deadlines. However, in the Sept. 11 grounding of planes, hotels generally waived penalties.

Leave the city center. Urban properties are usually more expensive. (For a rate rundown, see "Costly cities," this chapter.) If you don't mind staying outside the city, call some establishments in the surrounding areas.

Research preferred rates. You can only get these rates through a travel agency, travel club, booking organization, or corporate travel office that has negotiated them. Averaging 20 percent off rack rates (but varying from 10 percent to 40 percent), they're typically available on a "last room" basis. This means you get the discount as long as there are rooms available, even if the hotel is close to full.

However, preferred rates aren't available at every hotel. Your travel agent's latest "Hotel and Travel Index" and the current preferred-rate directory lists discounts. Agents can also access information online.

HOTEL BROKERS

These agencies provide a way for hotels to unload rooms they don't expect to sell at full price.

Wholesale brokers. This type of broker generally contracts with hotels on a yearly basis to sell rooms at a discounted price—many "own" a certain number of rooms. Some are tour operators who sell rooms to independent travelers at the same rates they offer in package tours.

Expect to pay a wholesaler for your entire visit; you'll then receive a room voucher or, if the trip is on short notice, one will be waiting for you at the hotel. (Note that wholesalers often can't accommodate last-minute bookings at all.) Wholesaler rates typically include all tax and service charges. But beware: Some brokers quote prices on a per-person rather than a per-room basis. Since most give commissions, your regular travel agent can deal with them for you.

Like preferred rates, wholesaler discounts generally average 10 to 40 percent, although occasionally they're higher. Brokers may be able to get you a room when a hotel says it has nothing available. However, if rooms are tight, the wholesale broker may offer no discount whatsoever.

HOTELS

In addition, some of these brokers offer a limited selection of hotels, and deals may be confined to fairly upscale properties. If you have to cancel or change your plans close to travel time, you will probably forfeit one night's room charge—even brokers who don't ask you to prepay may impose a cancellation charge. Always confirm all policies and terms when you book.

Online brokers. Advertising themselves as "discounters," such brokers simply act as the middleman in your transaction. Although they can usually provide some markdowns, they don't always offer the best deal. You may do better by calling hotels directly.

In spring 2001, *Consumer Reports Travel Letter* visited the web

---

COMPARING RATES

Hotels vs. brokers

The figures shown are based on 200 quotes for 100 hotels in Boston, Chicago, New York City, San Francisco, and Washington, D.C., obtained from the web sites of five travel brokers. After getting quotes, we then checked with each hotel directly to find out its best rate for the same accommodations. Result: The hotels usually offered a better deal. Savings listed are an average of those we obtained and exclude booking fees and taxes.

BROKER	SCOPE	FEES		BROKER BEATS HOTEL	
		BOOK	CANCEL	HOW OFTEN	SAVINGS
Travelocity	20,000 U.S. and international cities, 50,000 hotels	None	$50	65% of the time	$54 per night
Accommodations Express	190 U.S. cities, 1,300 hotels	$5	25	60	32
Hotel Discounts	90 U.S. and international cities, 2,500 hotels	None	50	33	37
Expedia	4,000 U.S. and international cities, 40,000 hotels	None	10	28	31
1-800-USA-Hotels	1,499 U.S. and international cities, 15,000 hotels and bed & breakfast inns	None	None	28	20

---

sites of five "discount" travel brokers to find the least-expensive weekend accommodations for a trip about a month away. Then we then called each hotel and requested the best rate for the same rooms. We found that the hotels themselves may offer a better deal about half the time overall. And when they did, the savings were high—an average of $79 per night. (See "Hotels vs. brokers," this chapter, for details on our findings.)

Our recommendation: Shop around, via both phone and Internet. Do call hotels more than once; you may score better the second time. And however you book, always ask about fees and confirm the cancellation policy.

HALF-PRICE HOTEL PROGRAMS

All the major half-price programs offer the same basic terms. The big differences are in quantity and geographic spread—the more hotels and locations a program lists, the better your chances of getting discounted rooms when and where you want them.

Program directories generally also include a laundry list of other discounts and deals, from airfare discounts to reduced greens fees, which can net additional savings.

The drill. Once you've enrolled in a club or bought the discount directory, you must contact the hotel directly to see if the listed discount is available when you want it. If no half-price rate is available on your dates, the hotel may offer you a lesser discount. Alternatively, you can try for a different date or check with another hotel. You must usually call at least a few hours ahead for a reservation—not just show up at the desk.

On checking in, you show your program's valid ID card. (You won't get a deal just by mentioning the program name.) Pay when you leave, by either cash or charge card. Note that the half-price ID covers only one room a night. If your party requires two or more rooms, assume you must have a separate membership for each.

Caveats. Don't join a program thinking you'll get a deal on every single hotel stay. First, your real-life discount might be less than a full 50 percent. Also remember that the baseline for "half-price" is the artificially high rack rate. And although half-price rates are supposed to be accessible on any day of the year, they're subject to availability, which means no discount when a hotel expects to be more than about 80 percent full, or when seasonal blackouts apply. Peak-season discounts are often obtainable only on weekdays in resort areas and on weekends in cities. A few hotels impose a minimum or maximum stay.

Listed hotels have dropped out of the program, and there's a substantial turnover in properties. You typically cannot combine a half-price discount with any other reduction—a senior or weekend rate, say. Carefully check program directories for restrictions. Still, even getting a substantial rate reduction on one hotel stay could pay your program costs. Some half-price directory resources are listed in "Programs that can trim room rates," this chapter.

HOTELS AT HALF PRICE

Programs that can trim room rates

Entertainment Publications (800-445-4137; *www.entertainment.com;* $24.95 to $64.95; AE, Disc, MC, V.) This program offers a catalog of directories for U.S. and foreign hotels, plus local discount books. The "Hotels & Travel Ultimate Savings Directory" covers prime destinations and includes discounts on airfares, car rentals, and cruises. ID cards valid for 12 to 18 months.

Encore (800-444-9800; *www.preferredtraveler.com;* $69.95; AE, Disc, MC, V.) Besides hotel listings, this one also features a separate section of small inns and bed-and-breakfasts. Expect discounts on airfares, car rentals, cruises, and admission to visitor attractions.

Great American Traveler (800-548-2812; *www.memberweb.com;* Total Portfolio Package, $99.95, $49.95 to renew; Great American Traveler hotel program, $49.95, $29.95 to renew; AE, Disc, MC, V.) In addition to hotel discounts, the program offers reductions on condo rentals, percent-off greens fees at many golf courses, and amusement-park and ski-resort discounts.

Quest (800-742-3543; $99; quarterly hotel updates, $4 a year; AE, Disc, MC, V.) Expect only small discounts on hotels, airfares, and cruises, with some deals on condo and car rentals. (Quest is often discounted via associations and credit cards.)

FREQUENT-STAY PROGRAMS

These programs can deliver a decent return in free stays and other payoffs, even if you spend as few as eight to 10 nights a year in hotels. Membership in most hotel programs is free. Some allow unlimited time to earn a reward; others specify a one-year time frame.

The more earning opportunities, the better. Certain programs give credit for all money spent, not just the room cost. Payoff counts, too. The midpriced and budget chains generally run the most-generous programs. A program that provides benefits you can use right away may be preferable to one that requires a minimum number of stays to qualify.

Point-based programs. Most give points or some other credit based on what you spend at the hotel, in many cases going beyond the room charge to include food, room service, merchandise, and other onsite purchases. Some also allow credit for rooms occupied at a preferred, senior, half-price, or other discounted or promotional rate (though they may not give credit for the deepest discounts).

The others typically limit credit to travelers who pay rack rate or the hotel's published corporate rate. If program literature specifies that earnings are confined to "qualifying" rates, check when you reserve as to whether your rate entitles you to credit.

Some programs give points for using car-rental or airline partners, usually during the time of a hotel stay. And some also allow you to "double dip"—to earn both hotel and airline credit for the same stay.

Several offer one or more levels of very-frequent stay (VFS) status, similar to an airline's very-frequent flier status. VFS provides faster earning and/or more generous benefits.

The typical minimum award is one free night—at any time in some programs, during a weekend (or an off-peak night at some resort locations) in others. Most let you redeem points for a wide range of other travel services as well as merchandise. However, certain big chains offer only a "customer recognition" program—no free stays, just membership benefits, such as late checkout and room upgrades. Others may give a 10 percent discount on each stay.

HOTELS

How to have a safe hotel stay

Working with local authorities, some U.S.-based hotel chains have heightened security at their properties in the U.S. and abroad in the wake of the Sept. 11 attacks. Differences aren't obvious, though. Hotel officials say most changes are behind the scenes. Do your part to stay safe and secure, too.

• Don't choose a hotel simply by name; investigate the neighborhood. A property catering to savvier business travelers, rather than vacationers and tour groups, is less likely to be targeted by criminals.

• Request a room on a lower floor, but not the ground floor. Ground-floor rooms are less secure; rooms above floor six are too high for most conventional fire equipment to reach. Book closer to the elevator than the stairs for a shorter walk to your door. Make sure the hotel has electronic keys, dead bolts, door peepholes, and 24-hour security.

• Keep your identity private. A woman traveling alone should use only first initials and last name when booking and checking in. If the desk clerk says your room number so others can hear, consider requesting a different room.

• If driving in late at night, ask to be met in the parking lot by a staff member. Have a valet handle your car throughout your stay.

• Once in your room, locate fire escapes and plan an emergency route out. Lock all windows and doors. Travel with a small flashlight, rubber doorstop, and personal alarm for protection.

• Ask room service to call you right before they come up. Don't open the door to any unidentified visitors.

• Lock valuables in the in-room safe or in a front-desk safe-deposit box. Don't trust them to a locked suitcase.

• When leaving your hotel room, leave the "do not disturb" sign on your door (assuming your room has been cleaned), lights on, and TV tuned to the local language station. But not too loudly, so as to avoid disturbing neighboring guests. Unwelcome guests will assume you are a local and you are in. Upon returning, have your key ready so you can quickly open the door.

Night-based programs. Basically, staying the required number of nights—generally eight to 12—earns you a free night's stay. Many programs also offer some worthwhile benefits even if you never earn a free stay: room discounts, free breakfast, late checkout, free local calls, and priority reservations or a special reservation phone line.

HOTEL VALUE

If you aren't pleased with the hotel, a great price doesn't mean much. To evaluate what you can get for your money, CONSUMER REPORTS conducts a periodic hotel survey. Our latest overview was based on 41,000 responses from readers who collectively had spent more than 166,000 nights at 46 hotel chains between January 1999 and the spring of 2000. The resulting Ratings are on page 319. Here's a round-up of what we found:

Luxury wins out. For our survey, we grouped hotels into four cat-egories—luxury (costing a median of about $150 per night), upscale (about $110), moderate (about $70), and budget (about $50)—on the basis of both the price paid and the amenities offered.

The highest marks for overall satisfaction went to luxury chains. On the whole, upscale hotels received slightly lower scores, moderate slightly lower still, and budget hotels the lowest of all. Moreover, while about 30 percent of readers cited luxury, upscale, and moderate hotels as an excellent value, only 24 percent said the same of budget hotels. A hotel in the moderate or upscale category may be an espe-cially good choice, because some charge near-bargain rates and many offer amenities once found only in the most expensive lodgings.

Among the extras prized by readers who stay at more-expensive hotels are an onsite restaurant, business facilities, room service, a concierge, and a pool or gym.

But each category has winners. At each level, a few hotels stood out. This implies that the high-rated budget hotels supplied the basics that travelers want—a clean room that is made up promptly and is well stocked with soap and towels—and that the high-rated, pricier hotels fulfilled the expectations people have when spending more.

HOTELS

COMPARING HOTEL RATES

Costly Cities

Here's a look at the rates in 11 major U.S. cities.

CITY	AVERAGE ROOM RATE	OCCUPANCY RATE
New York	$240	84%
Boston	201	78
San Francisco	174	83
Santa Barbara, Calif.	157	76
Philadelphia	146	63
Chicago	141	75
Scottsdale, Ariz.	138	66
Washington, D.C.	136	74
Seattle	135	73
Miami, Fla.	126	75
New Orleans	125	75

Source: PKF Consulting, for the year 2000

Problems happen. When asked about 14 specific complaints, such as inadequate lighting, an uncomfortable bed, and a noisy room, 32 percent of survey repondents said they encountered at least one. Guests at budget hotels found more cause for complaint, citing at least one glitch during about 40 percent of their visits. (The figure for luxury hotels was 25 percent.)

Upkeep, which was closely allied to traveler satisfaction, fell substantially as the category of hotel went from luxury to budget. Only 5 percent of those who stayed at luxury hotels found the upkeep fair, poor, or very poor, but 23 percent who stayed at budget hotels felt that way.

Perks have multiplied. "Amenities creep"—the hotel industry's term for the trickling-down of conveniences such as coffeemakers, pools, and fitness rooms—has brought fancier extras to even modest hotels. And it has also resulted in really fancy extras at some luxury hotels, such as high-quality restaurants, a technology concierge (for when your laptop goes on the blink), a personal butler, or a massage service.

Prices keep climbing. Since the mid-1990s, room rates have generally exceeded the inflation rate by 2 to 3 percentage points a year.

BED AND BREAKFAST INNS

Are they for you?

Although size and personality vary with each establishment (as do decor, comfort, and prices) these inns share characteristics that beguile some travelers–and drive away others. On the plus side, B&Bs offer charm, a peaceful atmosphere, hospitality, good home cooking, and conversation with fellow guests. But living in someone else's dwelling isn't for everyone. And there are generally no discounted rates. A B&B is worth trying if you:

- Like meeting people.

- Enjoy eating a big breakfast–and discussing the day's plans with strangers at the breakfast table.

- Savor touches such as afternoon tea.

- Don't mind sharing a bathroom (necessary in some inns), or leaving your room unlocked (doors may not lock from the outside).

- Aren't bothered by "finger-wagging" notes like "Our towels don't go to the beach."

- Can do without a coffee maker, refrigerator, or microwave oven in the room–and probably a TV as well, although some inns have a communal set.

- Are willing to wait for service. You may not be prepared to wake the innkeeper to have the heat adjusted in the middle of the night.

- Can leave young kids at home, since some inns don't allow children under a certain age.

Friends and relatives can offer B&B recommendations. Or try some of the hundreds of web sites representing regional, state, and local innkeepers' groups. Among those we found helpful: *www.ibbp.com, www.inndirectory.com, www.bbonline.com, www.inncrawler.com,* and *www.travelguides.com.*

HOTELS

Based on a comparison of our 1997 and 2000 lodging surveys, CONSUMER REPORTS found that the rates people paid have increased the most at luxury hotels—20 percent over four years.

STEALTH FEES

Another consideration is whether that good rate will still look good when you add in the extras. With taxes, parking fees, and hotel surcharges on just a few phone calls, a room bill of $100 can balloon to $150.

Some add-ons can be avoided; others can't. The trick is to know what to expect (ask questions when you reserve) so you can budget accordingly and look for ways to save. Here are five "gotchas":

Taxes and surcharges. Levied to fund everything from ballparks to schools, taxes can add as much as 14.9 percent to the final tab. Tariffs are highest in major cities: Chicago leads, with 14.9 percent, but Washington, San Francisco, Los Angeles, Atlanta, and New York are close behind.

Parking. You expect free parking (and get it) at most motels. However, if you stay in a city, all bets are off. The parking fees quoted to us by big-city luxury and upscale hoteliers ranged from $12 to $47 a day. (Bypassing the valet to park the car yourself saves some money, if the location seems quite safe.)

Phone calls. Surcharges on long-distance calls made from a hotel room can go as high as 50 percent, especially at luxury and upscale hotels. Bring along a phone card, and ask if a surcharge applies for these card calls. Using the lobby phone for long distance may also save. Many chains charge nothing for local calls made from the room. (See "Phoning home" in the Reference section for more tips.)

Room service. Scan the room-service menu for fees, and add them to your bill. You'll pay tax on your meal, of course, but may also be assessed a delivery charge and, perhaps, a service fee in lieu of the tip. See if service is included before you tip the waiter.

Fitness center. The hotel provides all the latest equipment—but you may have to pay to use it.

CHAPTER 19

Hotel Ratings Explained

Is the cost difference between a "Superior Deluxe" and "Deluxe" hotel worth it? What defines "First Class" and "Tourist"? Here's a guide to industry ratings.

In the U.S. at least, the most widely used hotel grades are those found in the "Official Hotel Guide" (OHG)—which is published for the travel industry, not consumers. When a tour, brochure, or newspaper ad promises a certain grade of hotel, that claim is probably based on OHG classifications.

OHG ratings combine two elements: quality of lodgings, which refers to room size and standard of furnishings, and extent of facilities, covering the number and size of public and meeting rooms, restaurants, and shops. Handbooks geared primarily to consumers also rank hotels—some more candidly than the OHG. And around the world, some government agencies also assign ratings.

DECODING THE OHG RATINGS

The OHG divides hotels into three main categories—Deluxe, First Class, and Tourist—with subcategories under each. Here's what each of the rating terms really means (reprinted with the permission of the OHG).

Deluxe. These establishments range from ultra luxurious to less opulent, but still quite plush.

Superior Deluxe. Exclusive and expensive, often palatial, these hotels offer the highest standards of service, accommodations, and facilities, along with elegant and luxurious public rooms and a very prestigious address.

Deluxe. Outstanding and with many of the same features as Superior Deluxe, this type may be less grand—and more reasonable—than those above, yet just as satisfactory.

Moderate Deluxe. Accommodations or public areas may be less luxurious than fully Deluxe properties. In others, the hotel may be a well-established famous name, depending heavily on past reputation. The more-contemporary hotels may be heavily marketed to business clients, with fine accommodations and public rooms offering Deluxe standards in comfort, yet with less emphasis on atmosphere and/or personal service.

First class. This category runs the gamut from very high-quality accommodations to those that are much less luxurious (but more reasonably priced).

Superior First Class. Expect an above-average hotel, perhaps an exceptionally well-maintained older hotel, but more often a superior modern hotel specifically designed for the First Class market, with some outstanding features. Accommodations and public areas will be tastefully furnished and very comfortable. These can be good values, especially the commercial hotels.

First Class. The rating indicates a dependable, comfortable hotel with standardized rooms, amenities, and public areas—and maybe a superior executive level or wing. But don't look for luxurious facilities or special services.

Limited-Service First Class. Although the property offers full first-class accommodations, you'll have limited public areas, food service, and facilities. Usually moderate in size, these hotels often utilize a residential scale and architecture, and many offer complimentary breakfast and evening cocktails in the lobby or in a small, informal restaurant. This bracket is generally geared to the individual business or pleasure traveler.

Moderate First Class. These are essentially First-Class establishments with comfortable if somewhat simpler accommodations and public areas, and may lack desirable features such as a restaurant. While adequate, some rooms or public areas may tend toward basic and functional. But rates are also reasonable.

Tourist. Such a rating encompasses everything from budget hotels to some strictly "port-in-a-storm" properties. They include:

Superior Tourist Class. The top subcategory denotes a budget property with mostly well-kept, functional accommodations (some up to First-Class standards). Public rooms may be limited or nonexistent. Although often just a place to sleep, the hotel may have some charming or intimate features, and is usually a good value. The amenity/low-rate ratio may balance for individuals or groups who want to save money.

Tourist Class. Expect a purely budget operation with some facilities or features of Superior Tourist Class, but usually no First-Class accommodations. Use these places with caution.

Moderate Tourist Class. These low-budget operations, often quite old and sometimes not well kept, are feasible only if no other accommodations are available.

About the ratings. When you use OHG ratings—or any other hotel-classification system—be sensitive to the nuances of the report. The travel industry is reluctant to say flatly that any establishment is out-and-out bad, so the OHG and other sources often resort to code words and euphemisms. When the description says "may not be well kept" or "should be used only in a pinch," read it as "this hotel is a dog."

OVERSEAS RATINGS

Outside the U.S., a whole new world of hotel accommodations and ratings systems awaits you. Many travelers rely on the ratings in their

HOTELS

preferred guidebooks, but you can also mine other sources.

What's available. Government agencies assign hotel ratings in Australia, Austria, Belgium, France, Greece, Indonesia, Italy, Mexico, the Netherlands, New Zealand, Switzerland, and the United Kingdom. These ratings may be noted in hotel and tour brochures in place of, or in addition to, OHG ratings. Government systems tend to rely on statistical measures, such as dimensions of guest rooms or percentage of rooms with bath.

What's not. The governments of many important tourist countries (including Denmark, Finland, Germany, Japan, Norway, Sweden, and the U.S.) don't rate hotels. Travelers to those countries, as well as tour operators and travel agencies, have to rely on nongovernmental sources, such as guidebooks and, perhaps, web-site photographs of individual properties.

Ratings aren't everything. In many parts of the world, hotels more basic than those that the OHG rates can be quite adequate. In fact, OHG doesn't even list many low-end hotels. Budget travelers in Paris, for instance, may be perfectly happy in hotels with a government rating of only one or two stars—if they know what to expect. Similarly, travelers in the U.S. often find budget hostelries a great buy even at list price.

CHAPTER 20

Extended-Stay and All-Suites

These lodgings provide a home

away from home for a stay of more than

just a few days—usually at reasonable rates.

■

Traveling with your family to a wedding? Staying in one location for a long vacation? Or just want to enjoy more comforts of home while on the road? Then you'll appreciate an extended-stay or all-suite hotel.

In the past five years, the number of all-suite hotels in the U.S. has nearly doubled. Some 3,237 properties now offer almost 400,000 rooms, and all-suite hotels have a higher average occupancy rate industrywide than nonsuite properties.

SUITE FEATURES

A suite usually offers more space than a standard hotel room (and costs an average of 10 to 15 percent more). However, the word "suite" has varied meanings among different hotel companies, and hotel chains' individual suites also may vary among locations.

Suite design. Ideally, a suite's bedroom is separated from the living area by a full wall and a door that closes. But in a 2001 *Consumer*

Reports Travel Letter survey of 30 of the largest U.S. all-suite and extended-stay properties, we found that more than one-third of the suites had either a partial wall only—or no wall at all dividing the space. A number of properties also offer "studio suites," although studios are by definition single, undivided rooms.

Whatever the suite's size, the unit may (or may not) include a couch (often a sofa bed), recliner, kitchen or minikitchen, and/or work area.

Choices. You have two types of properties to consider. Upscale all-suite hotels, such as Hilton Suites and Embassy Suites, offer conventional hotel conveniences—room service, a hotel restaurant, and daily housekeeping—and often feature a swimming pool, hot tub, and fitness center. Although these suites usually do have an actual wall separating the bedroom from the living room, they usually lack a full kitchen. Instead, expect a minikitchen with a wet bar, coffee maker, refrigerator, and sometimes a microwave.

Midprice all-suite hotels have fewer conveniences, and they may not always offer a separate bedroom.

EXTENDED-STAY HOTELS

Catering primarily to guests who plan to remain for some time, these properties also welcome short-term stays, from a single night to a few nights to a week. They often combine hotel conveniences with separate apartment-style suites. Higher-end establishments typically cater to business travelers.

Most extended-stay properties attempt to cultivate a home-away-from-home atmosphere, with a full kitchen complete with stove, full-sized refrigerator, and sometimes even a dishwasher. Some include outdoor amenities such as barbecue areas and swimming pools. Certain extended-stay properties offer laundry facilities and dry-cleaning services, as well as onsite convenience stores.

Less-expensive extended-stay properties tend toward fewer frills, with less-frequent housekeeping (weekly instead of daily, for example) and no room service.

HOW TO CHOOSE

Whether the premium is worth the price depends on what kind of traveler you are, your expected service level, and whether you'll really use a suite's amenities.

Single travelers. Singles—or couples traveling without children —may find so-called studio suites a good value. They're typically economy properties with a single sleeping/sitting area, and often offer a full kitchen. But ask what you'll get; some have only a minikitchen. If you'll be sharing the accommodations with friends, the wide-open floor plan may not provide enough privacy.

Families. You'll want an entirely separate bedroom, a full kitchen, and daily housekeeping. Some hotels include breakfast. Be sure to ask if children stay free; chains frequently offer this perk.

Business travelers. Many properties provide amenities such as onsite business centers with computers, photocopiers, and fax machines, as well as in-room services—expanded ergonomic work areas, high-speed Internet access, voice mail, and multiple telephone lines. However, if you plan to hold an in-room meeting, find out if your suite will have a full wall between the bedroom and the "boardroom."

PRICE POINTS

Extra space can mean a lot when you're on an extended trip or traveling with a family—but you do pay a premium. And a regular hotel room may have many of the same suite amenities, such as telephones with data ports, and a refrigerator, minibar, and coffeemaker.

Properties often have discounted weekend rates, senior rates (many require AARP membership), AAA rates, or Internet specials. Rates also can vary tremendously by season and location within chains—and even at a single property during peak periods. So ask what's available. In certain destinations, there may be only a small price difference between suites and standard rooms, making an "upgrade" a feasible option. And stays may earn credit in frequent-guest programs.

Since many hotels are independently owned and operated, quality can (and will) vary widely, and even a familiar brand-name hotel

HOTELS

HOW SUITE IS THAT SUITE?

A quick look at what you'll get in some suites.

Hotel chain	Reservation	web site	Breakfast included
AmeriSuites	800-833-1516	www.amerisuites.com	hot buffet
Aston Hotels & Resorts Hawaii	800-922-7866	www.astonhotels.com	continental (a)
Best Western	800-937-8376	www.bestwestern.com	varies by hotel (c)
Candlewood Suites	888-226-3539	www.candlewoodsuites.com	none
Clarion Suites	800-252-7466	www.clarionhotel.com	continental
Comfort Suites	800-517-4000	www.comfortsuites.com	continental
Country Inns & Suites by Carlson	800-456-4000	www.countryinns.com	continental
Crossland Economy Studios	800-398-7829	www.extstay.com	no
Days Inn	800-329-7466	www.daysinn.com	continental
Doubletree Guest Suites	800-222-8733	www.doubletree.com	no
Embassy Suites Hotels	800-362-2779	www.embassysuites.com	hot buffet
Extended Stay America Efficiency Studios	800-398-7829	www.extstay.com	no
Hawthorn Suites/LTD (e)	800-527-1133	www.hawthorn.com	hot buffet
Hilton Suites	800-445-8667	www.hilton.com	hot buffet
Homewood Suites by Hilton	800-225-5466	www.homewoodsuites.com	continental
Intown Suites	(g)	www.intownsuites.com	no
MainStay Suites	800-660-6246	www.mainstaysuites.com	continental
Marriott Hotels, Resorts and Suites (h)	800-228-9290	www.marriott.com	no
Quality Suites	800-228-5151	www.qualityinn.com	hot buffet
Radisson Hotels & Resorts	800-333-3333	www.radisson.com	varies by hotel
Ramada	800-272-6232	www.ramada.com	varies by hotel
Residence Inn by Marriott	800-228-9290	www.residenceinn.com	hot buffet
Sheraton Suites	800-325-3535	www.sheraton.com	no
Sierra Suites Hotel	800-474-3772	www.sierrasuites.com	continental
Springhill Suites by Marriott	888-228-9290	www.springhillsuites.com	hot buffet
Staybridge Suites by Holiday Inn	800-238-8000	www.staybridge.com	hot buffet
StudioPLUS Deluxe Studios	800-398-7829	www.extstay.com	no
Summerfield Suites by Wyndham	800-996-3426	www.wyndham.com	hot buffet
TownePlace Suites by Marriott	800-228-9290	www.towneplacesuites.com	no
Wellesley Inn & Suites	800-444-8888	www.wellesleyinnandsuites.com	continental

(a) At some properties. (b) Not all suites have kitchens. (c) By 10/01 all Best Westerns will be required to make breakfast available on-site (there may or may not be a charge). (d) Hotel charges by room, not number of travelers. (e) Hawthorn Suites LTD are similar budget properties, with fewer amenities and about 20% smaller rooms; the chart reflects Hawthorn Suites. (f) Only 3 individuals allowed per room. (g) No central reservations

1 bedroom rack rate (daily unless noted)	Children free under age	VCR/VCP in room	Average size in sq. ft.	Kitchen
$ 79-119	18	yes	380	mini
$140-565	18	some	570-1,120	varies
$ 89-119	12	some	no requirement	varies (b)
$109-149	n/a (d)	yes	528	full
$ 85-300	19	no	343-514	varies
$ 69-160	19	no	402-804	mini
$ 78-98	18	some	390-432	mini
$169-199/wk.	none	no	227	full
$100-175	12	no	385	mini
$169-259	18	yes	300-450	mini
$161-229	18	no	473-506	mini
$199-299/wk.	none	no	300	full
$ 75-300	n/a (d)	yes	500	varies
$159-225	18	some	425-550	mini
$129-189	19	yes	396-472	full
$155-175/wk.	none (f)	no	288	full
$ 79-129	19	no	410-610	full
$100-235	n/a (d)	no (j)	420-500	(i)
$ 79-179	19	yes	minimum 522	mini
$ 99-269	19	most locations	400-440	varies
$ 69-189	18	some	432	mini
$ 90-120	n/a (d)	no	427	full
$199-249	18	some	456-740	varies (b)
$ 69-169	18	no (a)	350	full
$ 79-99	n/a (d)	no	332-396	mini
$ 75-130 (k)	n/a (d)	yes	501	full
$299-399/wk.	none	no	300-425	full
$129-279	18	yes	580	full
$ 60-80 80-125 (l)	n/a (d)	no	362	full
$ 49-89	18	no	450	full

number; individual property numbers listed on web site. **(h)** Chart only refers to all-suite properties. **(i)** No kitchen, suites have refrigerator and coffeemaker. **(j)** Generally VCRs are available to rent. **(k)** Rates vary by season, location, and length of stay; from $75/night for 30-night stays to $130/night for one night. **(l)** Only offering studio and two bedroom units.

HOTELS

may not deliver the same amenities at all locations nationwide. To get a sense of the accommodations—and avoid unpleasant surprises — check the web site. A number of these hotel sites feature detailed, three-dimensional floor plans, photographs, or 360-degree virtual tours of suites.

ALTERNATIVE ACCOMMODATIONS

Suites are not your only option for a long-term stay. In big U.S. cities, you may find apartment buildings converted to weekly or monthly rentals. Check the city newspaper classified ads and the phone book Yellow Pages. In resort areas, a condo or villa rental may be a better deal (see Chapter 22).

SUITE OR NOT?

What to ask before you book

To ensure that you get the accommodations you want, pin down the hotel's definition of a suite, then see what extras it offers. The web site can provide basic background. Calling the hotel directly enables you to ask key questions before booking.

• Are the bedroom and living area separated by a full wall with a door that closes?

• How large are the rooms? (Obtain specific dimensions.)

• Is there a full kitchen–or only a minikitchen? Are utensils and cookware provided? (Get details; you'll want more than a meager pot or two.)

• Is breakfast included in the room rate? Is it a continental breakfast, hot buffet, or other type?

• Is room service available? During what hours?

• How frequent are the hotel's housekeeping services?

• What type of business services are available onsite? And what type are obtainable for the suite?

• Are there cable TV, VCRs, and movie rentals?

• What amenities does the property offer–swimming pool, fitness center, laundry room, vending machines?

• How old is the building? If it is older, when was it last refurbished?

CHAPTER 21

Hotel Discounts Abroad

Overseas accommodations can be pretty

pricey these days. Here's how to find bargains.

———————————— ■ ————————————

You've snagged a true bargain airfare to Paris or London. But when you look for a hotel room, will you chalk up an equally appealing deal? Maybe—or maybe not. A night in a First Class or Deluxe hotel in London or Paris at rack (list) rate can easily set you back $300 to $400 these days. To save, you need to know all your options.

FOREIGN HOTELS AT HALF PRICE

The major half-price programs concentrate on North American and Caribbean hotels. Properties in Europe, Asia, and other popular destinations, if covered at all, are rather an afterthought. Still, a few top programs offer overseas listings.

Because a night in a First Class or Deluxe property in a major European city can be so costly, you can quickly offset the membership cost of even the stiffest half-price programs. And of course, your membership fee entitles you to discounts at participating U.S. hotels, too. Programs work the same overseas as they do in the U.S., but it's wise to reserve a month or two in advance.

FINDING A DEAL IN EUROPE

Although lodging costs in the major European cities can be notoriously high, travelers can find some bargains with a little advance planning. You simply need to consult the right resources and, if true savings are important to you, alter your definition of an acceptable room. In general, affordable rooms are smaller, with fewer of the amenities, such as minibar, room service, and hair dryer, that American travelers have come to expect from even mid-priced U.S. hotels. You can sort through your options via several channels.

The Internet. The web is a treasure trove of travel bargains. Lodging options are particularly diverse online, ranging from sites operated by international and country-specific hotel chains to

---

FRENCH-ACCENTED ACCOMMODATIONS

Cheap lodgings? Mais oui!

Rural France. The French countryside is full of small inns where you can often find accommodations in the same price range offered by sub-budget chains. However, very few of these inns are listed in guidebooks published in the U.S. The easiest way to find them, almost anywhere in France, is to study the current edition of the Red Michelin Guide:

Cottages. Many city tourist offices maintain lists of gîtes (cottages) available for rent in the nearby countryside. Although rentals are usually by the week, you can sometimes negotiate a deal for a shorter stay.

Restaurants. Countryside restaurants that are noted as "avec chambres" can sometimes offer better room deals, although the main business of these establishments is food service.

In the cities. Hotel booking offices, run by the local community or its tourist office, are located in most French cities (as well as in cities throughout the rest of Europe), usually in or near the main rail station. Stop to check room availability and make a reservation for one of the many inexpensive hotels using this system.

Hotels. Those listed with the guide's "quite comfortable" or "modest comfort" symbols (small cottage icons) often have rates as low as the sub-budgets.

---

those run by country or city tourist boards to the individual sites of small pensions, bed-and-breakfasts, and inns. You'll also find details on hostels—by far the cheapest places to stay.

Wholesalers and tour companies. Both types of travel providers buy up discounted blocks of hotel rooms in anticipation of filling them. Wholesalers, who advertise in Sunday-newspaper travel sections, frequently work with both travel agents and independent travelers to book these rooms. Discounts typically range from 20 to 40 percent. Tour companies expect to fill the rooms with travelers buying complete packages, but if they have excess capacity, they may sell you just the lodging at a full or partial discount.

A travel agent. Travel agencies often negotiate special deals directly with hotel chains or wholesalers. If your agency has nothing especially appealing, check around with some others. Depending on your travel dates and length of stay, someone may be able to turn up preferred rates (deeply discounted corporate rates) on select properties.

Promotions. The leading international hotel and resort chains will often offer weekend, holiday, and off-season sales, so you can stay at top properties for as much as 50 percent off.

Senior discounts. As in the U.S., hotels in Europe may offer discounts to over-50 travelers. Ask before you book.

Think small. Europe is full of small inns, many of which are family run, providing excellent value and a different type of travel experience. There's more information on these lodgings later in this chapter.

FINDING A DEAL IN ASIA

Locating lodgings in Asian cities can be tougher than finding rooms in Europe for obvious reasons: Language and time-zone barriers are more extreme, and currency conversions can be trickier. Several travel tools can assist you.

Half-price programs. Can you go the half-price route? Perhaps. But although the Asian offerings of half-price programs have greatly improved in recent years, they still remain pretty thin for some areas.

Wholesalers. Depending on your destination, you might instead

HOTELS

want to try a wholesale agency, basically a tour operator that guarantees suppliers a certain volume of bookings in exchange for price cuts.

When arranging your room, tell the agency where and when you're going, and indicate any preference for location or specific facilities. If you already have one or two favorite hotels, ask what deals the agency might have there. Otherwise, determine what's available in your price range.

You reserve in advance and prepay by check. The wholesale agency sends you a voucher that you present on arrival. (In some cases, the vouchers are sent directly to the hotel.) Cancel well before departure and you get a full refund, less a modest fee; cancel closer to departure and you forfeit the cost of one night's lodging. If you prefer to have a travel agent make the arrangements, some wholesaler listings are commissionable.

Be forewarned. As with any prepaid lodging, once you get past the cancellation deadline, you're locked into the deal. Book through a wholesale agency only if your travel plans are firm and you know the hotel where you'll be staying.

SMALL INNS AND BUDGET MOTELS

Two types of money-saving accommodations are plentiful overseas—and they could not differ more from one another.

Small inns. These individually run establishments—variously referred to as inns, guest houses, pensions, or bed-and-breakfasts —can provide a comfortable stay for budget travelers. You typically stay in an interesting, even historically important building or home. Breakfast, eaten communally with other guests, is included. Rooms may be small but are usually nicely decorated and quite clean.

But there are minuses. Not all rooms have a private bathroom. To get the cheapest prices, you may have to share a bathroom with several other guests. You will also forsake hotel services, and rooms are not likely to be air-conditioned.

Remember that some small inns are more exclusive than others; prices at these well-appointed establishments can rival those of First Class hotels.

Budget motels. Will you take efficiency over charm? Then budget motels, especially in Europe, are a great bargain.

For example, the U.K. has the Granada Inns chain, located next to Granada gas stations and restaurants along the motorways. Even cheaper are the Little Chef Lodges, affiliated with a U.K. fast-food chain.

You'll find the most budget-motel chains in France, in several classifications: sub-budget and another category a notch or two above. There's no real U.S. counterpart to the French sub-budget hotel. At somewhere near 100 square feet, the rooms are less than half the size of those you find at even bottom-end U.S. chains, and all lack air conditioning. They're furnished with one standard double bed (with, perhaps, an overhead bunk or a foldout minisingle as well). Bathrooms are tiny, with a shower down the hall. Check-in counters may be open for only a few hours in the morning and again in the evening. (At other times, guests can check themselves in automatically with a credit card.) But rooms are clean and serviceable.

In France, you must go upmarket two levels to find an establishment

HOTELS

TIGHT SQUEEZE

Assessing quaint accommodations

Small, atmospheric inns and pensions in Europe and other parts of the world can be challenging for travelers with some physical limitations. Charming and picturesque could also mean:

* Steep steps or an incline leading to the front door.

* Steep staircases (sometimes spiral) leading to upper-floor rooms. Such stairs are especially difficult to negotiate when you carry your own luggage.

* Extremely small in-room bathrooms (the larger facilities are usually shared).

* Tubs rather than showers. And the tubs often have very high sides, making getting in and out somewhat perilous.

When you book a small inn or pension, ask whether room access involves steep or narrow stairways. And get a clear description of the bathroom, including tub or shower.

resembling a U.S. budget motel. Chains such as Climat de France and Campanile approximate what you'd find at Motel 6. Even so, the rooms are smaller than those found in the U.S. chains—and cost more. The bath is similar to U.S. models, but air conditioning is relatively rare.

YOUR OTHER OPTIONS

Even dedicated discount shoppers are sometimes forced to reserve a room at rack rate. In those cases, you can still save yourself some money by comparing rates among different hotels in the same location. There are generally three ways to determine room availability and cost in overseas hotels with no U.S. reservation numbers.

Reserve by computer. Many hotels abroad are listed in the computer-reservation systems used by travel agents. You book these hotels the same way as you would a domestic hotel. For most agencies, the commission on a hotel booking for a few nights would never cover the costs of extensive comparison shopping. But once you've identified your preferred properties, a travel agent will probably agree to check the prices in a reservation computer—especially if you then book the accommodations through that agent.

Contact the hotel directly. International phone calls can be expensive and cumbersome—especially with time-zone and language barriers—but they may be your best bet. Although fax messages are convenient, they may be ignored by personnel at larger hotels when received from an unknown individual traveler. To minimize the phone charges, have specific dates and requirements ready when you call.

Check hotel reps. Many overseas hotels are represented in the U.S. by one or more hotel agents, independent booking services that will sell you a room at specific properties. Unfortunately, a representative is actually the least attractive option because you are often charged more than rack rate. But when the convenience is worth the extra cost, go ahead. Many reps list their rates in travel industry computer reservation systems and will also book overseas hotels through those systems. (A hotel is often listed more than once in a reservation system at different rates—in the hotel's own listing and through one or more representatives.)

Reps can usually issue immediate space and rate confirmations by phone. Most require a deposit (the cost of one to three nights) or a credit-card number to confirm reservations; others ask for full pre-payment. Also, some charge extra for last-minute reservations (booking one day ahead, say). Most impose cancellation limits—usually one night's charge for a no-show, but sometimes up to a three-night penalty. The resort-accommodations cancellation policy may be more stringent during the high season.

Payment procedures also vary. Some reps accept payment directly, either for one to three nights as a deposit or for the entire stay. In most cases, cash or credit cards are the currency, although a few reps accept personal checks. The advantage of paying a rep is that if you must cancel, your deposit is refundable from a U.S. organization. Also, a few reps accept a U.S. dollar payment at the booking-time exchange rate, then honor that rate regardless of any subsequent currency fluctuations.

Other hotel reps obtain credit-card guarantee information and forward it to the hotel. Your rate is computed and paid in foreign currency at the time you check out; any refunds due must come from the hotel.

Book a package. Airlines such as United and American offer air/hotel packages that may also include some sightseeing. Call the airlines or check their web sites for special deals. (Packages can save on airfare, too.) Once you get hotel specifics—deals may offer a choice of properties and luxury level—you can research the hotel on the web or in guidebooks to see exactly what you'll get.

HOTELS

CHAPTER 22

Villas, Condos, Home Exchanges

If you plan to be in one place for a week,

a month, or longer, a vacation rental or home exchange

can deliver more space for less money.

For extended stays (or even for shorter ones) a vacation rental can be an economical and enjoyable alternative to a standard hotel room. Vacation units range from rustic one-room cottages to estates accommodating a dozen or more people. Some are used exclusively as vacation rentals; others are owner-occupied and rented only occasionally.

A home exchange lets you stay in someone else's house while your exchange partner lives at your place. The "cost" is usually nothing more than a small membership fee in the home-exchange service, plus time to set up the exchange and clarify terms.

RENTAL/HOME EXCHANGE PLUSES

If you're in the mood for a relaxing vacation, a house or condo setting has some advantages.

A better price. You can often save a bundle. For example, many one-bedroom rentals include two double beds in the bedroom and a convertible sofa in the living area. That one rental could accommodate six people—a group that would require two or three hotel rooms. Such an arrangement is ideal for ski trips or other destination-oriented trips where you'll be out most of the day.

More space. A house or larger condo affords a lot of extra room, with completely separate living and sleeping quarters.

Lower living costs. A kitchen helps you cut food expenditures, always a plus for families or anyone on a budget. Most rentals or exchanges have a washer and dryer, too.

Added convenience. Properties frequently include access to private yards, pools, and other recreational facilities. In resort areas, rentals may be handier to beaches or ski slopes than hotels, and will usually have free onsite parking. You can also behave as casually as you do at home and dress as you like.

Local color. You can live like a local—shopping for food and other necessities and just exploring. In an overseas unit, you'll be able to hone your language skills as you immerse yourself in village or city life.

RENTAL/HOME EXCHANGE MINUSES

Vacationing in a house can also have a downside, which can prove both disappointing and expensive.

Minimum service. For some travelers, a resort hotel's amenities — daily maid service, fresh towels, onsite restaurants, room service—are what make a vacation enjoyable. Even if a rental provides access to some services, you usually pay extra. Many lack a TV or cable. Air conditioning isn't a given, even in warmer climates. Home-exchange means "at-home" conditions.

Housework. Spending time cooking, making beds, doing laundry, and cleaning isn't everyone's idea of a vacation.

Uncertainty. You can't always be sure of what you're getting. The only protection is whatever screening the rental agency may have done. If you rent directly from the owner, you're even more vulnerable. For home-exchange cautions, see "Ensuring a safe home exchange," later in this chapter.

HOTELS

179

Inflexibility. With a rental you typically have to reserve and pre-pay the full price far in advance—rather than the single-night deposit required by a hotel. If the property is unsatisfactory, you can't spend just one night, check out, and move elsewhere. Home-exchanges lock you into a specific time period.

Still, there are ways around most problems. If you want house-keeping services or another amenity, look for a rental that provides them as part of a package or an option. To avoid getting stuck with a lemon, check on the property conditions with someone who has rented there before. And look for a large complex catering to short-term renters, with an onsite manager. When swapping your home, carefully work out all details, duties, and perks in advance.

RENTAL MECCAS

Most of the action in the vacation-rental market centers around a few popular areas.

Resorts. U.S. vacation rentals seem to be concentrated in Florida, especially near Walt Disney World; in California, Colorado, Utah, and New England ski areas; and in Hawaii. You'll also find quite a few along the East Coast, near beach and golf centers.

Beaches. Outside the U.S., rentals concentrate in most highly developed, warm-water beach areas, especially in the Caribbean, Mexico, and along the coast of Spain.

Big cities. Rental apartments are increasingly popular in the world's major tourist cities, like London, New York, Paris, and San Francisco.

Rural Europe. The largest numbers are in France (particularly in Provence and the Dordogne), Italy (especially in Tuscany, Umbria, and the Northern lake region), and in England.

TIPS FOR HASSLE-FREE RENTING

Thinking about a vacation rental? These suggestions can make your stay less expensive and more fun.

Consider the season. Just like resort-hotel rates, vacation-rental costs go up and down seasonally. ("Travel seasons," in Chapter 6, shows some peak- and off-season times around the world.)

Time your stay. Many vacation rentals require a week's stay minimum. You may also have to rent on a fixed weekly schedule—usually Saturday to Saturday—and perhaps bend your itinerary. However, during low season, rental properties may be glad to have your business on your terms. Also consider extending your stay. Some accommodations offer reduced rates for long-term rentals (a month or more) or for large groups.

Book ahead. A vacation-rental booking usually requires a long lead time—as much as six months in advance for popular destinations at peak season. If space is still available, most agencies will work with shorter notice, but you may have to pay extra for phone calls or delivery of paperwork.

Negotiate. Feel free to haggle: List prices often aren't firm. Many vacation-rental brokers demand an up-front payment (as much as $50) as a "registration" fee or as a charge for brochures. You'll want to apply that fee to the rental cost.

Be prepared to pay. Beyond having to prepay the full rent in advance, even on fairly long rentals, you may also have to prepay for bedding or maid service. The agent may also ask for an additional cleaning or security deposit. Be aware that many brokers don't accept credit cards; you may have to write a check. Cancellation penalties can be stiff, especially if you cancel close to the occupancy date. Consider trip-cancellation insurance for any vacation rental (see Chapter 4).

Get move-in and property information. You may have to make an appointment with the property manager, local agent, or neighbor to obtain keys, turn on utilities, and arrange phone service. Note that rentals are not necessarily equipped with linens; ask about this.

Or wait until you get there. In an unfamiliar destination—but not during peak season—you may want to wait until after you arrive to arrange a vacation rental. Stay in a hotel for a few days, giving yourself enough time to scout out the rental options; then make a deal through a local realtor or the manager of a large rental complex.

Evaluate your options. For a last-minute choice or shorter-term stay, an apartment-style or all-suite hotel can provide many of the same advantages as a rental.

HOTELS

181

RENTAL AGENCIES

It's highly likely that you'll arrange your rental through one of the two main agency types specializing in vacation real estate.

Wholesale booking agencies. Such agencies focus primarily on developing extensive rental listings. Some large wholesalers publish elaborate, full-color brochures. Typically, wholesalers provide commissions to retail travel agencies that book their rentals, and some also act as retail bookers.

Retail booking agencies. These agencies will sometimes arrange

---

THE REALITY OF RENTALS

Quirky homes away from home

Consumer Reports Travel Letter staffers have sampled a variety of rentals around the globe—from Cape Cod to Florida to Scotland to Waikiki—and learned from experience.

* Assembly-line condos such as you'll find in Hawaii present few surprises or challenges. You get more space than in a hotel, but fewer services. Housekeeping is available if you want it.

* One-of-a-kind cottages or private apartments, on the other hand, can be unpredictable. At their best, they're superior to any but the most-elaborate hotel suites for privacy, peace, and living space. At their worst, they're weird—a Paris apartment, for example, where most of the beds were on "mezzanines" reached by climbing steep, spindly ladders.

* Be prepared to cope like a homeowner if something does go wrong. Someone in your group should be handy with basic tools. And never head out to a rental without at least a screwdriver and pliers. Also, you may have to figure out how to use appliances whose manuals have long since disappeared.

* Bring your own utensils. In all of our vacation rentals, we've yet to find a sharp kitchen knife or a frying pan with a flat bottom.

* You'll probably need a car. But remember that renting one can be very expensive in France or Italy.

* Rural rentals often have no phones. If a communications cutoff is a problem, take a cellular phone or rent one for the duration of the trip.

---

airline tickets and rental cars. Some retailers develop a portion of their listings; others simply sell from a wholesale catalog. For European rentals, quite a few U.S. retail booking agencies use wholesalers based in Europe.

Any good rental broker should be able to provide professional advice about destination areas and individual rentals.

OTHER OPTIONS

These rental sources might prove fruitful—and less expensive. However, ask questions and get an accurate description of the property and terms. (See "Cracking the code," this chapter.)

The web. Both vacation-rental agencies and individual owners are increasingly listing properties on the Internet. Track down listings by searching for a specific region plus the word "rental." Do remember, however, that there is no international trade organization that regulates web sites, so you would have to settle any disputes yourself.

The best sites are those geared to the U.S. market. Look for clear descriptions and photographs, and an easy reservation process. If you can e-mail the owner or rental representative, chances are this communication method will be easier—and less expensive—than phoning, especially if you're renting abroad and there are any language problems. (See Part Two for more information about travel and the web.)

Travel clubs. They may offer vacation rentals exclusively or as part of their larger mix of accommodations.

Half-price hotel programs. Some of these programs may claim to offer "discounts" on vacation rentals. But since many rental properties have no official published rate, you can't really tell whether a quoted rate is discounted or not. Travel clubs and half-price programs charge annual membership dues or fees for directories.

Tour operators. A number of companies sell package tours that include vacation-rental accommodations.

Realtors. In popular vacation areas, realtors often handle local rentals as a sideline.

Classified ads. Newspapers and magazines run ads for apartments,

HOTELS

cottages, and houses in all price ranges. Check Sunday newspaper travel sections and the side-column ads in city magazines. English weekend newspapers, found at newsstands stocking foreign publications, typically contain classified ads for a wide variety of vacation rentals—extensive listings for the United Kingdom and France, and scattered listings for many other countries.

Tourist offices. In some locations, tourist offices maintain lists of nearby vacation rentals. You can write ahead for those lists or get them when you arrive. In Europe, it's possible to find on-the-spot countryside vacation rentals available at very low prices (except during July and August).

Friends. Ask around to get recommendations—from friends, and friends of friends. Having a firsthand account of the property plus

---

IF YOU SWAP HOMES

Ensuring a smooth home exchange

The Internet has popularized home exchanges; online listings and e-mail provide convenient access and communication. Here, prudent precautions.

• Web-based home-exchange companies differ in membership costs (from $30 to $65 per year), and listings volume and variety. Review offerings before joining. (The Resource Guide lists home-exchange sites.)

• Pick home-exchange partners carefully. Companies don't screen members, so establish an ongoing dialogue with prospects. Openly discuss worries and expectations. Be sure that size, facilities, and local attractions are accurately explained. And agree on what "clean" means. Home-exchange personnel report varying standards of cleanliness as the biggest complaint.

• Put details in writing—signed by both partners. Include any special duties, such as pet care; arrangements for small household repairs; liability for possible damage; and any no-no's. (Valuables are safest stored in a locked closet or offsite.)

• Check insurance. Those staying for 30 days or less are usually considered guests and will probably be covered by your home insurance. Car insurance time limits are usually the same. Longer exchanges may require other arrangements.

special tips about the area (and any helpful people in the vicinity) can make your rental smoother.

CRACKING THE CODE

No matter how you rent, a primary source of information about individual properties is likely to be a brochure. Whether it's a simple photocopied tear sheet or an elaborate, full-color catalog, the brochure normally lists, at minimum, the location, number of rooms, and number and type of beds, and describes kitchen facilities. Many also include photographs, drawings, or floor plans.

But many brochures overaccentuate the positive. Look more closely to separate truth and exaggeration.

Photos. Compare the descriptions to the photos, and scrutinize both closely to get the hard facts. Clever wording can disguise a shack as a quaint cabin, and a wide-angle lens can make a broom closet look like a ballroom.

Sleeping specifics. The specified number of people a rental "sleeps" is often more appropriate to an army barracks than a comfortable vacation property. Unless you're willing to stack your travel party like cordwood, judge your space needs by the number of rooms and types of beds—not the number of people the brochure says you can shoehorn into the place.

Never assume. Don't expect anything that isn't specifically promised, especially in Europe. If a brochure doesn't actually say "shower," you're apt to have nothing more than a tub.

TIMESHARES: ARE THEY FOR YOU?

The concept of vacation ownership, also known as timesharing, primarily appeals to those seeking a vacation property that they can secure for many years or even a lifetime. In the U.S. today, more than 3 million owners now hold an interest in more than 1,700 timeshare resorts. Some properties are part of such well-known hotel chains as Disney, Hilton, Marriott, Radisson, and Starwood.

But carefully research any timeshare before you buy. High-pressure sales techniques and unscrupulous sellers can lure you into a deal

HOTELS

too quickly. Unclear terms may camouflage many flaws. And prohibitive costs and low resale value could turn your property into a financial burden.

Timeshare terms. You'll find two basic plans:

• The deeded purchase of an ownership interest in a piece of real estate, granting you shared ownership of a unit that can be bequeathed to heirs;

• A lease, license, or club membership that lets you use a property (such as a resort, hotel, or condominium unit) for a specific amount of time each year for a set number of years.

Generally, you purchase either "fixed" or "floating" time. A fixed-time plan secures a time slot during a specific travel period. Purchasers of floating time can schedule their week within a period of several months, and the time slot can change from year to year.

Timeshare owners also pay an annual maintenance fee, usually between $300 and $800, which may fluctuate over time. Most owners also opt to join either Interval International or Resort Condominiums International, the two major vacation-exchange companies—worthwhile if you want to vary your vacation locale each year, but membership adds another $100.

Sales subterfuge. Some salespeople may be less than truthful about a facility's physical condition and market value. They may make oral promises not covered in the written contract, or the contract may include fees and obligations not mentioned in the sales talk. And sometimes sellers may misrepresent the annual availability of a unit.

Financial drawbacks. The true cost may be higher than you think. Before you sign, add up mortgage payments and expenses, annual maintenance fees and taxes, closing costs, broker commissions, and finance charges. Even if the total seems reasonable, remember that owning a week in a timeshare may not be any cheaper than simply renting a condo or villa each year.

Some salespeople may tout a timeshare's potential appreciation value. In general, though, the market for resales is quite poor.

Timesharing tips. Remember these points when considering a timeshare purchase:

- Beware of faxes, e-mails, and mail offering free vacations. They may actually be promotions designed to entice you into visiting a timeshare resort. Once at your destination, you must often listen to a sales presentation.

- Watch out for bait-and-switch schemes. Properties may not actually be in promised locations, so always visit the facility.

- Never rush into a purchase. The property will likely still be available after 30 or 60 days, giving you time to research the company.

- Contact the state authorities and find out if any complaints have been filed against the company. Many states now have time-sharing statutes to ensure that vendors are registered and licensed, and to mandate escrow accounts. Some states also have offices providing assistance with consumer inquiries or complaints.

- Work with companies affiliated with the American Resort Development Association (ARDA), which has a code of standards and ethics for its members.

- Before signing, make sure the contract has a rescission period so that you can change your mind and get a full refund.

- If your timeshare deal includes annual maintenance fees, ask if there is a fee cap.

- Ask other owners or members about the property and its maintenance and upkeep.

- Don't hesitate to challenge sellers. In the U.S., the Federal Trade Commission (FTC) works against fraudulent, deceptive, and unfair business practices. For complaints, call 877-382-4357.

HOTELS

PART FIVE

Roads & Rails

CHAPTER 23

Renting a Car in the U.S.

Get the best rental-car deal by shopping around.

Research changes in road conditions to save time and trouble.

■

Airports aren't the only areas affected by increased security concerns. Motorists will also encounter checkpoints on the road, most notably at bridges, tunnels, major thoroughfares, and downtown areas. Perhaps for the first time, you may even be asked to show your ID or open the back of your vehicle.

But these new realities don't change the old car-renter's reality—how to get the most reasonable price for a problem-free rental.

GETTING THE BEST DEAL

In the spring of 2001, *Consumer Reports Travel Letter* surveyed prices of eight of the largest car-rental companies in 11 top U.S. and Canadian cities. We found that depending on the location, some car-rental firms charge up to $80 more per day than their least-expensive rivals for a similar car in the same city on the same dates. The add-ons that can add up on your rental bill—insurance, second-driver fees, underage surcharges, and inflated prices for refueling—also vary from one firm to another.

Our advice: Comparison shop before you book. Also search out deals, such as web-only bargains and promotional specials. (As of late 2001, rental firms were offering bargains to lure back travelers; but it's impossible to say how long these prices will last.) When you do book, ask plenty of questions of the rental agent so that you aren't "ambushed" at the rental counter by unexpected charges.

The survey, which covered eight firms—Alamo, Avis, Budget, Dollar, Enterprise, Hertz, National, and Thrifty—turned up a broad range of prices and policies. Although actual prices may change with the times, a firm's "pricing profile" will probably remain the same.

Rates are all over the map. Dollar and Thrifty emerged as low-cost leaders, but may not have locations or vehicles where you plan to rent. On the flip side, National and Avis were the highest. (Avis had the single highest rate, of $251.97 per day in New York City.)

Insurance revs up the bill. High-pressure tactics at the rental counter lead some unprepared renters to buy unnecessary coverage. But during our survey, not a single reservations agent offered information on insurance, even after we pressed them for details. So educate yourself on what you need and don't need. (See "Car-rental insurance overview," this chapter, for a step-by-step plan.) As far as insurance rates, Enterprise offered some of the lowest, while Thrifty quoted some of the highest.

Taxes take their toll. Depending on where you rent, taxes can dramatically inflate the total price. Travelers can't avoid the most costly add-ons: airport concession fees or charges for off-airport locations, and sales tax and surcharges to fund city projects such as convention centers. But you can budget for them. Ask the agent exactly what taxes will be charged.

Younger renters drive up costs. Drivers under 25 can expect to fork over a substantial daily surcharge, and they may be limited in the types of cars they can rent. The minimum age for a renter is at least 21 in most states. New York allows drivers 18 and over to rent—but at a substantial extra cost. Enterprise charges them $97 per day above the (already-high) New York base rates; other companies exact from $20 to $80 more per day.

CARS & TRAINS

None of the car-rental companies we surveyed impose a maximum age for drivers in the U.S. and Canada. However, older drivers may face restrictions overseas, depending on a given country's laws as well as other factors such as insurance costs. Check for limitations in specific countries when calling each individual firm.

An extra driver accelerates costs. Planning to split the driving? Ask about the second-driver fee, which can range from a nominal $3.99 to a whopping $25 per day. (Alamo offered the lowest charges, Avis the highest.) Although married couples aren't required to have the same last name in order to get the fee waived, those with different last names may have to show a copy of their marriage license. (And who routinely travels with that piece of paper?)

Some companies—Alamo, Hertz, and National—won't waive the fee for spouses. Dollar's policy varies by location. And *Consumer Reports Travel Letter* readers have reported that many firms usually insist on charging the fee for same-sex couples.

OTHER RENTAL CONSIDERATIONS

Once basic costs are handled, there are still other hurdles.

Debit-card policies. A number of car-rental companies won't accept reservations with a debit card—basically an ATM card bearing a Visa or Mastercard logo. Avis, Enterprise, Hertz, and National will accept them only for final payment, not to guarantee rentals. So you may need a charge card to rent.

PLAN B FOR BUMPING

When rental companies overbook

Rental-car companies typically overbook by 10 to 30 percent to account for no shows. If they run out of cars in your category, they'll usually give you an equal or better one. If they have no cars at all, insist that they arrange for a comparable rental, even it means going to a competing company. In any event, during busy travel time, it won't hurt to have a back-up plan, like taking a shuttle to your hotel and renting the next day from a less-busy off-airport vendor.

Child safety seats. Parents traveling with young children want to count on the child-safety seat they've reserved. However, of the companies we surveyed, only Alamo, Budget, and National guarantee child-safety seats with no exceptions. Hertz does not guarantee them at all. Charges usually run $5 or so per day, with some companies setting a maximum charge per rental of $40 or $50.

Ski racks. Only Avis, Budget, Enterprise, and National guarantee them without exceptions. Charges range from $3 to $10 per day.

Late returns. After the "grace period" of 59 or 60 minutes, you may start accruing hourly car-rental charges or be hit with another full-day charge. Always clarify the company's policy when you book.

Note that the grace period may not apply to child-safety seats or ski racks. Even if you're just a few minutes late—and therefore within the grace period for the vehicle—you may have to pay another full-day charge for the safety seat or ski rack.

All the rental firms we surveyed have similar late-return policies. Some companies may waive such fees on an ad hoc basis, but you can't plan on it. If you rent one of these add-ons, make the effort to get back on time.

Additional drop-off fees. Do you want to rent a car in one location and return it to another? Most companies have moved away from flat-rate drop-off surcharges; the cost is now typically built into higher daily rates instead. And if you return the rental car to a different location within the same city or even within a certain distance in the same geographic area, you may not incur either a drop-off fee or a higher daily rate.

However, if the return location is further afield, surcharges can soar up to hundreds of dollars. Make arrangements ahead of time with the car-rental company. Drop-off fees vary widely by location. Special promotions and seasonal deals can cut such "one-way rates."

Your driving record. Rental-car companies in certain states increasingly check driving records, a process that takes only a few seconds. (You probably won't even be aware that it's happening.) If the check turns up a record the company deems risky, the agent can refuse to rent to you.

THE COST OF FILLING UP

The Automobile Association of America (AAA) surveys over 60,000 self-serve stations in 50 states to compile The Daily Fuel Gauge Report. Check *www.aaa.com* for prices on regular, mid, premium, and diesel gasoline.

It pays to know just what's on your driving record. Usually, if you haven't had a ticket in the last three years, you're OK. Clean record? Rent from whichever company offers the best deal. Ditto if you have only a few problems or live in a state that doesn't disclose driving records. But those with problem records who live in states that permit screening may have to rent from a company that doesn't check records. Ask for company policies when you call around for comparison rates.

Your local DMV can provide your driving-record status. To see what will show up on a car-rental company's computer, you can contact TML Information Services, one company offering online data services (800-388-9099). For $9.95 plus

---

RENTAL-VEHICLE CHECKLIST

Inspect before you drive away

When you sign a rental-car agreement, you may be affirming that the car is in good condition, which may limit your recourse if you spot a defect later. You also want to make sure the vehicle has all the necessary equipment. So look at what you're getting.

* Check the tires (including the spare) for bulges, cuts, and excessive wear. Be sure there's a jack.

* Walk completely around the car (some rental companies now require this). Have any obvious body or mechanical damage noted on the contract to avoid being charged for it later.

* Test the windshield wipers, seat belts, seat adjustments, and all lights, including the brake lights. Note the gas level.

* Make sure there's an owner's manual (usually in the glove compartment). If not, have the agent demonstrate the use of important controls and convenience features.

* If at all possible, return the car during business hours (even if there's an express drop-off), and have the attendant review the car for damage.

tax, TML will screen your driving records against the criteria used by rental companies and mail you the report. The service, available for about 35 states, is prohibited for California or Pennsylvania drivers.

REFUELING CAN PUMP UP THE PRICE

Rental cars usually come with a full tank of gas. Travelers then typically have three refueling options:

- The company will refill the tank—at a premium, of course, sometimes as high as $4 per gallon.
- You can return the car with a full tank, and avoid this gouging. (This is usually the most economical option.)
- Or you can prepurchase a full tank of gas when picking up the rental, known as the fuel-purchase option (FPO).

All companies except Enterprise (and a few Dollar locations) now offer FPO. But although companies say their prices match or beat local pump prices, don't count on this tactic to save money.

Since the fuel charge is included in the rental's taxable subtotal, it's subject to sales tax and airport concession fees. And because there are no refunds for the unused gas left in the tank, you've got to bring the car back virtually empty to make the FPO "pay."

STEER YOUR WAY TO AN ECONOMICAL RENTAL

A strategic approach heads off unpleasant surprises.

Work out the details first. Determine in advance the type of vehicle, the exact length of the rental, who will drive it, and how you will pay. Know all the extras that could be assessed, such as taxes and fees at specific locations—these are what drive up rental costs.

Check the web. You can see who's charging what and get an idea of your possible tally. For the overall picture, compare rates from independent travel web sites with those of the rental companies themselves. Don't just accept a web "discount rate" at face value.

Talk to your travel agent. Some agencies have "override" bonus commission deals from rental firms. (See Chapter 3 for override details.) Such deals can work to your advantage when an agent can pass along a volume discount.

CARS & TRAINS

195

Ask about weekly and weekend rates. Both can yield substantial savings—as long as you observe the terms.

Weekly rates. Time periods actually range from five to seven days. Be aware that you must return the car on time (usually at the exact hour or anytime before) or get stuck with paying for extra hours, even a full day.

Weekend rates. Usually in effect from noon Thursday through noon the following Monday, these rates require a two- or three-day minimum rental. With some companies, missing the return deadline makes the entire weekend rental revert to the more expensive weekday rate.

Check for added discounts. There may be a break for members of AAA, AARP, the U.S. military, or other groups.

Inquire about loyalty points. Many of the leading car-rental firms are partnered with airlines and hotel chains.

Confirm all terms. Pin down the price, including all taxes, surcharges, fees, and terms. Ask for the story on second drivers, driver age requirements, drop-off fees, and the availability of child-safety seats, ski racks, and cell phones. Go over points several times if necessary, to clarify each detail. Request a confirmation with a number.

COMPUTER MAP-MAKING

Plotting your routes in advance

Computer mapping programs and mapping web sites are helpful for trip planning. But print out the directions before you hit the road, rather than trying to look at a screen while driving. Here are programs and sites to consider.

Computer programs cover the country. Rand McNally TripMaker Deluxe ($29.95) can pinpoint Mobil Travel Guide hotels and restaurants on detailed, interactive maps. AAA Map 'n' Go 7.0, from DeLorme ($30.00) has maps of the entire U.S., plus 66,000 AAA listings of lodgings and restaurants.

Internet maps are yours for the clicking. MapBlast (www.mapblast.com) provides interactive maps and driving directions, plus information on services and lodging. MapQuest (www.mapquest.com) lets you find a street map by address, intersection, zip code, or airport, and has info on scenic drives.

Settle the insurance question. Don't wait until you get to the rental counter. Despite what rental agents tell you, most drivers don't need to purchase the company's coverage. (For details, see "Car-rental insurance overview," this chapter.)

Leave time to refuel. If at all possible, fill the gas tank before returning the car, the best way to control rental fuel costs.

SECURITY PRECAUTIONS

Map out a plan for driving through a changed landscape.

Choose the right vehicle. On some roads, particularly in New York City, vans, recreational vehicles, and cars with tinted windows may be especially subject to inspection at checkpoints.

Assess road conditions. AAA has a trip-planning service that identifies travel hot spots. On the web, the Federal Highway Administration's site provides links to local road authorities. See "Plotting your routes in advance," earlier in this chapter, for Internet mapping sites. And ask the rental agent for maps, directions, and special local traffic tips when you pick up your car.

Allow time at the rental counter. You may not notice security measures at most car-rental locations. But companies are advising customers to allow extra time for pick-up and drop-off, especially at airport locations.

Avoid airport-access roads. Airport roads, including highways that double as access roads to airports, may be more backed up than usual, given added security and constraints on terminal parking.

Be aware of border policies. If you are crossing into or out of Canada or Mexico, expect long lines at the checkpoints. U.S. Customs officers are searching everyone and everything entering the U.S. Carry proper documentation: A valid passport could help to speed up processing. For updated information and estimated waiting times, go to *www.customs.ustreas.gov/travel/travel.htm*.

Driving a rental car across the borders into Canada or Mexico, however, is not allowed by some rental firms. Other companies charge added fees and limit a mile radius near the border. You may also be required to purchase special insurance.

CAR-RENTAL INSURANCE OVERVIEW

Sales pressure to purchase additional insurance is often intense, since this product is so profitable for car-rental companies. (One study found that such coverage increases the base rental price by an average of 46 percent a day.) Rental agents usually get a commission for selling the industry's "alphabet soup" of offerings. Here's what they'll pitch to you. (See "Insurance at a glance," this chapter, for a quick summary.)

Collision damage waiver/loss damage waiver. Not really insurance, the "CDW/LDW" waiver simply releases you from financial responsibility for physical damage to the car, and for theft and vandalism. Purchase CDW only if your own auto insurance is inadequate to cover the rental. (Some car-rental companies offer cheaper versions for only the first $500 to $3,000 in damages, an option if your own auto insurance is good for your rental and you just want to cover your deductible.)

Supplemental liability insurance. Providing up to $1 million in coverage, this protects against liability incurred in any accident that causes injury or death to others and/or physical damage to another's property. Your own auto insurance policy usually covers rental cars under the policy's standard liability provisions.

Personal accident insurance. This insures you and your passengers for accidental death or any bodily injury incurred during the rental.

Personal effects coverage (PEC). Designed to insure personal items belonging to you and your passengers against theft and vandalism, this may duplicate your homeowners or apartment-rental policy. But high deductibles on personal policies (and the risk of a rate increase for a claim) might make this coverage a feasible alternative.

YOUR CAR-RENTAL INSURANCE STRATEGY

Plan ahead—waiting until you get to the rental counter could mean spur-of-the-moment decisions and unnecessary expense.

Check your own auto-policy coverage. Call your insurance agent to clarify coverage. About 60 percent of all auto-insurance policies do cover rentals—but remember that they offer only what you have for your own car. So if your personal vehicle lacks comprehensive or collision insurance, so will your rental car. However, if at least one car on your personal policy has complete coverage, that umbrella will also apply to your rental.

Investigate credit-card insurance coverage. Many credit-card companies provide CDW coverage (but not liability coverage). To activate it, decline the rental firm's coverage and pay for your rental with your charge card. Charge-card coverage is typically "secondary," meaning you must submit any claim to your own insurance carrier(s) first. (For those with no personal insurance coverage, however, it becomes primary.)

CAR-RENTAL INSURANCE AT A GLANCE

TYPE/PRICE PER DAY	WHAT IT COVERS	DO YOU NEED IT?
Collision damage waiver/loss damage waiver $9 to $25	Typically releases you from financial responsibility for the rented vehicle in the event of theft, vandalism, or damage.	Only if your own insurance is inadequate.
Supplemental liability insurance $6 to $15	Provides coverage against liability incurred in any accident causing injury or death to others and/or property damage.	It's not a bad idea. And get more if you have sizable assets. [1]
Personal accident insurance $1 to $10	Protects you in the case of accidental death or injury during the rental. Passengers are covered if injured while inside the rental car or while getting in or out.	Not if you have your own medical or travel insurance.
Personal effects coverage $1 to $8	Insures your personal items and those of passengers against theft and vandalism.	It may be less expensive than relying on your homeowner's or apartment-rental policy.

[1] Personal auto policy usually covers rental cars under standard liability provisions for non-owned cars. No major charge-card company includes liability insurance in basic car-rental plans. Non-car-owners might consider a non-owner liability policy, typically $200 to $300 per year for up to $1 million in coverage.

Although charge-card coverage is usually valid in the U.S., it may not be usable in all international locations. (See Chapter 24 for overseas cautions.)

Buy rental-car insurance only if necessary. However, since your tolerance for risk might be lower away from home, when faced with unfamiliar or larger vehicles, strange roads, or different driving procedures, you may want additional coverage.

Car-rental companies are required to provide only the minimum amount of liability coverage called for by a particular state. But CONSUMER REPORTS recommends you exceed state recommendations, either with the rental firm's coverage or your own. We advise minimum liability insurance of $100,000 for bodily injury, per person; $300,000 for bodily injury, all persons; and $100,000 for property damage. If you have sizable assets, we suggest increasing bodily injury coverage to $150,000 per person and $500,000 per accident.

Be aware of possible exclusions. Whether provided by the car-rental company or your charge card, all coverage is peppered with exclusions. Standard in most rental-car contracts are clauses that void coverage if you drive off-road or under the influence of alcohol or narcotics, or allow anyone but an authorized driver to operate the car. Most notable among the charge-card exclusions are losses not reported within certain limits (wait too long and you lose the right to claim them) and coverage of certain "exotic" or expensive models. The bottom line: Get a written list of terms from your charge-card company and read all contracts.

CHAPTER 24

Renting Around the World

If you rent a car overseas, you'll have to

consider currency conversions and language barriers,

as well as foreign road signs and rules.

━━━━━━━━━━━━━━ ■ ━━━━━━━━━━━━━━

Renting a car can be the most cost-effective and convenient way to tour a foreign country. Shop around as you would in the U.S.

CONSIDERATIONS WHEN RENTING ABROAD

Here are suggestions that can smooth your ride.

Choose a U.S. or large multinational company. At gateway airports worldwide, you'll see many familiar logos of multinational rental companies or their affiliates, such as Alamo, Avis, Budget, Dollar, Hertz, National, and Thrifty. Renting from a known company confers two big advantages.

Agents probably speak English. While there's no guarantee, employees of a U.S.-based company will usually have at least a basic knowledge of English. If you do have difficulty understanding an employee at a rental desk, ask to talk to a supervisor. If there's still a problem, request the company's customer-service number.

You'll resolve disputes more easily when home. Should you have a billing or damage-liability dispute, you (or your insurance and/or credit-card company) will probably settle it more quickly with a U.S. company than with a foreign one. Local rental-car company rates might be lower than those of a large multinational company, but vehicles, service, and maintenance may not measure up to what you're used to at home.

Book before you leave. Researching and booking your rental before departure can save money. Comparing costs on your own via phone or Internet, or through a travel agent, can uncover special promotions or upgrade deals. Reserving a car guarantees you a car upon arrival, so you won't have to scramble from counter to counter.

Read the contract thoroughly. Make sure the specific rate you were quoted when you reserved matches the rate on the contract you sign. Do a quick calculation; rates will be in local currency. And question any extra charges, such as taxes or fees. (See Chapter 23 for more on charges and fees.)

Learn local driving rules. Even when driving in an English-speaking country, you'll find the rules of the road to be quite different from those at home.

Right or left? Your comfort level with "reverse driving" may influence your decision to rent at all. (See "Driving on the left," later in this chapter.)

Speed limits. In many countries, the speed limit is higher than it is in the U.S. In Germany, France, and Italy, for example, cars in the fast lane often zip along at over 100 mph. Maximum speed limits also vary greatly from open highways to urban areas.

Mph or kph? Depending on the country, speed limits and distances will be indicated in either miles or kilometers. Determine which it is before setting out.

Seat belts. Wearing one is compulsory in an increasing number of countries around the world.

Child-safety seats. Are they required—and available—and for children up to what age? Some countries also prohibit young children from sitting in the front seat of vehicles.

Traffic conditions. In some foreign countries, roads are extremely congested; in others, they are notoriously dangerous—as a result of reckless drivers, poor conditions, or a combination of both. Guidebooks usually indicate if driving is even a viable option.

Weigh the language barrier. Many Americans safely rent cars in non-English-speaking countries in Europe, getting by with rudimentary language skills and good maps. Navigating in a country with a language based on unfamiliar characters or symbols, such as Japan, Korea, China, Russia, or most of the Middle East, can be decidedly more difficult. Again, guidebooks can tell you whether it's feasible to rent a car. (In some countries, you can "rent" both a car and a driver, often your best bet, although it costs more.)

The CDW/LDW overseas. You may find it especially tough to avoid CDW/LDW when renting overseas. Many foreign-based rental companies apparently continue to rely on CDW/LDW for profits; some may threaten to put a hold on your card to cover possible damage if you decline their coverage. (If you carry more than one credit card, you could charge your rental on one card and put day-to-day expenses on the other.) Your best defense is to prearrange the rental through a U.S. office or agency. Specify when you reserve and rent that you intend to use your credit card for collision protection and won't buy the CDW/LDW.

However, charge-card coverage may not be valid in all countries. Ireland, Italy, Jamaica, Australia, and New Zealand are frequently excluded. Eastern European and Latin American countries may present problems due to high car-theft rates. Consult your charge-card company for terms and conditions before you leave.

RENTING AND DRIVING IN CANADA

You must meet certain requirements, whether you're renting or visiting with your own car.

Renting in Canada. You'll need a driver's license, a charge card, and an insurance card. The rental company should give you a card disclosing its provided liability coverage for the vehicle. Coverage may be below Canadian requirements, so do get the nonresident inter-

CARS & TRAINS

provincial card from your own insurance company.

Collision insurance, covering damage to the car when you're driving, isn't legally required. But unless the rental is an old wreck, it's wise. Your own policy's collision coverage probably applies in Canada; check before you leave home.

Credit-card collision coverage works in Canada the same way it does in the U.S. If your own auto insurance includes Canada, the card provides additional, secondary coverage. (It may also pick up any liability not covered by your car insurance, up to a stated limit. Check with your charge-card company.) And should your personal auto insurance exclude Canada, your card's collision coverage becomes primary.

Documents. You need only a valid U.S. driver's license, proof of liability insurance, and the vehicle's registration to drive. But to return to this country you must show proof of U.S. citizenship or legal residence. Your driver's license won't do—you need a passport, green card, or certified copy of your birth certificate, especially now that border security is so much tighter..

Liability insurance. Whether driving your own car or a rental, you must carry coverage against damage to someone else's property or person. The legal minimum is C$200,000 (U.S., about $125,000); in Quebec it's C$50,000 (U.S., about $31,000). If involved in an accident, you must show proof of insurance.

Liability coverage for Canada, on your own car or a rental, is probably included in your regular automobile insurance. But before you leave, check with your insurance representative—if you aren't covered, you'll need to buy a separate add-on policy. If you are covered, ask your company to send you a Canadian nonresident interprovince motor vehicle liability insurance card, which certifies that you carry the statutory minimum liability coverage.

However, some rental car companies may require you to buy supplemental liability insurance whether you need it or not.

Driving a U.S. rental car. The rental contract serves as the rental-car company's official permission to drive a car into Canada. But many local rental offices establish additional limits of their own. For example, Seattle car-rental offices may limit Canadian driving to British Columbia only. (If you have an accident or a mechanical problem outside the allowable driving area, you're liable for towing and repair.) Some U.S. rental-car companies impose mileage caps on Canadian driving. Others won't allow you to cross the border.

Border checkpoints. Security at all U.S. borders has tightened dramatically since the events of Sept. 11. Expect searches, questions, and long lines. Have your documentation ready and all baggage easily accessible.

RENTING AND DRIVING IN MEXICO

Driving in Mexico—either your own car or a rental—always involved bureaucracy. Now the borders are backed up, too.

Documents. Crossing the border in either direction requires proof of U.S. citizenship or residence. To drive, you need a valid U.S. driver's license and a Spanish translation of it. (Get an international driving permit. Details are in this chapter.)

Whenever you travel beyond the immediate border areas (Tijuana, Tecate, Mexicali, or Baja, California) or stay in Mexico more than 72 hours, you'll also need a Mexican tourist card (*tarjeta de turista*), free at Mexican consulates and tourist offices, and upon arrival from most airlines serving Mexico. The tourist card is valid for stays of up to 180 days and must be used within 90 days of its issuance. Visitors must carry it at all times while in Mexico or risk incurring a fine.

Insurance. U.S. insurance rarely covers liability in Mexico. Whether you drive your own car or a rental, you'll almost certainly need to buy separate Mexican liability insurance, widely available from independent agencies in border-crossing areas, through border-area AAA offices or, if you rent, through a rental agency. Some liability coverage is included in Mexican car rentals; it varies by location and company. If the amount isn't close to what you carry in the U.S., buy extra.

Your U.S. insurance probably won't cover you for collision, either. If you don't want to buy the collision-damage waiver from the rental company, use credit-card coverage. Should your own insurance exclude Mexico (as it most likely does), the card's coverage will be primary. (Check with your credit-card company before you rent for any exclusions and conditions.)

Driving a private car. No special procedures are required if you confine your driving to a "free zone," typically within 20 miles of the border but including most of Baja California. Just arrange your insurance and go.

You'll need a temporary car-importation permit to drive beyond the free zone, however. To obtain the permit, you must present both the original and a copy of your vehicle's title certificate and registration at a border station, about 12 to 16 miles below the border.

The permit fee (about $22) is payable only by a credit card issued in your name by a bank outside Mexico; cash or traveler's checks aren't accepted. A hologram is then applied to the inside of the vehicle's windshield and must be removed by Mexican border officials when you return to the U.S.

Driving a U.S. rental car. Company policies vary, so confirm when you rent. Some offices near the border may prohibit any driving in Mexico; others may limit how far below the border you can go or cap the distance you can drive in Mexico before you start paying per-mile charges.

Mexico puts you through the same car-permit rigmarole with a rental car as with your own car. However, the rental company provides the necessary proof of ownership. Be sure to let the rental agent know you intend to drive into Mexico.

Crossing the border. Like the borders with Canada, those with Mexico are now under heightened security—and plagued with increased congestion. At press time, waits of several hours were not uncommon. Since many people living along the border "commute" from one country to another, the best crossing time might be mid-day, rather than during the morning or late afternoon hours. Have all documentation at hand and luggage ready to be easily searched.

Renting in Mexico. All you need is a valid driver's license, a credit card, and Mexican insurance sold by the rental company. But be aware that Mexican rental costs can be substantially higher than they are in the U.S.

RENTING AND DRIVING IN EUROPE

Driving in Europe affords flexibility and can allow you to roam beyond the big cities, enjoying smaller towns and stunning country-side—along with unfamiliar roads and traffic rules. Also consider safety. Some areas do pose dangers to American travelers. Check the public announcements issued by the U.S. State Department before you decide whether to rent and drive yourself. (Details are in the Reference Section.)

If safety is not an issue, cost can be a useful tiebreaker if you're torn between renting a car and traveling by rail. For two people touring Europe, a car rental beats train travel in all countries but Italy, where car-rental rates are high, and France, where both modes of travel cost about the same. A solo traveler, however, would do better traveling by train except on a short trip in the Europass area (France, Germany, Italy, Spain, and Switzerland) and in the U.K., where car and train costs are about even. However, factor in gasoline prices, too. (See "A gallon of gas costs how much?" this chapter.) Here's what to expect if you choose to travel Europe by rental car.

Documents. At the rental counter, you'll need a reservation confirmation or voucher (reserving in advance reduces problems), a valid U.S. driver's license, a credit card, and your passport. An international driving permit isn't required in any country but Italy, but is recommended for travel in Austria, Germany, Spain, Eastern Europe, and the Middle East.

Rental-company choices in Europe. Arriving at one of Europe's gateway airports is almost like landing at a major U.S. airport. The major multinational companies are all represented, including Alamo, Avis, Budget, Hertz, National, Payless, and Thrifty. In addition, you'll find Eurocar, an affiliate of U.S.-based Dollar, as well as three European-based renters—Kenning, Town & Country, and Woods—all of which have U.S. representatives.

The wholesale-tour-operator option. You can also rent a car from

CARS & TRAINS

several U.S.-based wholesale tour operators: Auto Europe, AutoNet, DER Car, Europe by Car, European Car Reservations (ECR), International Travel Services (ITS), and Kemwel Holiday Autos. All arrange rentals through various Europe-based renters, multinational as well as local.

Payment alternatives. The multinational car-rental companies offer a choice between prepayment at a rate guaranteed in U.S. dollars and payment in local currency when the car is returned. (Unless the prepaid price is significantly lower, choose the pay-at-return option. It's less hassle if your plans change.) Tour operators usually require payment upfront.

Car decisions. Rental car prices are keyed to a car's letter code—but with little consistency. One country's B-class car may be another country's C-class car. In fact, a single company may class the same model as an A in one country and a B in another. For that reason, it's smart to shop by car model—when reserving, ask for cars by specific model, not letter code.

Standard subcompacts. These are the smallest cars comfortable for two touring adults. Typically, these cars are two- or three-door models, which can accommodate two people and their baggage—but have rear-seat room suitable for infants or small children.

Standard midsized cars. Midsized models are the smallest cars

---

WHEN IS RENTING A GOOD DEAL?

Some countries are very expensive

Rental car prices in Europe vary greatly from one country and company to another. When deciding between car and train travel, you'll want to compare prices. (See Chapter 25 for rail guidelines.) To help, we've listed which countries generally offer good-value rental-car rates and which are notably expensive.

Good value: Austria, Belgium, France, Germany, Luxembourg, the Netherlands, Portugal, Spain, Switzerland.

Expensive: Bulgaria, Czech Republic, Denmark, Finland, Hungary, Iceland, Ireland, Italy, Norway, Poland, Romania, Slovenia, Sweden, the United Kingdom.

---

that will comfortably accommodate three or four adults or two adults with larger children. They're usually four-door sedans, two classifications up from standard subcompacts, with adequate rear seat room for two adults.

Rental companies (and tour packagers that offer rental cars) often push four-door models of some of the roomier subcompacts or compacts as adequate for four travelers. But you'll probably find those cars are too tight for rear-seat passengers.

Cheap come-ons. Some rental companies feature cramped, severely underpowered subcompacts at lowball prices. While these models may be fine for tooling around town, they're unsuitable for the open highway.

Economical automatics. Now fairly common in many European countries, automatics are often just one category up from the standard subcompact group—fine for two, but skimpy for four. In some countries, however, you'll find an automatic transmission only in large, luxury cars.

Air conditioning. Air conditioning is now more common—and less expensive—especially in warmer European countries. If it's important to you, check availability when you reserve your car.

Recreational vehicles. Minivans and campers have also become popular in Europe. The rental rates for these vehicles are high, however, especially in summer.

The best deal. No single company is consistently either the cheapest or the most expensive from country to country—or for all models within the same country. But some rates are better than others.

Weekly touring rates. These are usually the top bargains you can book in the U.S. for summer driving in Europe. (Longer rentals are usually prorated at a per-day rate of one-seventh the weekly price.) Typically, you must keep your car five days to qualify. Return the car early and the company may recalculate at the local daily rate, which can often run up your bill.

Basic prices are usually uniform throughout each country. But you can expect to pay a surcharge at many large airports; rates in Greece and Spain may vary at island locations.

CARS & TRAINS

You'll generally be able to find deals in Europe that include unlimited mileage. In a few countries, costs are higher in July and August. However, rates are always subject to change, with some company's charges more volatile than others—check exact rates for exact dates before you depart.

Can't set your itinerary in advance? If you decide to rent after you arrive in Europe, a local rental office will probably quote you a much higher price than you would have gotten by reserving in advance—maybe with a mileage cap, too. Unless you are renting for just a day or two, don't pay that extra amount. You can probably get the weekly touring rate by calling a multinational rental company's North American reservation office or your travel agent back home.

One-way rentals. Most companies don't charge extra for a rent-it-here, leave-it-there rental within a single country. However, to rent in one country and return in another, check first with the multinationals—some provide one-way rentals between a few adjoining countries at no extra cost. (You pay the originating country's rate and tax.)

Change gateway? Most tourists pick up their rental car in the country in which they arrive. So you may find it worthwhile to choose your gateway country for its low car-rental rates. In past surveys of rental rates, both Belgium and Germany offered low rates. And airfares to these destinations from the U.S. and Canada were generally at least as good as to neighboring countries. Other low-rate countries were the Netherlands, Portugal, Spain, and Switzerland.

Extras and limitations. European rentals have add-ons and restrictions. Some you can't avoid—but a few you can.

VAT. European auto rentals are subject to value-added tax (VAT), which can boost your rental cost by as much as 25 percent. Note that rental-brochure rates usually exclude VAT, so always ask how much it will add when reserving. Services such as car rentals are "consumed" locally, so in most European countries, travelers can't claim the VAT refunds available on goods bought locally but "exported" outside Europe. While most rental companies list identical VAT rates, a few tour operators apparently manage to get a partial VAT refund—which they then pass along to customers—because they're "exporting" car rentals to travelers who live in North America.

Airport expenses. Quite a few European airports impose fees that rental companies pass along to renters. Most are trivial—in total, they might add up to less than the cost of a taxi from the airport to a downtown rental office. But in Austria, Belgium, Italy, Luxembourg, Switzerland, and the U.K., renting from an airport location can add as much as 10 to 14 percent to the total cost—enough to make you consider dealing with an off-airport office. (The fees don't apply to cars that you simply return at an airport.)

Highway charges. Any car driven in Austria or Switzerland must have a sticker indicating payment of that country's highway fee. Local rental cars normally have that sticker. But if you rent in an adjacent country, you (not the rental company) must buy the sticker or pay a stiff fine. Rental cars in such border-area cities as Milan and Munich often have a sticker already—ask for one if you plan to drive in Austria or Switzerland.

Geographic limits. At some locations, car-rental companies

A GALLON OF GAS COSTS HOW MUCH?

When renting abroad, remember to factor in fuel costs. Here are the 10 highest gasoline prices worldwide and the 10 lowest, as of December 2001.

HIGHEST GAS PRICES		LOWEST GAS PRICES	
Hong Kong	$5.20	Jakarta	$0.38
London	4.02	Caracas	.51
Espoo, Finland	4.02	Kuwait City	.74
Oslo	3.97	Manama, Bahrain	.80
Tokyo	3.92	Riyadh	.91
Jerusalem	3.90	Cairo	.98
Amsterdam	3.88	Almaty	1.14
Paris	3.85	Kuala Lumpur	1.16
Seoul	3.84	Kiev	1.17
Berlin	3.74	Moscow	1.21

Source: Runzheimer International, a Wisconsin-based consulting firm.

CARS & TRAINS

restrict your driving destinations. The most common ban is on driving Western European rentals into Eastern Europe, with some exceptions (cars rented in Austria and Germany can often be driven into the Czech Republic, Hungary, and Slovakia). Whenever you reserve a rental car in Europe, ask if your entire itinerary is acceptable. When it's not, check with other rental companies.

Age restrictions. Minimum and, occasionally, maximum age limits vary by country and company. Should your party include an under-25 or over-70 driver, be sure to check age restrictions when you reserve.

DRIVING ON THE LEFT

Before arranging to rent a car in a foreign country, read guidebooks to establish whether traffic circulates on the left or the right. In countries adhering to the British system—United Kingdom (England, Scotland, Wales), Ireland, Malta, Gibraltar, Australia, New Zealand, South Africa, India, the British Virgin Islands, Grenada, Jamaica, Hong Kong, Fiji, the Cook Islands, and Tonga—be ready for the experience of driving on the left.

Know the basics. Cars built to drive on the left are the mirror

---

MORE DOCUMENTS

An international driver's permit

Some countries, predominantly those where English is spoken, will allow you to rent a car using a valid U.S. driver's license. Many others require that you have what is known as an International Driver's Permit (IDP). Valid in over 150 countries, the IDP contains your name, photo, and driver information, translated into 10 languages.

If you travel a lot and enjoy the flexibility allowed by renting a car, the IDP is a worthwhile investment. And you can easily obtain one through any AAA office. Bring your valid U.S. driver's license, two original passport-size photos, and $10. You can also print out an application at the AAA web site *(www. aaa.com)* and apply by mail using a photocopy of your U.S. driver's license.

opposite of those driven on the right. The driver's seat is on the right side of the car, so you'll look to the left to view the rearview mirror. The turn signal and window-wiper controls are also reversed. If the car has a manual transmission, you will shift gears with your left hand rather than your right.

Avoid renting in a downtown location. An airport pickup is preferable to starting out in the heart of a traffic-congested city, because you're likely to first experience local roads or highways rather than crowded, narrow (and often one-way) streets.

Give yourself time to adjust. Before venturing onto roads that require attentive driving skills—busy city streets, curving mountain or coastal roads—drive around in less-crowded areas, such as back roads and residential neighborhoods.

Avoid manual-shift cars on your first rental. Although a rental car with a manual transmission will save you money (quite a bit in some countries), it can greatly increase the frustration factor for novice left-hand drivers. Having to shift gears—with your left hand, no less—while still adjusting to the disorientation of driving on the left and navigating unfamiliar streets and highways, is difficult at best. If you've never driven on the left, reserve an automatic transmission, even if you favor a stick and drive one at home.

CHAPTER 25

Taking the Train or the Bus

A train or bus ride can be practical, economical, and scenic.

Both transportation modes have enhanced security.

Many Americans ride commuter trains or light-rail trains to work every day, but as a vacation option—either in the U.S. or overseas—flying or renting a car has usually been the first choice. After Sept. 11, travelers began to consider the train a more viable alternative.

U.S. motorcoach bus lines, which carried about 200 million more passengers in 2000 than the airlines and more than double the load of Amtrak and commuter rail lines combined, saw a sharp dip in ridership after Sept. 11. But ridership may rebound as more travelers seek an alternative to flying.

TRAIN TRAVEL IN NORTH AMERICA

Amtrak, the company that has controlled intercity domestic rail travel since it was created by the government in 1971, can get you to most places (more than 500 cities in 45 states) on trips ranging from under an hour to three full days. Most Amtrak trains offer comfortable seating and plenty of legroom. Many overnight trains have a full-service dining room and a two-level sightseeing lounge car open to all passengers. Sleeping berths are also available on longer trips. You must make reservations well in advance for peak summer travel. By May, it may be too late to book your preferred route.

The newest Amtrak service is the high-speed (and pricier) Acela train, with such amenities as personal audio programming, and tray tables sized for a laptop: Acela Express between Washington and Boston, Acela Regional in New England, and Acela Commuter from Philadelphia and western New Jersey to Newark and New York.

Amtrak has also introduced a Guest Rewards program, awarding points for train travel that can be spent with Amtrak or its travel partners as well as some retailers.

In Canada, intercity rail travel is controlled by VIA Rail Canada. The company, founded in 1978, services the majority of Canada's provinces with routes to 450 cities—although 85 percent of its ridership is concentrated in the Quebec/Windsor corridor, which includes the cities of Montréal and Quebec.

Time factors. Trains can be faster than traveling by car, since you needn't factor in traffic and rest stops. Train travel can actually be as fast as air travel on some short, intercity trips like New York to Washington, D.C., or Portland to Seattle. Getting to and from less-than-accessible airports tags on almost the same amount of time as the train trip itself, and airport lines can add extra delays. In contrast, train stations are conveniently located in city centers.

On longer trips, you can expect to spend eight to 10 times as many hours on the rails as in the air. For example, a flight from New York to Miami takes about three hours, while the trip by train takes 24 to 28 hours.

Cost factors. Train travel is not cheap. Costs rise when the trip covers several days and requires sleeping accommodations. On journeys of 12 to 20 hours, many people opt to sit for the entire trip rather than book a sleeper berth. The cost of a coach fare on a train is about the same as some low-fare airline prices.

Train travel is almost always more costly per person than auto travel, even when rental-car costs are figured in, especially when two or more are traveling. However, there are discounts and good deals available, depending on the traveler's age and itinerary. (See "Rail passes and discounts," this chapter.)

New protection policies. Amtrak passengers now are required to show a photo ID when buying a ticket from station ticket agents or when checking baggage on long-distance trains. You must have a ticket to board an Amtrak train anywhere between Washington,

RAIL PASSES & DISCOUNTS

Bargain fares in the U.S. and Canada, as of December 2001 (in U.S. dollars).

RAIL PASSES	DISCOUNTS	SPECIAL DEALS
AMTRAK CALIFORNIA RAILPASS allows seven days of rail travel within a 21-day period on any Amtrak train or bus route; adults, $159; children ages 2 to 15, $80.	50 percent for children ages 2 to 15 accompanied by a paying adult; 15 percent for full-time students, seniors over 62, and the disabled.	Check Rail Sale at *http://tickets.amtrak. com* for discounts on one-way travel between selected cities; other special fares listed each Monday.
VIA RAIL CANADA CANRAILPASS allows 12 days of unlimited travel in a 30-day period to any stop; $658 peak season, $411 off-peak.	$592 peak season for children and seniors, $370 off peak; 35 percent for full-time students with International Student Identity (ISIC) card.	Super-Saver fares in low season with advance purchase; with VIA Preference, get ticket-earning bonus points.
NORTH AMERICAN RAIL PASS, offered by Amtrak in conjunction with VIA Rail Canada, allows 30 consecutive days of travel to 900 destinations in U.S. and Canada; peak season (June 1 to October 15), $674; off-peak (October 16 to May 31), $471.	No featured discounts.	No special deals featured.

D.C., and Boston, even a nonreserved train. In other areas of the country, you may still purchase tickets from conductors on the train, but will need to show a photo ID.

Amtrak has added uniformed police in rail stations and on trains and, at press time, was soliciting federal help to beef up existing patrols of rail crossing and bridge and tunnel tracks.

VIA Rail has increased track patrols near borders and heightened security at major stations and facilities. Be ready for inspections between the U.S. and Canada, and take a valid passport, if you have one. Call your rail line or visit the web site for the latest information. Phone numbers and web addresses are in the Reference Section.

MOTORCOACH SECURITY

Bus lines have also instituted tighter rules. Greyhound hired off-duty police officers and other security personnel to conduct random searches of passengers at bus terminals in major metropolitan areas, including close searches with metal-detecting wands at boarding. Riders may now be asked to open their checked baggage as well as any hand-carried items. Many terminals now prominently post lists of banned items, such as knives and other cutting tools, firearms and ammunition, and mace.

At press time, the American Bus Association had proposed additional measures, such as new baggage-screening techniques, metal-detector wanding, and secured waiting areas. However, there were no plans to require advance reservations, although many bus lines prohibit ticket purchase onboard. Contact the line before you travel to resolve questions.

EUROPEAN TRAIN TRAVEL

Trains often make more sense than renting a car in Western Europe. They are generally faster and eliminate traffic or parking worries. Fares are also quite affordable, especially compared with air fare, which can be very expensive unless you get special coupons (see Chapter 17 for more information on these deals).

Train travel in Europe is especially smart if you're traveling alone, are

CARS & TRAINS

staying mainly in big city centers where parking can be a nightmare, or plan to rack up a lot of mileage—say on a multiweek, multicountry trip. Plus, on the train, you won't have to decipher foreign-language road signs.

Many European countries already had strict security at railroads, airports, and other vulnerable areas. But at press time, measures had been stepped up. Along with a greater police presence at stations and onboard trains, there may be metal detectors, more frequent luggage checks (searches as well as x-ray screening), and earlier check-ins. So even with a Eurailpass and a reservation, don't expect to hop on the train at the last minute. And don't walk away from your bags—all abandoned luggage and parcels will be destroyed.

TICKETS AND PASSES IN EUROPE

Rail travelers in Europe have many choices, from simple one-way tickets to multiweek passes. Students and those over 65 may also qualify for discounts.

One-way and round-trip tickets. If you plan to take a train from one major European city to another, a single one-way ticket is your best bet. You can choose either a first- or second-class ticket as well as the type of train—classified in each country by such standards as speed or number of stops. A first-class ticket generally costs about one-third more than a second-class ticket. Second-class cars in most European countries are perfectly comfortable, but more crowded.

Multinational passes. There are currently about a dozen multinational pass options available to overseas travelers in Europe, the most well known being the Eurailpass. Note, however, that all multinational passes must be purchased in the U.S. prior to departure.

The Eurailpass. The classic Eurailpass allows unlimited first-class travel plus free or reduced fares on many suburban trains, long-distance buses, and boat and ferry lines in the following 18 countries: Austria, Belgium, Denmark, Finland, France, Germany, Greece, Holland, Hungary, Ireland, Italy, Luxembourg, the Netherlands, Norway, Portugal, Spain, Sweden, and Switzerland. It is the most expensive but least restrictive option available. ("European train passes," this chapter has details and prices.) If you have questions about what is covered by a Eurailpass, contact Rail Europe, the official Eurailpass representative in the U.S.

Limited multinational passes. Groups of countries also offer regional passes, with travel limited to the participating countries. Two examples in Western Europe are the Benelux Pass (Belgium, the Netherlands, and Luxembourg) and the Scanrail Pass (Denmark, Finland, Norway, and Sweden). In Eastern Europe, two regional passes are the European East Pass, which covers Austria, the Czech Republic, Hungary, Poland, and Slovakia, and the Balkan Flexipass, covering Bulgaria, Greece, Macedonia, Romania, Serbia, Montenegro, and Turkey.

National passes. Most or all of the countries that participate in the Eurailpass also offer their own national passes, practical if you confine your travels largely to one country; a national pass will almost always be cheaper than a multinational pass of the same length. And unlike all but the student-discount type of Eurailpass, many national passes are available in second class. National passes are especially good deals in France, Italy, Switzerland, and the Netherlands.

Great Britain does not participate in the Eurailpass program but offers its own BritRail pass. In addition, BritRail offers the BritRail Party Pass, which offers reduced-price packages for three or four adults traveling together. Up to two children travel free with BritRail Family Pass.

Although a national pass may not have all the extras of a multinational pass, some offer perks or features of their own. The Swiss pass, for example, provides free or discounted travel on important private railroads that Eurailpass excludes.

Discounts for seniors. Since most European railroads give reductions to senior travelers, those over 65 may do better with individual tickets (usually discounted 30 to 50 percent) than with travel-all-you-want rail passes. Here are a few deals:

• Seniors who show ID (typically a passport) can get discounts on tickets in Denmark, Finland, Norway, and Portugal, but travel may be blacked out on peak days or at peak times.

CARS & TRAINS

EUROPEAN TRAIN PASSES

Rail passes can be the way to go, depending on the duration of your stay and where you are going within Europe. Here are some sample passes. Prices are current as of December 2001.

PASS	DURATION/COST
EURAILPASS Unlimited first-class travel in all 18 Eurailpass countries.	15 days: $554; 21 days: $718 1 month: $890; 2 months: $1,260; 3 months: $1,558
EURAIL SAVERPASS Unlimited first-class travel in all Eurailpass countries for 2 to 5 people traveling together for duration of pass; prices per person; 15 percent less than standard Eurailpass.	15 days: $470; 21 days: $610; 1 month: $756; 2 months: $1,072; 3 months: $1,324;
EURAIL YOUTHPASS Unlimited second-class travel in all Eurailpass countries for anyone under 26; 30 percent less than standard Eurailpass.	15 days: $388; 21 days: $499; 1 month: $623; 2 months: $882; 3 months: $1,089; 10 days: $654; 15 days: $862
EURAIL FLEXIPASS First-class travel for set number of consecutive days over 2- month period.	10 days: $654; 15 days: $862
EURAIL SAVER FLEXIPASS First-class travel on Flexipass terms for 2 to 5 people traveling together for duration of pass; prices per person; 15 percent less than standard Flexipass.	10 days: $556; 15 days: $732
EURAIL YOUTH FLEXIPASS Second-class travel on Flexipass terms for anyone under 26; 30 percent less than standard Flexipass.	10 days: $458; 15 days: $599
EUROPASS First-class travel for set number of nonconsecutive days over 2-month period in France, Germany, Italy, Spain, and Switzerland; choose 2 more countries from Austria/Hungary, Belgium, the Netherlands, Luxembourg, Greece, and Portugal for additional fees.	5 days: $348; 15 days: $688 (More options are available.)
EUROPASS SAVERPASS First-class travel on Europass terms, in Europass areas, for 2 to 5 people traveling together for duration of pass; prices per person; 15 percent less than standard Europass.	5 days: $296 15 days: $586 (More options are available.)
EURO YOUTHPASS Second-class travel on Europass terms, in Europass areas, for anyone under 26; 30 percent less than standard Europass.	5 days: $244 15 days: $482

• In Austria, France, Greece, and Sweden, seniors who buy an official ID from the railroad (good for a year) get discounts, too. You can have an ID card issued on the spot at a main rail station booking office. In most cases, you'll need a passport-sized photo—but many stations have photo machines. Austrian cards are also available in advance by mail.

Still, a Eurailpass may prove more convenient for multicountry rail trips, since it cuts out time-consuming waits in ticket lines for each leg of a trip.

TRAIN RESERVATIONS

Many Americans may find the need for reservations on European trains confusing. Both a ticket and a pass entitle you to board a train, but neither will guarantee you a seat. To be certain you have a seat on many popular trains, you need a reservation—which "assigns" you a specific seat in a specific car on the train for which you hold a ticket.

Reservations, which generally cost from $5 to $8 depending on the country and the train (sleeper-car reservations are more expensive), are made at a separate counter. So once you've purchased a ticket, you must then wait in another line to reserve a seat. If you have a Eurailpass, you need only wait in the reservation line—but since reservations are not included in the price of a Eurailpass, you'll pay the same reservation fee as non-passholders.

You can also make reservations in the U.S. through Rail Europe before departure. But the service costs $11 per standard reservation, so it's no bargain—although you will avoid waiting in line at assorted stations. Advance reservations may be wise for certain highly popular routes during peak travel season.

Do you really need reservations? The answer is yes and no. On certain high-speed day trains—such as the TGV, ICE, AVE, X2000, and Eurostar—and on all overnight trains, you are required to reserve a seat, couchette, or sleeper. And on certain InterCity and EuroCity trains (which are popular because they are faster and make fewer stops), reservations are also a must. Reservations are not available in Belgium, the Netherlands, Luxembourg, or Sweden unless the train is going to another country. On most other trains, seat reservations are generally not required. You simply sit wherever you find an unreserved seat in a car designated by the class of your ticket—either first-class or second. For a reservation strategy, see Chapter 26.

TRAIN TRAVEL AROUND THE WORLD

In general, most comprehensive guidebooks—especially those geared to budget travel—will give you an overview of the status of a country's rail system. For example, you will learn that you can take a comfortable, super-speed rail journey in Japan but that in Turkey the bus system is much more modern and reliable. Or you'll discover that a rail trip in New Zealand delivers superb sightseeing and pleasant surroundings, but one in India will combine vistas with delays and uncomfortable conditions. As you've surmised, trains aren't always the best option for long-distance travel.

Decide if you want to go the distance. It might sound romantic to take a rail journey across the Australian outback from Sydney to Perth. The reality, however, is 65 hours of hot, rolling landscape. And with a series of affordable air-pass coupons from either of Australia's domestic airlines, you could make the trip in about six hours—like a transcontinental U.S. flight. If you've always wanted to take a leisurely, scenic journey across a country, do it. But research the setting first and, on a long trip, be prepared to pay a premium for sleeper accommodations.

Try a mix of transport types. A particularly scenic region of a country is a prime candidate for train travel. But you might consider pairing train trips with flights to save time. Or, if you arrive by ship in a port city, a day or overnight trip by train could be an ideal way to see the countryside.

CHAPTER 26

More Rail Miles For Your Money

Get the best from your rail pass with

careful planning and rail smarts.

■

The following strategies will help you squeeze every penny from a rail pass without wasting time or sacrificing convenience.

MAP OUT YOUR ROUTE

Whether you're traveling in the U.S. or abroad, plot to save both time and money.

A strategy for Europe. A Eurailpass can go farther than you think. For example, it's possible to stretch a one-month Eurailpass into transportation for a six-week journey. Follow these tips:

Have a firm itinerary. On longer trips (a month or more), if you'll mainly travel from one city to another, you can save about 20 to 25 percent by purchasing a two-month Eurail Flexipass. It allows either 10 or 15 days of travel during that time period rather than the unlimited travel of the more expensive Eurailpass.

Don't backtrack. Plan your route so you progress from country to country without doubling back. It's often desirable to start in either a northern city (such as Amsterdam) or a southern one (such as Rome) and work your way in the opposite direction. This course will take you the farthest distance in the least amount of time.

Validate wisely. Choose as your rail departure point a city that you want to visit for three to five days. Then don't have your pass validated until the exact day you actually leave that city—even if you make your seat reservation a day or so earlier.

Perfect your endgame. If you plan to visit Great Britain, which does not participate in Eurailpass, end your train travels in a city with affordable access to London by plane or ferry.

Travel with a companion. Traveling with another person will allow you to purchase a Eurail Saverpass, which is 15 percent cheaper than a standard Eurailpass.

A strategy for North America. In the U.S. and Canada, longer distances between cities require more planning to get the most miles with an Amtrak or VIA Rail Canada North American Rail Pass.

Choose sightseeing spots. With the 30-day North American pass, don't try to see too much or you'll spend more time in transit than enjoying the places you visit. Concentrate your travels in a particular region of the U.S. and/or Canada.

Divide the trip. Shape your itinerary so you take your train travel in short- to medium-distance (300 to 800 mile) segments. You'll then sit no more than 12 hours on the train at a time and avoid the cost of sleeper accommodations. Plan to spend only one-half to one full day on the train every three to five days, a reasonable pace.

VALIDATING A EURAILPASS

After you purchase a Eurailpass in the U.S. (they must be bought prior to your departure for Europe), the pass will not be usable until it has been "validated" by a Eurail representative at your first departure station. (Look for the Eurail office or window at the station.) Validation is simply a stamp on the pass that records the first day of usage—and thus also forecasts the day it expires.

Because station lines during peak travel periods can be long—sometimes requiring up to an hour of waiting—you may want to have your pass validated prior to the first day of train travel. After you get settled at your hotel, visit the train station and find the Eurail office. But make sure you tell the representative to validate your pass for the date you first plan to use it, not that day's date. Don't assume all agents will speak English, although a good number do. It's always smart to have your request written in whatever language is spoken locally. At the very minimum, write out the date for which you want your pass valid. If that's June 1, 2002, write it like a European— 1/6/2002—the day first, then the month.

Once you have a validated pass, familiarize yourself with the station. European train stations are notorious for long lines, so don't wait until the last minute to make your train reservation, should one be required.

WHEN YOU DON'T HAVE RESERVATIONS

The matter of reservations is one of the trickier questions facing anyone with a Eurailpass. Yes, you already have your ticket, but a ticket doesn't guarantee a seat. Certain trains require reservations, which cost an extra fee. These guidelines can help you get a seat without reserving.

IT'S ONE-THIRD MORE

Go First Class?

Should you pay one-third more to travel the rails first class? If you get a Eurailpass–and you're over age 26–you don't need to make that decision. All "adult" Eurailpasses are good for first-class travel. But if you are taking only a few train trips during your stay and so are buying individual tickets, you'll be asked "Which class?" at time of purchase.

First class generally means more-comfortable, less -crowded train cars–the first-class compartments seat six passengers, for example, while those in second class seat eight. (Cars are clearly marked on the outside with either a 1 or a 2.) You may want to consider first class on longer journeys, but if you're on a tight budget, most second-class cars are perfectly adequate.

CARS & TRAINS

Pack light. The fewer pieces of luggage you have to haul through the train, the easier it is to spot and claim an unreserved seat.

Arrive early. You'll have plenty of time to find the platform and the appropriate first- or second-class cars.

Find the train configuration chart. Most stations in Europe have charts either at the head of each track or along the platform that show where the first- and second-class cars will be located. The cars correspond with letters (A, B, C) along the platform. You can then situate yourself next to the appropriate car and be one of the first to board.

Look for reservation markers. Reserved seats will have a slip of paper either on or above the seat, so look for unmarked seats. If no one shows up to claim a reserved seat right away, don't be tempted—even if the seat is better than the one you have. The reserving party will probably get on at a future stop.

LEARN INSIDER TIPS

After a few weeks of riding the rails in the Europe, you'll be an old pro. Until then, a few tips can avert hassles.

Look ahead. For example, upon arriving at your destination, make plans for your departure. Consult train schedules and choose a train and a time. Decide if you'll need a reservation—then make it, so you won't have to wait in lines later.

Mark your territory. When visiting the lavatory or the dining car, leave a newspaper or magazine to alert other passengers that the seat is taken. Take precautions and you won't have to call the conductor to oust an interloper.

Watch for smoking and nonsmoking cars. Unlike the U.S., Europe has much looser restrictions on smoking. However, trains do feature both smoking and nonsmoking cars. If smoke bothers you, make sure you're not in a smoking car when you grab that unreserved window seat.

Keep your ticket. Never discard your ticket until you've left your arrival station. Eurailpass-holders needn't worry—you'll keep your pass for the duration of your trip. But those riding with one-way or round-trip tickets must hold onto them, since you may be asked to show your ticket as you exit the station platform. If you've thrown it away, you might be required to buy a new one.

COMBINE NATIONAL PASSES

The Eurailpass generally proves cost-effective on trips to multiple countries over a period of a few weeks. For shorter trips, or for those that include only two countries, a combination of rail passes may be more economical, especially since you'll have the option of choosing a cheaper second-class pass.

Before deciding which pass or passes to buy, go over your route and compare costs. In some instances—if you'll take three or four long trips between major cities over the course of two weeks, for example—buying separate tickets may save money, especially if you're entitled to a senior-citizen discount, given by most countries to single-ticket purchasers but not to Eurailpass holders.

TAKE ADVANTAGE OF EXTRAS

Many Eurailpass holders don't realize the pass provides extras, including free trips or reduced fares on a number of boats, buses, and private railways. For example, in Austria the Eurailpass covers a free cruise on the Danube between Vienna and Passau. In Belgium, Denmark, Finland, and Sweden, numerous ferry and boat trips are free or 50 percent off. In Switzerland, there's a fare reduction on several scenic cable car lines. And in Germany, a pass entitles you to a free sightseeing cruise on the Rhine between Cologne and Mainz.

Not all these bonuses are detailed in the Eurailpass brochure you'll receive with your pass. To get every freebie or reduction available, show your Eurailpass whenever you purchase a bus, boat, ferry, train, or cable-car ticket during your trip.

CARS & TRAINS

PART SIX

Tours & Cruises

CHAPTER 27

Pointers on Package Tours

Tours—prepackaged vacations lasting from a few

days to several weeks—can be an economical way to see many

faraway places in a short amount of time.

———————————————————— ■ ————————————————————

A tour provides travel for an all-in-one price, along with ease, security, and structure. But tours can be notoriously regimented, and may seem stifling to travelers used to setting their own pace and choosing their own sights. However, there are tours that include just travel from place to place plus lodging, and then leave you to explore on your own. Decide what suits your own travel style.

THE ABCS OF PACKAGE TOURS

Package deals or tours are put together by organizations known as wholesalers or tour operators and combine two or more travel elements, such as air transportation, lodging, meals, ground transportation, entertainment, car rental, airport transfers, and sightseeing. The tour menu has steadily become richer and more varied, now ranging from golfing jaunts in Scotland to trekking journeys in Nepal to bicycling trips through Italy.

Interested? Your travel agent has plenty of information, including the "Official Tour Directory." Also check newspaper travel-section ads, travel magazines, and web sites. Friends who've taken such trips are another useful source.

You'll find several tour types, each with pros and cons.

Basic package deals. If you're off to a city (London, Paris, Hong Kong) or sun-and-surf locale (Florida, Hawaii, the Caribbean, or Mexico), these are often good deals. Your price break comes from the packager's ability to buy airfare, hotel rooms, ground transfers, and sightseeing in bulk.

Such packages, widely available from tour operators and from major airlines and hotel chains, typically provide airfare, hotel, air-port transfers, and perhaps a rental car, as well as limited sightseeing options or discounts. Savings with flexibility to set your own agenda.

Escorted tours. On these jaunts, virtually everything is handled for you, including what you see, eat, and do at your destination. Most local touring is done by bus, with either a local guide or an escort who accompanies you throughout the trip.

On the plus side, an escorted tour delivers travel with minimal effort and fuss (unless you get a bad tour), and provides camaraderie (unless you have little in common with fellow travelers). You pay lower prices—especially at hotels—and may also get special access, since a tour is often the only way to take part in certain activities or go places otherwise off-limits to tourists. Generally, the facilities and itinerary have been carefully selected and prescreened. And all trans-portation and baggage handling are arranged—you simply put your luggage outside your hotel-room door at a predetermined time.

But escorted tours also have certain disadvantages. The tour's "flavor" and success very much depend on the quality of the tour guide and on the personalities of your fellow travelers—both out of your control. The strict schedules may prove annoying. Depending on the tour, you may be required to wear a name tag or a badge. And the pace is generally only as fast as the slowest person on the tour. Your whole trip is also prepaid. So you're locked in even if things turn out to be unsatisfactory.

A la carte options. Since many people don't need—or even like—handholding when they travel, many tour operators provide à la carte options that let you travel independently once you reach your destination, but still save on airfare and accommodations. Or you can always have a travel agent or tour operator tailor a trip to your specifications, though that's the most expensive way to travel.

READING THE BROCHURES

Once you've gathered brochures about a few potential tours, make sure you read the fine print, which spells out what's included and what's not, as well as important requirements and restrictions. Since some tour operators aren't completely frank about their offers, what you don't know can hurt you.

The brochure's tiny-type sections normally apply to all tours listed. So some copy covers official corporate names and tour numbers as well as purchase conditions, such as required paperwork and cancellation provisions. Beyond those basics, provisions seem designed mainly to protect the operator in case things go wrong, although some tour operators also try to inform the traveler of potential problems. To protect yourself, get out your magnifying glass and look for vital details.

Changing prices. The fine (sometimes barely legible) print will almost always note that brochure prices are subject to change—reasonable enough, since prices are set far in advance. But ascertain the actual price and conditions before buying the tour. The terms may also protect the operator's right to increase the price or modify what a tour provides *after* a traveler has paid a deposit or even paid in full (with some changes specifically ruled out as grounds for a full refund). Avoid such tours if possible. Some operators will, however, guarantee the price in the brochure.

The airfare. Although airfare affects price, most brochures never list an airfare. Some quote a package price with a firm airfare; others may list the lowest airfare available at the time the brochure was printed, adding that it's subject to change if the airline raises fares.

Charter vs. scheduled airline. Know which one you'll get. U.S.

regulations are stricter for charters (and tours based on charter flights) than for scheduled airlines. With a charter, a traveler must be given a full refund if the operator imposes any major change before departure: a price increase of 10 percent or more, say, or a switch in departure or return dates. But many important changes aren't deemed "major." A price increase of less than 10 percent, a different departure time, or a rerouting to pick up passengers in another city, for example, don't entitle you to an automatic refund on a charter-based tour.

Which airline you'll fly. If an airline sponsors a tour, you'll generally fly that carrier. Independent tour operators may list several airlines (any one of which could be used on a given tour) or a single airline (with the provision that it's subject to change). Whenever there's no promise of a specific airline or if the airline can be switched, you may wind up with below-average (and cramped) economy service.

Transportation to your destination. Air transportation from one or more U.S. gateway cities (usually those with major international airports, such as New York, Los Angeles, or San Francisco) is usually included. If you don't live near the gateway, you'll need to make arrangements to get there. Tour operators may offer prearranged add-on airfares—frequently a good value, so ask about this option.

Types of accommodations. You'll be told the level of accommodations; many brochures also list the actual hotels. However, tour operators generally reserve the right to substitute "comparable" or "equivalent" hotels for those featured in the brochure at any time. Some make specific promises, perhaps limiting substitutions to hotels of at least the same rating as those featured in the brochure. Other brochures promise not only comparable quality but a similar location, definitely a plus.

The basis for the rating may also be stated (a government system in Europe, for example). If not, the rating is often taken from the "Official Hotel Guide," a standard industry reference (see Chapter 19). But remember that many hotel-rating systems in foreign countries are not based on the U.S. standards: A four-star hotel in a country like Turkey may be more like a two- or three-star establishment here. If you doubt that a tour company is up-front about accommodation standards, check guidebooks for hotel evaluations.

If nothing is said about room quality and location, you're usually assigned a run-of-the-house room, which can be anything with the promised number of beds and type of bath facilities. When not guaranteed anything better, be prepared for the hotel's worst room.

Food caliber. Evaluate the meal policy by reading between the lines. Interpret "continental breakfast" to mean self-service coffee, tea, and bread. Unless a brochure specifically promises lunch and dinner choices from a menu, you may face assembly-line, dollop-it-out meals or a box lunch on the bus.

Tours generally include two meals a day, but dinner policies vary, from all dinners to some to none. When all meals are included, expect dinner to be at a mass seating in the hotel restaurant or a pre-selected restaurant, with the possibility of a few tourist-oriented dinner shows. A few premium operators include alcoholic beverages on some occasions, but most don't.

If you have special dietary requests, discuss them with the operator before you book.

Itinerary alterations. Usually, the small type adds nothing to the tour description in the front of the brochure. But a few have some specific disclaimers, including the right to make minor adjustments in sightseeing itineraries and to vary the order of cities or attractions visited in a multistop tour.

Necessary documents. A few operators state exactly when they will send tickets or vouchers to you. Making a reservation within the final month before travel may incur an additional delivery charge. Some operators include a section describing the required documents for the trip (passport, visas, medical certificates, and so forth) and disavow any responsibility for conditions arising from your failure to bring such paperwork with you.

Inclusions and exclusions. Most tour brochures explain policy on specific expenses that might be questioned. Some packages include services you might consider a given, such as tips to airport and hotel porters. Other items being equal, the more inclusions the better.

Most exclusions are unsurprising: charges for excess baggage, telephone calls, room service, or laundry. Ski-tour operators may disclaim responsibility for lack of snow. Some brochures commit operators to refunds for services that were promised but not delivered. But others allow the operator to make minor changes without a refund—and the operator is the judge of what is minor.

Cancellations and changes. Brochures should spell out the terms. Typically, travelers who cancel well in advance are eligible for full refunds (minus a fee). After a cutoff date (15 to 60 days before departure), there's commonly a sliding scale of penalties. But on many tours, there's no refund at all. A few operators impose especially stringent cancellation provisions for tours during seasonal events at popular destinations—Carnival in Rio, say, or Christmas in Hawaii. (See Chapter 4 for information on trip-cancellation insurance.)

Many operators let you alter travel dates or accommodations, subject to availability, for an additional $20 to $100 per change; a few waive the fee for the first change.

Smoking or not? If you want to avoid secondhand smoke, choose a no-smoking tour. No ban in the brochure? You may find a smoking section on the bus. Ask in advance.

Complaints and refunds. Some operators specify a maximum period in which to file complaints and refund requests; they may also delineate the method for resolving conflicts and complaints. Although these provisions may not be legally binding, they're often intimidating.

WHAT WILL IT COST?

Tours come in all price ranges, from budget-oriented "let's all pitch the tent" types running just a few hundred dollars a week to ultra-luxurious tours that skimp on nothing and cost thousands. Operators Cosmos and Trafalgar specialize in low-cost, no-frills travel, while operations like Abercrombie & Kent, Mountain Travel Sobek, and Linblad Special Expeditions are known for their premium high-end adventures.

If you spot a tour too pricey for your budget, you might investigate further to find other operators offering similar itineraries for less.

However, you usually won't dig up big discounts on tours—except on cruises, which have become highly promotional in some locations—since margins are thin. At best, you can get a rebate of 5 percent or so through a discount travel agency.

With careful shopping, you can sometimes discover a smaller tour operator that's a real gem. Small firms may specialize in a particular destination, run offbeat tours, or find interesting lodgings that don't accept large groups.

The single supplement. Standard rates for tours are "per person, double occupancy." If you want a room to yourself, you must usually pay a single supplement. In general, tour operators charge an additional 15 to 50 percent for that single room, although charges can run higher. However, one operator, Saga Holidays, offers single rooms (some are very small, but some are standard) at no additional charge on 40 percent of its European and educational itineraries. But book early, since these rooms are limited and sell out within a month or two of the tour brochure's publication.

EXAMINE THE ITINERARY

The vast majority of large commercial tours are oriented to two things —sightseeing and shopping—a lot of both, with little free time. Others are specialized, focusing on such areas as history, ecology, architecture, or ornithology. And adventure tours are also gaining in popularity. Whatever type you pick, be sure the itinerary gives you all you want.

The sights you'll see. Is everything you want to visit included? Generally, there's little free time to sneak in spots not covered.

Chances to shop. Many tour operators are under some obligation to stop by certain "shopping" areas, be they markets, tourist shops, or factories. Any time you see a "factory visit" or "handicraft demonstration" listed on an itinerary, you can be certain of a shopping opportunity. If hitting the stores is important to you, find out how much real shopping time you'll get.

Transportation mode. Will you be traveling by plane, train, bus, or other means? If transport isn't clearly spelled out on the itinerary, ask the operator for specifics.

Evening activities. Some tours include evening activities—cultural performances, plays, or music. Others leave you to your own devices after dinner.

EVALUATE THE PACE

Trying to cover eight European countries in 21 days, or both Australia and New Zealand in 24, means a hectic schedule with lots of time in transit. Different tours move at different paces, although most try to cram in as much as possible. Check these keynotes to locate a tour that won't require a vacation just to recuperate—or simply bore you beyond words.

Daily schedule. How much time will you actually spend at each stop? Are those limits enough to satisfy you? Most tours linger no

MAKING A PERFECT MATCH

IF YOU'RE LOOKING FOR...	TAKE A TOUR TO . . .
Art and European history	Austria, France, Italy, Great Britain, Greece, Russia, Spain, or the Netherlands
Ancient civilization and architecture	China, Egypt, Greece, Japan, Mexico, Peru, or Turkey
Good food	France, Hong Kong, Italy, Montreal, New Orleans, New York, San Francisco/Wine Country, or Thailand
Wildlife habitats	Africa, Alaska, Antarctica, Australia, Belize, Costa Rica, Galapagos Islands, Indonesia, or the Seychelles
Incredible scenery	Canada, Chile, Iceland, New Zealand, Scandinavia, Switzerland, the U.S. Pacific Coast, or Wyoming
Exotic cultures	The Amazon, India, Morocco, Nepal, South Pacific, Tibet, Tunisia, or Vietnam
Water recreation	Australia, the Caribbean, coastal New England, Florida, or Hawaii
Golf	Arizona, Bermuda, California, North and South Carolina, or Scotland

TOURS & CRUISES

more than a day or two in each city—three in some major ones—and just a few hours at each tourist sight.

Morning hours. Unless you're an early riser, you may cringe at typical start times: up, packed, and fed before 8 a.m., so you can hit the sights, then press on to the next destination.

Travel time. On some tours, more time is spent in getting to sights than in seeing them. Make sure the pace is such that hours in transit don't become overly tedious. Note, however, that on some tours through extremely scenic regions, travel time can be quite enjoyable.

Physical exertion. Scan descriptions of daily excursions, looking for such phrases as "a short walk," "a hike with some exertion required," or "over challenging terrain." Ask the operator what's involved physically and if any alternative activities are available.

CHECK TOUR GROUP PROFILES

Ask the operator about the age range, traveler type, and group size. Generally, tours appeal to a slightly older crowd, because this travel mode is so convenient. In fact, some operators, such as Saga and Golden Circle, specify you must be over 50 to join the tour.

Although budget- or adventure-oriented packages may welcome all ages, they typically attract a younger crowd. (Contiki Tours has an upper age-limit of 35.) Other tours are designed for specific groups, such as singles, women only, or gay travelers.

The tour operator should be able to estimate group size for you when you sign up, then confirm the number prior to your departure. Find out if the company reserves the right to cancel the tour without a minimum number of travelers.

Small groups. Some operators specialize in small-group tours of six to 10 people. Although these tours may cost more, they can also provide more personal attention. Small groups generally travel in small vans or buses, and may stay in hotels not available to larger groups. Mealtimes may be less "assembly-line," and allow you to experience more local color. Small groups also offer a chance of flexibility. You might be able to depart from a set itinerary if all group members can agree.

Large groups. Most tours move at least 20 travelers en masse, with everyone assembling at a certain hour, then adhering to a preset schedule all day. You'll travel in a large tour bus—or by plane, if covering a large area. Sometimes guides will split a larger tour into two or three smaller groups based on pace and interests.

VET THE TOUR GUIDES

Guides are a critical tour component. An inexperienced or unprofessional guide can turn even the best itinerary into a bad experience. Quiz the tour operator or your travel agent.

What does the company require of guides? An operator should be able to offer details about their guides' backgrounds and experience as they pertain to the tour's itinerary. For example, are they trained in specific areas, such as history or archeology, that might contribute to their expertise—and your enjoyment?

Is the guide an American? Many U.S. travelers prefer an American guide. Others want English-speaking local guides who might provide a more personal insight into their native country.

If foreign, is the guide fluent in English? Speaking English and being fluent are two different things. If you can't properly understand your guide, you may miss important details or feel frustrated by communication difficulties.

Will you have the same guide for the entire tour? Some fully escorted tours provide a single guide for the entire trip, even if it covers several countries, as many European and some Asian and South American tours do. Others have a series of guides who meet you at specific destinations (usually at the airport). If you'd rather have one guide for your entire trip, ask the tour operator if this is the plan. However, some tour operators reserve the right to guarantee a single guide only if a minimum number of travelers sign up; if the minimum is not met, they may substitute locals.

RESEARCH THE OPERATOR'S REPUTATION

Reputation can be hard to pin down. But an investigation can help determine whether a tour operator delivers on its promises. And with travel bookings down due to security worries, you'll want a stable, dependable operator that won't disappear due to economic woes.

Ask your travel agent. If booking through an agent, see whether other travelers have raved (or complained) about the tour you're considering.

Use web forums. Most major travel sites and some large guidebook sites have a forum feature, where individuals can pose questions to be answered by other travelers. Ask others who have taken tours with the operator to "review" their experiences. (For more on travel and the web, see Part Two.)

Reread the brochure. Again, those small-type sections can reveal a lot about a tour operator's procedures. For example, you might investigate what happens if a part of the tour needs to be canceled because of some condition like bad weather. Will the operator issue a refund?

AN ADVENTURE ON THE AGENDA

If your idea of a dream vacation is rafting down a river in the Yukon territory (rather than riding around Rome on a bus), then "adventure" travel might be right for you. If so, you'll be among the tens of millions of U.S. adults of all ages questing for less-conventional vacations, from the rough to the plush.

What's available? A wide range of activities falls under the description "adventure travel," with tours that can be divided into two types.

Soft adventure. By far the most popular, these trips involve moderately strenuous activities, such as camping, easy day hikes, and casual horseback excursions.

Hard adventure. Anticipate more daring and physically demanding activities, such as mountain trekking and white-water rafting. These trips typically attract the hard-core adventurer—but are growing in popularity.

Travel conditions. Some trips require you to share a tent with other travelers, use pit toilets, and eat very basic camp chow. Others offer electric-lighted tents and flush toilets as well as gourmet food.

Cost factors. Many prices run fairly low, about $150 a day, including all transportation during the tour in the continental U.S.

Because of the added transportation costs, however, travelers to Alaska can expect to pay at least twice that. Specialty trips and super-luxury trips cost far more.

Risk potential. Though no industry-wide statistics are available, anecdotal evidence suggests that most injuries suffered on adventure tours are minor, ranging from cuts and bruises to sprained ankles. But travelers can be seriously hurt or even killed. Some mishaps can be blamed on inexperienced tour operators or travelers who ignore safety warnings. And faulty equipment, poor physical conditioning, dangerous animals, an untamed river, or an unexpected storm can all lead to disaster. So follow some advice to play it safe.

Judge your limitations. You should receive an application that

CONSUMER PROTECTION FOR TOURS

Save your investment if an operator fails

In the past, it was difficult to amend or cancel package-tour arrangements without some sort of penalty; if customers bailed within a month of departure, they could generally expect to forfeit their entire payment. But since Sept. 11, tour operators have become more flexible about changed plans. However, operators are not regulated, and policies are voluntary. The U.S. Tour Operators Association (USTOA) has this advice:

• Check with the individual operator for the details of what will be covered and what will not.

• Thoroughly investigate the bond and escrow provisions of tour-operator contracts and what protection you have (if any) should the company suddenly shut down. (USTOA requires its member to post minimum bonds of $1 million as a safety measure for consumers.)

• Pay any deposits with a charge card to facilitate refunds.

• Buy trip-cancellation insurance, preferably from an independent insurance provider. Be sure "supplier-default" coverage is included. (See Chapter 4.) This coverage is even more vital in light of the travel and economic slowdown, which could push some suppliers out of business. If you do buy from the tour operator, watch out for unexpected insurance charges added in with the rest of the tour.

includes important questions about your health and physical abilities. Have you ever participated in this activity before? What's your fitness level? Do you require a special diet? Are you allergic to bee stings? Are you diabetic? Do you have asthma?

If the outfitter fails to ask an important question, discuss your particular health issues with a company representative. (It's wise to go over these issues with your doctor, too.)

Ask about serious accidents. Any outfitter should be willing to discuss past accidents, how they were handled, and what procedures are now in place to prevent future problems.

Pack your medications. Your family physician can tell you what shots and pills you'll need; you can also get health information from the Centers for Disease Control and Prevention (see "Health tips for travelers," in the Reference Section).

Outfitter expertise. Narrow your selection to companies specializing in your kind of tour; pin down details before sending a deposit.

Interview the outfitter. How long has the company been in business? Exactly what is included in the price? What size is the travel group? How flexible is the tour operator? And will you get any instruction or training?

SUGGESTIONS FOR RESOLUTION

Dealing with tour problems

Try to resolve any tour problems as they appear. Complain promptly to your tour guide or other company representative (if you're on an escorted tour), to the tour headquarters, or your travel agency back home. Keep your cool, and be specific about the problem and what resolution you desire.

If no solution is possible, bailing out may be best. Although an expensive option, leaving may strengthen your case for a refund or chargeback (a credit from your charge-card issuer for the disputed amount). To obtain either, you'll have to pursue your complaints in writing, detailing the difficulty and your expected resolution. As a last resort, consider filing a formal complaint with USTOA or NTA (for tour operators) or ASTA (for travel agencies).

Ask about the guides. Most outfitters and travelers consider a capable guide the most important element of a safe and enjoyable adventure. Find out the qualifications of guides assigned to your trip and ask how long they've worked for the outfitter. Make sure they've had advanced first-aid training.

Get client references. If a tour operator isn't willing to provide you with the names and phone numbers of clients, don't walk away—run away. Request referrals, then call them yourself.

Read your contract. What are the outfitter's refund and cancellation policies? What risks are you accepting—and what rights are you waiving?

Buy trip insurance. Most companies will send you a trip insurance policy, but buy your own policy from an independent insurance company—and make sure you understand all the terms and what the policy covers. You want adequate medical coverage plus protection should the travel supplier default. (See Chapter 4 for more on trip insurance.)

Check for liability insurance and permits. In the U.S., most outfitters carry a $300,000 to $500,000 liability policy for biking, horseback riding, river rafting, and other such activities. Such a policy ensures that if the company is grossly negligent, you can sue and collect damages. Also, make sure the tour company is legally in business and that it has the required insurance and permits to operate where it does.

CHAPTER 28

How to Choose a Cruise

A cruise is an "all-in-one" vacation package.

Consult experts and do your research

to ensure smooth sailing.

■

If you haven't taken a vacation at sea yet, the cruise industry has been betting that you will. Scores of new ships have been built and ordered. In fact, cruises have been the fastest-growing segment of the travel industry.

With the Sept. 11 attacks, however, bookings dropped as jittery would-be cruisers reconsidered their plans. And some cruise lines, such as Renaissance, went out of business, making travel insurance —purchased from a separate company, not the cruise line—a must. (See Chapter 4.)

To assuage passengers' concerns, several cruise lines have rerouted ships away from Europe, particularly the Eastern Mediterranean. Many instead scheduled cruises in and around the Caribbean, Mexico, Alaska, and New England/Canada. Some lines have also increased departures from U.S. ports, so U.S travelers could drive to departure points instead of flying.

On the brighter side, expect to see many cruise bargains. And one factor remains the same: You still need to plan ahead and make smart decisions. Here's how to navigate your way.

DETERMINE THE SHIP'S PERSONALITY

Your first priority is to select a line and a ship that attracts cruisers with whom you'll be simpatico, whether they're seniors, honeymooners, young singles, families, same-sex partners, or any other group.

For example, Carnival promotes a "festive-yet-casual atmosphere," while Celebrity and Princess tout themselves as attracting a "premium" clientele. Individual ships also have different personalities, based on such factors as age (many ships were built in the 1990s, but some are 20, 30, or even 40 years old, although renovated); the crew; and the facilities, such as pools, casinos, and cocktail lounges.

Some ships are also more family-friendly. Disney Cruise Line provides separate areas and activities for adults, teens, and kids: quiet dining, massage cabanas, and such events as a wine-tasting for parents; a teens-only coffee bar called "Common Grounds" plus teen sports activities; and most of a deck devoted to age-specific children's programs. Other cruises (Seabourn, for example) are strictly dress-for-dinner, adults-only affairs.

Carefully read the cruise lines' marketing material, check their web sites, and consult with experts—travel agents and cruise specialists—to get a feel for the clientele and the onboard atmosphere. Also talk to any experienced cruisers you know for the inside story.

CONSIDER THE SIZE

The trend in cruise ships these days is big. How big? Colossal. The Grand Princess and the Carnival Triumph each accommodate more than 2,600 passengers. Even larger ships are on the way. Carnival, Costa, Norwegian, Princess, and Royal Caribbean all have added or will add megaships with more than 2,000 berths—and some Royal Caribbean behemoths can carry up to 3,800 passengers.

Some people enjoy being onboard with more than several thousand strangers; the experience is like visiting a vacation resort with lots facilities to explore. But these boats are not for everyone.

Want a smaller ship? There are some scaled-down ships already on the seas or about to join major cruise-line fleets. A medium-sized ship carries between 1,000 and 1,700 passengers. Smaller vessels, which accommodate 600 to 800, can often get into some ports the biggest ships can't (some giant ships also cannot traverse the Panama Canal). Certain of the more expensive cruise lines, such as Seabourn and Silversea, also have "intimate" ships that carry just 200 to 300 passengers—for a price, of course.

Smaller still. A few cruise operators offer "tall-ship" or "windjammer" excursions, carrying fewer than 100 passengers.

Casual and barefoot. The "windjammer" experience—sailing aboard a restored tall-masted ship—is generally low-cost and casual, with a mix of passengers of all ages. Activities center around a port (or ports) and include lots of beach and snorkeling time. Miami-based Windjammer Barefoot Cruises is one of the largest providers.

Pampered and personal. Several luxury sailing vessels ply the Caribbean, Mediterranean, and South Pacific, operated by, among others, Windstar and Club Med. Ships are new, and trips cost much more than those on a traditional windjammer ship.

Chartered and carefree. A third sailing option is to charter a captain, small crew (usually a mate and cook), and a sailboat accommodating anywhere from six to 12 passengers. Depending on how many people split the cost, chartering can be either expensive or economical. Unless you splurge for a plush yacht, expect relatively basic, cramped cabins and shared shower/toilet facilities.

Or big, but uncrowded. A 47,000-ton ship, ample staff, and only six passengers sounds like a royal excursion, but it's actually a freighter cruise. Most freighters carry a maximum of 12 passengers, excluding crew. And accommodations are comfortable, with private bathrooms, showers, TVs, and VCRs. Expect a common lounge, videos and books, perhaps a small outdoor pool, and an elevator. Passengers dine with the officers and can purchase alcohol and cigarettes onboard.

But trips are generally long and uneventful; freighters stop in working ports, and there are no casinos, ballrooms, or entertainers.

Freighter travel is also expensive, depending on the length of the voyage, although all meals are included. Talk to your travel agent.

CHOOSE THE PRICE RANGE

Everything about the vessel, from the operating cruise line to ship size and age, is a factor in pricing. Certain cruise lines (notably Cunard, Norwegian, Silversea, and Seabourn), known for top-flight amenities, also command premium pricing. Others (particularly Carnival, Holland America, Premier, and Royal Caribbean) offer a wide range of accommodations, from relatively basic bunkbed-style cabins to luxurious suites.

Itinerary and amenities. The longer the cruise, the more expensive. But both the region a ship cruises and its ports of call can also affect pricing. Many Caribbean and Mediterranean itineraries are quite affordable; cruises to the South Pacific, Alaska, and Antarctica are generally steeper. And what you'll enjoy onboard, from food to entertainment to activities, also enters the equation.

Cabin type. Most ships offer about a dozen cabin categories, some even more. More expensive cabins are larger, outside (with windows), and on the more desirable mid and upper decks. The lowest-priced cabins can be about one-quarter the cost, but may be small, inside (no windows), and located on the lowest decks.

What's included. Typically, a quoted cruise price delivers this: cabin (double occupancy); port charges (since 1997, most cruise lines have included them in advertised rates); taxes (some may be extra, depending on the cruise line and the itinerary); airfare from select gateway cities, but check the fine print; all meals (you can eat all day); onboard entertainment (daytime music, nighttime shows); and certain onboard activities (pools, games). The number of single cabins is limited. Frequently cramped and undesirable, they also carry an often substantial single supplement.

What's not included. Certain items will cost you extra: shore excursions (easily $30 to $40 per person per port, so consider making your own arrangements once you arrive in port); liquor (almost always extra, though sometimes wine will be served at a special dinner);

Know the score on ship sanitation

The U.S. Centers for Disease Control (CDC) regularly sends unannounced inspectors to check cruise ships that call at U.S. ports, scrutinizing water supplies; food preparation and storage; potential food contamination; and general cleanliness, storage, and repair. Passing grade is 86—but a score in the 90s is better. Failing ships get a follow-up inspection.

Scores are updated every two weeks in the "Green Sheet." Visit *www.cdc.gov/nceh/vsp/vsp.htm* to download the Green Sheet, and to check your ship's actual inspection report and health history (past scores). For a fax-back copy of current scores only, call 888-232-3299; ask for Document 510051. Or write the Vessel Sanitation Program, National Center for Environmental Health, Centers for Disease Control and Prevention, 4770 Buford Highway, NE, Mail Stop F16, Atlanta, Ga. 30341.

souvenir photos (these snapshots are expensive memories).

You will also be responsible for laundry (prices generally comparable to hotel laundry prices); spa treatments (as high or higher than land-based ones); phone calls (to avoid these costly calls, use a calling card from a pay phone in port, a cell phone, or e-mail); onboard purchases (shopping or gambling can quickly add up); and any gratuities (can easily add $10 a day per person).

ONLINE BOOKING—OR AGENCY BOOKING?

Although cruise-ship reservations are handled mainly by travel agents, the number of online cruise bookings is growing. However, many consumers choose to complete the transaction by phone, rather than staying solely with the automated booking process.

Even if you'd rather not book such a big-ticket item online, you can mine the web for cruise-savvy information. The big travel web sites let you browse by destination or cruise line, view first-time cruiser FAQs, and post questions to the message board. Cruise-line sites—often really online brochures—allow you to investigate cruise-ship deck plans; choose your deck, cabin category, and cabin;

view a photo of a cabin or take a 360-degree virtual tour; and compare cruises side-by-side. (See Chapter 9 for e-Ratings of several cruise-line web sites.)

When selecting an agent (which we recommend, especially for first-time cruisers) go with a cruise specialist at a high-volume agency that sells many cruises.

Vet the agency. Ask if the agency maintains any "preferred supplier" deals or "override" or incentive commission programs with a specific cruise line, so you're aware of any biases. However, such agreements may work to your advantage; volume business may enable the agency get you a cabin upgrade or other amenities.

CRUISE-SHIP MEDICAL CARE

Staying healthy on the high seas

Standards for onboard medical facilities are not required by either international or U.S. law. But most lines serving the North American market have voluntarily created them, according to the International Council of Cruise Lines (ICCL), which has issued its own guidelines (available at *www.iccl.com*). Still, ships cannot offer the range of services available ashore. Help protect yourself.

• Buy insurance. Clarify current medical coverage. Then get a comprehensive travel insurance policy, including medical evacuation coverage. (See Chapter 4.) Pack a copy of the policy plus insurance-company contact information.

• Bring a detailed note explaining any medical conditions, a copy of recent test results (such as an EKG), and the name of primary and specialist physicians, plus complete contact information. Alert the medical staff to your situation at the start of the cruise.

• Pack enough medication to last the entire cruise, plus a list of all medications and dosages. Put medications and supplies (such as syringes) in hand baggage, split between two bags. If one is lost, you can continue treatment while ordering replacements.

• Have any surgery done prior to the cruise; allow enough recovery time. Check with your doctor about the safety of a longer cruise. Pregnant women may require special care not readily available.

Be sure your chosen agency is affiliated with either CLIA or the National Association of Cruise Oriented Agencies (NACOA); both include travel agents experienced in selling cruise vacations.

With an in-depth knowledge of the industry and the vessels, such agents should be able to guide you to the ship and itinerary that best suits your particular budget and interests, as well as the most congenial cabin. (First-time cruisers, usually unaware of problems with cabin location, are especially advised to work with an agent.) A cruise specialist can also provide information on any cruise discounts, such as last-minute savings opportunities.

Always book as early as possible. Cruise specialists advise reserving at least four to six months in advance to get the cabin of your choice. Early-bird buyers may also find savings: early-booking prices (generally a discount of 20 percent or more), two-for-one specials, kids-free programs, unpublicized reductions for prior customers, credit for shipboard purchases, and free hotel accommodations before or after the cruise.

Booking at a guaranteed rate, however—a frequent choice of budget-conscious travelers—means you leave the cabin choice to the cruise line's discretion and may result in an undesirable location.

Last-minute bargains may also be available, a month or less before sailing if ships aren't full. Also ask about "repositioning" cruises—between-season trips when a ship moves from one region to another, say, from summer in Alaska to winter in the Caribbean.

CHOOSE YOUR CABIN

Getting the just-right cabin is not a simple task, especially on one of the huge ships. You and your agent should consider a number of factors.

Size. Cabins are no longer sorted into "classes" that restrict your access to certain parts of the ship. But they're definitely divided up by size, usually measured in square feet: A small or "economy" room is usually less than 150 square feet; an average-sized or "standard" room is about 180 square feet. Deluxe rooms can be more than 250 square feet, and are often outfitted with separate sitting areas, as well as verandas or balconies.

Noise. Potentially noisy cabins are those near housekeeping stations or service elevators, or next to self-service laundries and ice machines. Also bypass cabins located under or above loud public areas, such as nightclubs, discos, theaters, and gyms. Promenade-deck cabins may expose you to the noise of walkers and joggers, especially early in the morning.

The sound of the anchor being raised and lowered is most audible in cabins near the front of the ship.

Engine vibration. The engine room is most likely to affect cabins in the far aft section, particularly on the lowest decks.

Excessive motion. One of the biggest fears for first-time cruisers is seasickness. Many newer ships are equipped with state-of-the-art stabilizers to maintain a steady ride. But even a mammoth cruise ship may feel the effects of rough seas.

Book as close as possible to midships (the center) and select a middle or lower deck. Those nearest the front or aft of the vessel are most likely to encounter up-and-down pitching motions, while cabins on higher decks are more prone to side-to-side rolling movements.

Itinerary matters, too. You are more liable to encounter stormy weather crossing vast stretches of open ocean. The Caribbean is usually calmer, but beware of hurricane season—June 1 to November 30. Those prone to motion sickness may want to opt for more "port-intensive" itineraries, which means less time sailing. (Chapter 29 has anti-seasickness tips.)

Views. Cabins with windows are indicated in the cruise brochure and on the web site as being "outside" rooms. And, of course, they cost more. But with some ocean-view cabins, that pricey view is partially or totally obscured by lifeboats hanging off the side of the ship (although some lifeboats are secured away from windows).

View-obstructed cabins are usually indicated in a brochure's deck plan. When booking, tell your agent you want to avoid them. Or, if a view is unimportant to you, ask if you will pay less.

Hallway traffic. Although cabins near stairs or across from elevators are convenient, you may have to sacrifice some privacy because the surrounding areas are subject to heavy foot traffic. When entering or leaving your cabin, you may often encounter passengers milling around the elevator or your door.

Access for the disabled. In June 2000, a federal court ruled that cruise ships registered in foreign countries and docking in the U.S. must adhere to the Americans with Disabilities Act (ADA) regulations. For details, see "Access for disabled travelers," in the Reference section.

ASK ABOUT CABIN UPGRADES

Upgrades become available when a cruise ship sells a higher percentage of inexpensive cabins than expensive accommodations—a fairly common occurrence. Rather than turn down customers wanting inexpensive but sold-out cabins, the cruise line may offer to upgrade passengers currently holding those accommodations.

Upgrades may be rewards for repeat customers. Or they may be incentives to early bookers. A line won't reassign an early booker unless that traveler really wants an upgrade. So if you do, have your agent add a specific notation in your reservation file.

DON'T MISS THE BOAT

An "air-sea package," including airfare to the ship's departure city, provides one-stop shopping and (sometimes) a cheaper airfare. But the arrangement doesn't mean the cruise line is responsible for your connection.

If you miss the ship due to a flight delay, the cruise line (and sometimes the airline) will usually try to help you reach the ship. But whether either will pay the costs is another matter. Read the cruise brochure's fine print. (After Sept. 11, some lines offered full credits for future trips; a few waived cancellation fees or offered full or partial refunds.)

Whether you book your own flight or buy a package, allow ample time to get to the ship in case of delays. And invest in travel insurance (see Chapter 4).

CHAPTER 29

What to Expect Onboard

Learn what you'll likely experience as you board

the ship and set sail on your journey.

━━━━━━━━━━━━━━━ ■ ━━━━━━━━━━━━━━━

Cruise lines have worked closely with law-enforcement officials and federal agencies, including the U.S. Coast Guard, the U.S. Immigration and Naturalization Service, and the FBI, to enhance security at sea.

Cruise lines now require passengers to identify themselves by showing a passport or birth certificate plus a government-issued photo ID prior to embarkation. (Request details from your cruise line.) Passengers can now expect increased inspection of luggage and carry-on articles (metal detectors and dogs are possibilities), and additional security personnel on board. Only ticketed passengers will be allowed past checkpoints. Anticipate searches of people and packages following any shore excursions.

Remember that these new security procedures, although time-consuming, are for your safety. Then relax and enjoy the cruise.

GETTING THERE AND BOARDING

If airfare is included in the cost of the cruise, you may be traveling with other passengers, on either a charter or a commercial flight.

Otherwise, you are responsible for reaching the port city and the correct pier. As you make your travel arrangements, remember these tips.

Arrive early. When scheduling your flight, always allow plenty of time—at least six hours, preferably more—between your arrival in the port city and your ship's departure. If your flight is delayed, the ship will leave without you. Some cruise lines recommend that you arrive a day ahead and spend a night at a hotel in the port, especially wise in the winter, when bad weather can cause flight delays and even cancellations.

Know your pier. Large ports like Miami and San Juan have literally dozens of cruise ships docked, an overwhelming and confusing sight. Don't expect to simply tell a cab driver, "The Sea Princess, please." Some drivers may know where certain ships are docked—most won't. Give the driver the pier number; if you're leaving from a foreign port where English isn't spoken, write down the pier number to show the driver.

PORT CITIES

Points of departure

Before you take your cruise, you've got to get to your ship. Depending on the itinerary, here's where it might be docked.

Caribbean: Miami, Fort Lauderdale, Port Canaveral, Tampa, or San Juan

Alaska: Vancouver

Mexico: Los Angeles (Pacific) or Miami (Gulf)

Mediterranean: Athens or Barcelona

Aegean/Adriatic/Baltic: Venice or Istanbul

Transatlantic: New York, Fort Lauderdale, or Miami

South America/Panama Canal: Miami, Fort Lauderdale, or San Juan

Hawaii: Honolulu or Los Angeles

South Pacific: Hong Kong, Sydney, or Papeete

Scandinavia: Amsterdam, Copenhagen, or Southampton

Antarctica: Buenos Aires or Ushuaia, Argentina

Board early. You'll avoid major delays as several thousand passengers try to clear immigration (if required) and comply with new security requirements. Most cruise lines offer a boarding period of several hours and try to make the process as easy as possible. Call your cruise line for specifics.

MEALS AT SEA

Most cruise specialists and some travel agents should be able to steer you in the right food direction. And some cruise line web sites offer morsels of menu information.

For dinner, you'll typically be asked to choose the first or second sitting; if you don't like to eat after 8 p.m., sign up for the first. You may also have the option of sitting with the same table mates the entire cruise or switching night after night. Some cruises also offer private seating (one couple per table).

SHIPBOARD AMENITIES

Today's modern cruise ships have been called "floating cities," and that's no misnomer. You'll find almost everything onboard that you might encounter in a small town or resort community.

Entertainment opportunities. Most ships have at least a few bars and lounges. Gambling facilities are possible, too. You may also find a theater showing first-run movies and/or documentaries about your ports of call, plus a library providing books to read by the pool.

Exercise and relaxation. Gym facilities are increasingly common (you can work off those midnight buffets); outdoor tracks for walking or running are a possibility; some ships have a spa. There may be one or more pools, although not Olympic-size.

Ships do provide enough deck chairs to go around, but the prized locations—near the pool, in a spot sheltered from the wind—will be snapped up first.

Shipboard commerce. Expect a variety of boutiques selling apparel and souvenirs. You can get money or exchange currency at the ship's bank, mail letters and postcards at the shipboard post office, or visit the onboard hair salon.

COPING WITH SEASICKNESS

Motion sickness occurs when you're subjected to accelerated movement in different directions, or when you lose visual sight of the horizon. Symptoms are generally dizziness, fatigue, and nausea, which may lead to vomiting. You might be prone if you have ever experienced motion sickness when in a car, plane, or other moving vehicle, or have middle-ear problems.

The tips under "Excessive motion," Chapter 28, can help you avoid some effects of rough seas. There are also a number of treatments available.

Anti-seasickness pills. Dimenhydrinate (Dramamine) or meclizine (Bonine), both sold over the counter and also typically available in cruise ship infirmaries, provide an antinausea effect for up to several hours. For full benefits, take at least an hour prior to sailing; repeat if necessary.

Anti-seasickness patches. A scopolamine (Transderm-Scop) patch is placed behind the ear several hours before the effect is needed, and can be worn up to 72 hours at a time.

Wristbands. Working on the principle of acupressure, the wristband's plastic button presses against the inner portion of the wrist. Some users report symptom relief.

Ginger. Several small studies have found ginger to be comparable to the OTC drugs discussed above, and it is registered as an OTC drug for use in nausea and travel sickness in several European countries. Because ginger has been shown to have some blood-thinning effects, individuals taking blood-thinning medications, such as aspirin or warfarin (Coumadin), shouldn't take ginger.

Antinausea drugs. If you need immediate relief from vomiting, the ship's doctor may administer an injection of an antinausea drug such as promethazine (Pherergan or Shogan) that brings relief within 30 to 40 minutes.

Wellness tips. These may help you avoid or limit discomfort:
• Stay in the middle of the ship, both vertically and horizontally. But avoid lying down in your cabin, if you can.
• Try to get out in the fresh air, and breathe deeply.

- Keep your eyes on the horizon, not on the water.
- Avoid heavy meals and limit alcohol.

PORTS OF CALL

The itinerary indicates which ports the ship will enter, and there is usually little deviation. But unforeseen circumstances, such as bad weather or local conflicts, can necessitate skipping a destination of or substituting another.

In such cases, unfortunately, disappointed passengers get little if any compensation. Typically the cruise line retains the right to change the itinerary, based on passenger safety and security—without recompense. Reasons include local or international political situations or potentially severe weather—not always predictable. But check with your travel agent or cruise representative to see if your cruise's itinerary has been changed in the past. (Also see "How to complain effectively," in the Reference section.)

The amount of time in each port is also specified in the brochure. Most ships stop for just a day (sometimes two on longer cruises). You usually arrive in the middle of the night, then have a full or half day to explore before the ship sails again in the evening.

SHORE EXCURSIONS

Virtually all cruises have pre-arranged tours in each port, generally priced higher than tours you can arrange yourself once ashore. Bypass the ship's excursions in all but a few cases: during peak tourist season in very popular ports (onshore tours could be booked); when time is very limited and the ship's trip includes sights you want to see; or if stopping in a non-English-speaking country or one where travel warnings have been issued to lone tourists.

Outside these instances, your own plans will probably be more satisfying. You have several options.

Rent a car—or a car and driver. Depending on the port, this approach is either quite affordable or quite overpriced. If cost is an issue, try to find another person or couple to split the costs.

Go by taxi or public transportation. Most cities have navigable and affordable buses or underground transport. You can also make your way on foot.

Take a tour. If you like the security of a structured tour, you should be able to book at one of many tour operations located dockside. Reputable tour operators are generally listed in major travel guidebooks. Check first.

Book a guide. Individual guides, available for hire, will approach you as you leave the ship. Some are quite personable and provide a unique insight into a city or island. But before you head off with someone, ask to see his or her credentials (local tourist offices often issue ID to reputable guides). And if a port is known for hustlers or scam artists, ask the ship's shore-excursion coordinator whether other passengers have had bad experiences with local guides.

Whatever you choose, allow enough time to get back to the dock before the ship sails—it *will* leave without you.

DISEMBARKATION

Individual ships operate differently, but usually an announcement is made or distributed the day before the cruise ends outlining procedures: how to clear up onboard charges (for alcohol, shore excursions, or purchases); when and where to leave your luggage so it can be taken off the ship; and what the customs/immigration drill will be.

Expect to wait in a few lines. You can simplify by having all your paperwork filled in. Once off the ship, you will be asked to claim your luggage and proceed through customs. Typically, there are lines of taxis waiting to ferry passengers from the pier to the airport for the flight home.

REFERENCE SECTION

Essential information for travelers

A roundup of facts and tips you need
to know before you travel.

YOUR PRE-TRIP CHECKLIST

Travel is exciting, alluring—and dependent on a multitude of details. Overlooking even one can mean canceled plans, hassles or delays at customs, or a scramble to find new accommodations—not exactly the stuff of dream vacations.

Make a list. If you're traveling abroad, get started at least two months in advance. List everything you must have before you leave—passport, an additional photo ID for possible security requirements, visas, reservations, immunizations (see "Health tips for travelers" later in the Reference Section)—then post the list where you can cross off each item as it's finished.

Check tickets and reservations. Always examine everything when it arrives, either from your agent or the travel supplier.

• See that listed flights—and airports—are the ones you booked, and look over flight departure and arrival information.

• Always reconfirm hotel and rental-car reservations. Be sure you have solid bookings—a reservation confirmation number from your rental-car company and a mailed or faxed confirmation from your hotel. If you've made an e-booking, you'll want a printed copy of your confirmation to take with you.

• Confirmations are especially important if you'll travel during peak season, when so many travel services sell out.

Consolidate your documents. At least one week before you travel, all your documents should be in a neat package, put together by either you or your travel agency.

• Be sure you have brought all trip-related documents home from the office. Many people plan trips during working hours, then leave vital papers in a desk drawer or briefcase.

• A leather or plastic document holder is ideal. You can keep it in a secure pouch or hotel safe as you travel.

• Photocopy your passport. Should it be lost or stolen, a photocopy will greatly speed up the replacement process. Make two or three copies and keep one in each bag.

• Keep documents someplace where they will not be disturbed or thrown out during pretrip turmoil—but not in a location where they'll be forgotten.

Type an itinerary. Include all relevant information: flight numbers and arrival times; airline ticket number; hotel names, addresses, phone numbers, and rates; rental-car confirmation numbers and rates.

• This will act as a guide as you travel and a "tracking memo" in case there's an emergency.

• Put one copy in each piece of luggage, and one where you can easily access it—pocket or purse. Give another copy to relatives.

• Confirm all international flight connections. If you are flying on an international carrier, then transferring once you land to a local carrier, call to confirm 72 hours in advance—three days before your international flight.

OTHER SMART GROUNDWORK

Language arts. Many people connected with the travel industry speak English. But on foreign turf, you're sure to encounter people who don't. Brushing up on basic words can help you out in a pinch.

• At Travlang (*www.travlang.com*), you'll find electronic translators and translating dictionaries as well as books for learning more than 180 languages. You can also learn a new word every day via the web or free by e-mail.

• Fodors, the guidebook publisher, has a Languages for Travelers series—pocket-sized phrasebooks with pronunciation keys, and Audio Sets (phrasebook, two cassettes, and an audioscript). Visit *www.fodors.com/books/key.html* for details.

• Lonely Planet, of the guidebooks and cable TV series, also has pocket-size phrasebooks and audiocassettes. Check out *www.lonelyplanet.com*.

• Berlitz (*www.berlitz.com*), the familiar language teacher, sells its books, tapes, and CD-ROMs online.

Plotting your route. Guidebooks feature maps and transportation information. But you may want to go into more detail.

• The Airport Transit Guide has the details you need on how to travel into town and back from over 450 airports around the world—routes, times, frequencies, costs, and more. It includes disabled accessibility info and airport web sites. The 144-page, pocket sized book is $9.95. Go to *www.airporttransitguide.com* for information and sample pages.

• If you want more detailed maps than your guidebook provides, Internet map sites can help. Check DeLorme (*www.delorme.com/cybermaps*), MapQuest (*www.mapquest.com*), and MapBlast (*www.mapblast.com*).

Weather watch. Will it rain in Spain or sizzle in Paris? Your guidebook will tell you generally what to expect. (Also see "World weather," Chapter 6.) You can also get three- to five-day forecasts for almost any place on earth at three weather web sites: CNN Weather (*www.cnn.com/ WEATHER*), MSNBC Weather (*www.msnbc.com/news/WEA_Front.asp*), and the Weather Channel (*www.weather.com*).

Go smoke free. Attitudes toward smoking are different around the world than they are in the U.S. and you may encounter secondhand smoke almost everywhere you go. At *www.smokefreeworld .com,* you can surf for smoke-free locations worldwide. And if you know of havens for nonsmokers (especially a friendly exception in a smoky town), you can send a review to the web site.

TRAVEL DOCUMENTS

Passports. Apply or renew several months in advance to avoid potential hassles and extra fees. The busiest time is January to July, as people prepare for peak-season travel.

• For passport information, call The National Passport Information Center (NPIC) at 900-225-5674 (automated calls, 35 cents per minute; operator-assisted, $1.05 per minute) or 888-362-8668 (flat $4.95 charge to Visa, MasterCard, or American Express).

• Or visit the NPIC web site *(www.travel.state.gov/passport _services.html),* where you can print out a passport application, and find answers to frequently asked passport questions—such as advice on getting your birth certificate.

• U.S. passports, good for 10 years (five years for ages 15 and under), are issued only to U.S. citizens or nationals. First-time adult applicants must appear in person. Some renewals may be made by mail, but call NPIC to be sure you qualify and have the necessary documentation.

• Each application must be accompanied by proof of U.S. citizenship, proof of identity, two passport-size (2" X 2") photographs, and required fees.

• Fees for routine service—normally, a new passport within about six weeks—are $60 for those 16 and older ($45 passport fee; $15 execution fee); and under age 16, $40 ($25 passport fee; $15 execution fee).

• For expedited service—when you need to get your passport within about two weeks—add $35 per application. In this case, NPIC also strongly suggests that you arrange overnight delivery service for sending your passport application and having your passport returned to you. Contact the NPIC directly if you have what the agency terms a "life or death emergency."

• If you aren't eligible for mail-in service, passports are issued at passport agencies (usually by appointment only) and at some post offices, in addition to other locations. For where to apply for a passport nationwide, call NPIC or check the web site. Also determine what form of payment is accepted: Mail-in applications may be made with a personal check or money order only. Passport agencies accept certain credit and debit cards; other locations may not.

• Twelve major cities, including Boston, Miami, and San Francisco, now have automated numbers that let travelers make appointments for last-minute passports. You will need to show proof that international travel, or a foreign visa, is required within 21 days. Call NPIC or visit *www.travel.state.gov/agencies_list.html* for a list.

Visas. If your destination requires a visa, you must obtain it directly from the embassy or nearest consulate of the country you plan to visit.

• For which country requires what, visit *http://travel.state.gov/ foreignentryreqs.html.* The web site also lists locations and phone numbers of embassies and consulates in large U.S. cities.

• The U.S. State Department advises that you begin the visa process as soon as possible after planning your trip, since delays are not uncommon.

• In some cases, a traveler may be required to obtain visas from a local consular office. Check "Foreign Consular Offices in the United States" at *www.state.gov.* for nationwide listings.

• Certain passport agencies (many of those listed in the web site directly above) will assist travelers who need visas. Check directly with the passport agency. Your travel agent may also be able to help.

• Many countries require that your U.S. passport be valid at least six months or longer beyond the dates of your trip. If your passport expires sooner, you'll have to apply for a new one.

• Travel Document Services (TDS) provides visa services for U.S. citizens for most countries requiring an entry visa. TDS also expedites U.S. passports. Very urgent passports may be obtained the same day if you must depart on short notice. For information, call 800-874-5100 or visit *www.traveldocs.com.* Fees may be stiff.

Essential information for travelers

ESSENTIALS

GOVERNMENT SAFETY ALERTS

In light of recent terrorist activity and increased threats against Americans abroad, it's wise to check the worldwide cautionary information provided by the U.S. State Department.

You can access all public announcements on the State Department web site *(http://travel.state.gov)*. Or call the department's automated phone system, 202-647-5225. For fax-back service, call 202-647-3000.

Travel warnings. The strongest pronouncements issued, these recommend that Americans avoid travel to a particular country. They may also warn that the U.S. Embassy has removed or reduced its presence, minimizing its ability to assist Americans if anything should happen. (Countries not recommended for travel will have both a Travel Warning and a Consular Information Sheet; see the latter category below.)

Public announcements. These communiqués, which may be country-specific, cover a region, or be a worldwide caution, are made when there is a perceived threat to American travelers.

• They concern fast-breaking news, cover a short, finite time period, and have expiration dates. In an uncertain situation, such as political upheaval, that date may extend as far as three months ahead.

• In the past, Public Announcements have concerned short-term coups, bomb threats to airlines, violence by terrorists, and anniversary dates of specific terrorist events.

Consular information sheets. Available for every country in the world, Consular Information Sheets are issued once a year, but revised as conditions change.

• They provide an overview of the location, including such information as location of the U.S. Embassy or Consulate; health conditions; unusual immigration practices, currency regulations, or entry requirements; minor political disturbances; crime and security information; and drug penalties.

• If an unstable condition exists in a country, but it is not severe enough to warrant a Travel Warning, a rundown of the situation may be included under an optional section entitled "Safety/Security."

• Consular Information Sheets generally do not contain advice per se for travelers. They instead present the facts, allowing each traveler to make the decision. But read them carefully, since they can often present a disturbing picture, revealing serious problems such as car theft, violent assaults, and armed robbery.

• You may also find important caveats, such as the necessity of taking a taxi after dark, the danger of pickpockets, or overbilling of tourists in restaurants.

NON-GOVERNMENT INFORMATION SOURCES

Road conditions. The Association for Safe International Road Travel (ASIRT) provides road-safety data for 155 countries in its publication, "Road Travel Reports," available for donations starting at $5. Call 301-983-5252; fax 301-983-3663. Or visit *www.asirt.org*, which offers free travel tips and a sample report.

Destination data. The Worldcue Traveler Service division of iJET Travel Intelligence provides destination-specific information such as entry/exit requirements, safety and security, health, transportation, and weather. Based on input from more than 5,000 sources, updates are delivered via a personalized web page, which you can also access over the Internet as you travel. Fee is $25. Call 877-606-4538 or visit *www.ijet.com.*

CUSTOMS INFORMATION

The information here was current at press time. However, security may necessitate changes in regulations. For a fact-filled pamphlet, "Know Before You Go," visit *www.customs.treas,* or contact U.S. Customs at 877-287-8667 or 202-354-1000. (You may also get personal assistance on this line.) For information on Canadian customs, call 800-461-9999 (in Canada) or 204-983-3500 (from all other locations).

What to declare. When you return to the U.S., you must declare everything you brought back that you did not take with you. And you must state on the Customs declaration what you paid for the item (or the value, if you received it as a gift) in U.S. currency. To avoid hassles, save all receipts and have them handy when you go through customs.

The personal exemption. All U.S. residents are entitled to a $400 exemption—if they carry the purchased items with them, bought everything for their personal use, and haven't used the exemption within the past 30 days.

• Travelers returning from any of 24 Caribbean-basin countries may claim up to $600; travelers returning directly to the U.S. from the American possessions of American Samoa, Guam, and the U.S. Virgin Islands may bring in up to $1,200 worth of goods duty free.

• You may include up to 100 cigars and up to 200 cigarettes in the exemption; you are also allowed one liter of alcohol.

• Families and/or couples may fill out joint declarations—meaning that if one spouse spent $200 and the other spent $600, the couple is still within the exemption limit. Children and infants have the same exemption as adults; alcoholic beverages are excluded.

• If you have used your $400 exemption within the past 30 days, you are still eligible for a $200 exemption; families may not use a joint declaration. (The tobacco/alcohol limit is also reduced.)

• Beyond your exempted amount, you must pay a flat 3 percent duty on the next $1,000 worth (1.5 percent duty if traveling from U.S. possessions) and various duty rates for any additional items.

Restricted items. You may need a permit or a license (or not be allowed) to bring in the following: Absinthe and liquors made with Artemisia absinthium; copies of copyrighted items, such as books and videotapes; cultural artifacts and cultural property; drugs and drug paraphernalia; food products, fruits, vegetables, meat, and poultry; game and hunting trophies; medications; merchandise from embargoed countries; and plants. Also restricted are pets; fish, wildlife, and any products made from them; trademarked items (certain cameras, watches, perfumes); firearms and ammunition; and hazardous materials.

Currency. You may take out or bring in as much money as you like. For $10,000 or more, you'll have to file a permit with U.S. Customs.

Gifts. You may send gifts worth up to $100 to friends and relatives in the U.S., duty free. Mark the wrapper "Unsolicited gift" and list the total value of the package. You can't send a "gift" to yourself. And traveling companions may not send gifts to each other.

"Duty-free." Travelers who buy items at duty-free shops may think they won't have to pay taxes on their purchases when clearing U.S. Customs upon return. But "duty-free" purchases are only duty-free in the country where you bought them. They're still subject to duty in the U.S. if your purchases exceed your exemption, and are subject to all of the previous restrictions.

Foreign-made personal items. If you travel with valuable foreign-made items—say, a camera, watch, or laptop—register them with the U.S. Customs Service before you leave.

Baggage searches. U.S. Customs has always been permitted to search baggage and to detain incoming passengers, if necessary. Be especially ready to exhibit the contents of your baggage now, and cooperate by answering all questions.

Baggage notes

How to choose the right bags, pack smartly, and other baggage handling tips.

CHOOSING LUGGAGE

CONSUMER REPORTS regularly rates luggage, based on tests of durability, ease of use, and other factors. Ratings of five luggage types—wheeled carry-ons, large wheeled uprights, large wheeled duffels, wheeled garment bags, and conventional garment bags—appear on page 313.

Today's new travel procedures—uneven access to curbside check-in, frequent luggage searches, and long lines and waits boarding planes, trains, buses, and ships—mean more "baggage wrangling" for travelers than ever. You'll want luggage that's light yet sturdy, as well as easy to move and manage. Keep these tips in mind as you shop.

Durability. Nylon fabric held up best in our tests. Corner protectors add strength.

Stability. Wheeled carry-ons or garment bags may topple easily, especially with a briefcase or purse strapped on; large upright bags proved much more stable. Wheeled duffel bags with feet or a stiff panel at the wheeled end—or both—were more likely to stand upright.

Handles and straps. The handle should lock in a closed position to avoid damage in transit. Some handles lock open at two lengths. Which length is best for you depends on your height. Try before you buy if you can.

• If a bag bumps your heels as you roll it, the handle is too short.

• A side handle should be positioned so you can grasp it with your stronger hand.

• End handles on a wheeled duffel make it easier to lift.

• A piggyback strap will secure your purse or briefcase; a simple hook lets it dangle. (But large bags have a greater tendency to tip when extra pieces are strapped on.)

• Check all handles and straps for padding, comfort, and fit.

Wheels and feet. Wheels like those on inline skates help make a bag easier to pull. Here are desirable characteristics:

• Recessed wheels should withstand damage well; feet add stability.

• Stair skids—plastic shields on the back of the bag near the wheels—help a bag slide over stairs or curbs more easily.

Extras. Pockets, zippers, and gussets influence convenience.

• Inside mesh pockets keep contents visible. Those made of water-resistant materials hold cosmetics and damp clothing.

• Exterior pockets are handy, but look for double zippers with pull tabs you can lock together.

• The easiest duffel zippers open across the top and down the side.

• An expansion gusset—an extra flap of fabric held in by a zipper—enlarges the bag's capacity. However, an expanded carry-on may no longer fit airline size limits.

PACKING TIPS

Travel light. A baggage search and/or scan will be faster if you carry less in your suitcases.

• Choose lightweight, washable, no-wrinkle layers in coordinated colors (preferably dirt-deflecting dark tones).

• Wear your bulkiest items—an all-purpose jacket or sweater—in transit. Pack one lightweight waterproof outer layer in your bags, along with a small-size umbrella. Try to take only two pairs of footwear—walking shoes and a dressier pair.

• Use travel-sized toiletries. Take a compact hair dryer; if going abroad, you'll need a two-in-one adapter/converter (available at hardware stores).

Pack smart. Plan ahead to prevent headaches later.

• New FAA regulations permit one carry-on and one "personal bag"—a purse, briefcase, backpack, diaper bag, laptop, etc. Don't expect to sneak by with more than this allowance.

• When packing your carry-on, include only things that you would need on the plane, valuable items you do not want to trust to checked baggage (such as jewelry, cameras, cash, prescription medications, eyeglasses, house keys, and passports and other travel documents), or anything perishable or breakable. You might also want to put in a 48-hour supply of essentials.

• According to the FAA at press time, the following cannot be taken beyond the security checkpoint and so are banned from carry-ons: knives of any length, composition, or description; cutting instruments of any composition or description, including carpet and box cutters (and spare blades); any device with a folding or retractable blade; ice picks; straight razors; metal scissors; metal nail files; corkscrews; baseball bats; golf clubs; ski poles; and hockey sticks.

• Anything that might ignite a fire and/or generate fumes is also prohibited: lighter fluid, strike-anywhere matches, hair spray, butane fuels such as curling-iron refills, and self-defense sprays such as mace.

• The FAA states that the following are allowed: walking canes, umbrellas, nail clippers, safety razors, syringes (with documentation of medical need), and tweezers and eyelash curlers. Traveler information is available at the FAA web site, *www.faa.gov.*

• An airline may exceed minimum FAA requirements, and passengers have found that their carrier may, in fact, veto some items—tweezers, knitting and sewing needles, and even safety pins have been blocked. You may be able to transfer them to checked baggage. Or they may be confiscated (and "confiscated" means you won't get the article back). If you have doubts about anything, check with your carrier before you travel.

• Child car seats that meet FAA specifications (see Chapter 11) may be carried on the plane. However, strollers must be checked.

• Don't overstuff bags. Remove or stow any straps and hooks; they can get caught in baggage-handling machinery.

SPECIAL HANDLING

Cameras, camcorders, and film. All such equipment is being carefully examined, so allow extra time.

• Always pack your camera or camcorder in your carry-on, preferably in a cushioned case. Riding in checked baggage can be too rough for the lenses and mechanism. Or use a separate camera bag —but only if it won't exceed the "one carry-on, one personal bag" allowance.

• High dosage airport security scanners can leave a stripe or line on undeveloped film. (Processed slides and prints are not affected.) Use protective pouches specifically designed for the scanners (available in photo-supply stores) for film or loaded cameras in both checked and carry-on luggage.

• If you plan to request hand-inspection, contact your carrier in advance for any special advice. And plan on getting to the airport extra early.

• Should you have more than 20 rolls of film, or motion picture film, call your carrier well in advance to arrange a hand-inspection appointment.

Laptops. Remember that your laptop counts as the "personal bag," so don't expect your notebook computer to be "an extra."

• Do carry on your laptop. In a checked bag, it can be damaged by rough baggage handling, even if it's well-padded with clothing. Invest in a padded or hard-sided carry-on case.

• Laptops may be hand-inspected in some airports, and x-rayed in others, depending on the equipment available at the checkpoint. New airport security scanners won't harm computer hard drives or floppies. (Scanners in small overseas airports might erase disks; if in doubt, request hand inspection.)

• "Explosive-trace detection systems" at some screening locations allow airport personnel to inspect electronic devices without them being powered up. (Screeners rub hand-carried items with a swab and put it in the system for analysis.)

• Since it's hard to predict inspection methods—especially if screeners want to give your laptop a second look—allow plenty of time for all procedures, including booting up.

• Never leave your laptop unattended. Theft is a very real risk. And under new regulations, unattended bags may be searched and/or removed by airport security personnel.

• Onboard, it's safest to stow the laptop under the seat in front of you. When placing it overhead, make sure it's resting on the bottom of the bin, below the lip of the door. If put on top of another bag, it could fall out when the bin is opened.

BAGGAGE ALLOWANCES

Checked luggage. Most airlines allow three pieces. Anything beyond that number is considered excess baggage, and usually subject to an additional charge. But also remember that you may not have access to curbside check-in at all airports and baggage may be subjected to time-consuming searches. So the fewer bags you have to check, the easier it will be for you to get to the gate on time.

• If carrying more than six bags, you might pay $75 to $150 *per bag.* Those who must travel with lots of gear should consider sending some of it ahead with an express delivery service.

• Airlines also charge a fee, usually $75, for an oversized or overweight bag. Most set the limit at 70 pounds and 62 linear inches; as a rule, luggage weighing more than 100 pounds is shipped as cargo. If flying on more than one airline, you may pay an excess-baggage charge to each. Call your carrier to get its rules on such baggage. Do not wait to resolve the issue until you arrive at the airport.

• Expect separate rules and fees for sports equipment and other odd-shaped items. Again, call your carrier in advance of travel.

Carry-ons. Generally, a carry-on bag must not exceed 40 pounds and 45 linear inches, a total of the height, width, and depth of the bag—usually 22x9x14 inches. Some airlines may allow up to 50 inches; rules are not uniform carrier to carrier.

• Frames and displays near many airport check-in counters show size limits. But always check with your carrier when you book; an airline has the right to modify its rules at any time. If a particular flight or aircraft does not have sufficient storage space for all the carry-on baggage passengers may want to bring aboard, the airline may restrict some carry-ons. Carrier web sites also have additional information (see Resource Guide for telephone numbers and web sites).

CHECKING YOUR LUGGAGE

Keep an eye on your baggage. In this country and abroad, always put your luggage into the taxi or limo trunk by yourself after the driver gets out and opens the trunk for you—or at least watch carefully as luggage is loaded. When you arrive at the airport, observe your luggage again as it is unloaded.

Get there early. The sooner you arrive at the airport, the better the chance both you and your bags will get on your flight.

• Airlines may have a "baggage cut-off time," after which you cannot get your bags on the plane. Limits vary, depending on such factors as terminal location at a specific airport and the use of automated baggage-sorting systems. Call the airline for specifics at the airport you'll use.

• A "late check" tag is automatically generated if you get to the counter after the cut-off time. When your delayed bags arrive at the destination, airline policies vary on how, when, and where you can claim them.

• Note that FAA regulations stipulate that no "unattached" bags are allowed on international flights. You and your luggage must fly on the same plane.

Fly straight through. Stopping or connecting can increase the likelihood of misplaced bags. If you must switch planes, watch out for "short checks"—a tag indicating the interim destination, but not the final one.

Use safeguards. Some simple but vital tips.

• Put your name and address inside as well as on the outside tag. Include a copy of destination information (address, phone number) and a flight itinerary in the bag.

- Remove any old airport checking tags, and lock your luggage.
- Watch as bags are tagged to be sure they carry the right destination airport code.
- Keep carry-ons with you. Take them along if you stop over; your plane may be switched. Since carry-ons often contain valuables, they're a target for thieves, so never leave them unattended. (Right now, unattended bags will be taken by airport security.)

AIRLINE BAGGAGE LIABILITY

Domestic trips. The U.S. Department of Transportation (DOT) raised liability for checked baggage to $2,500 per person (from $1,250) early in 2000. This amount covers luggage loss or damage, and theft of packed items.

- According to DOT statistics, the reported rate of mishandled luggage domestically averages about 5 per 1,000 passengers. This includes damage, delay, and pilferage as well as loss. Baggage is more likely to be delayed than truly missing; some 98 percent of "lost" bags are returned to passengers within a few hours.
- Although airlines aren't required to compensate for delays, some offer free kits of overnight supplies. A carrier may also reimburse the cost of personal-care products plus some clothing basics. Buy nothing without airline authorization, however, and save receipts. If baggage is delayed more than a day, ask the airline to allow additional purchases.
- Travelers in a pinch may qualify for more recompense. If you're attending an important meeting or special event, for example, airline personnel may authorize a replacement for clothes caught in luggage limbo—but you must ask first.
- Most airlines assume no liability for carry-ons, since this baggage should remain in your possession. If a carry-on is lost, however, the airline may give you a small advance for supplies and toiletries while it searches for your bag.

International flights. Maximum baggage compensation is set by treaty at $20 a kilogram of checked baggage weight (or about $9 per pound).

- According to the DOT, claims are seldom based on actual weight. Most airlines serving the U.S. on international routes (both U.S. and foreign carriers) have filed tariffs stating they will assume every lost or damaged bag equals the maximum weight limit, usually 32 kilos (around 70 pounds), making the allowance $640 per bag, regardless of weight.

- The airline is liable only for depreciated value, not replacement value or original purchase price.

Claims. Report loss or damage before leaving the airport.

- The DOT cannot force airlines to reimburse you. But most carriers voluntarily accept valid claims up to the allowed amount.

- Always negotiate with the airline on which you arrived. Even if another carrier is involved—if, say, the domestic code-share partner will actually trace the baggage or pay for it—the airline landing at your destination initiates the process.

- If a bag is simply damaged, you may be able to get repairs done on the spot or get a replacement bag.

- Airlines will issue cash or a check at their baggage service centers. A carrier may offer you a free ticket for a future flight in lieu of compensation. If that doesn't meet your needs, demand cash instead.

- If you do not get satisfaction for loss or damage, pursue your request in writing.

Insurance. Cover the difference between the value of your personal effects and the maximum airline payment with a year-round personal-property policy, separate baggage insurance policy, insurance offered by your credit card, or excess-valuation coverage.

Money matters

Smart ways to handle your money, avoid excess taxes, and phone home.

CURRENCY

Check the exchange rate. You can better plan expenses before you go and assess prices once you arrive. The Universal Currency Converter *(www.xe.net/ucc)* has instant conversion rates. Your own bank may also be able to supply rates. (A mini-calculator will help you switch from one currency to another as you travel.)

Welcome the euro. The euro (at press time worth about 89 cents) enters circulation on January 1, 2002, when local banks and major retail outlets will begin issuing euro bank notes and coins, and taking national currencies out of circulation. The exchange will be completed by March 1.

• The euro replaces the Austrian schilling, Belgian franc, Finnish markka, French franc, German deutschmark, Greek drachma, Irish punt, Italian lira, Luxembourg franc, Netherlands guilder, Portuguese escudo, and Spanish peseta. When traveling among these countries, you won't need to swap currency.

• However, three of the 15 EU nations—Britain, Denmark, and Sweden—will continue to use their own independent currencies for now. So you will need to exchange currency if including them in your European travel plans.

Exchange some currency before you leave. Just $20 to $50 will allow you to bypass long lines and lousy rates at most airport exchange booths. No time or opportunity before you leave? Once you clear Customs in your destination, look for a bank-affiliated ATM (increasingly common at airports) and convert that same small amount.

Use charge cards. You probably plan to pay for tickets, hotels, car rentals, and the like with plastic. But using your card for meals and shopping is also a wise move. American Express, Visa, and Mastercard are widely accepted overseas.

• You'll avoid the conversion fee (sometimes as high as 10 percent) that many stores and restaurants may charge when you pay in U.S. dollars or traveler's checks.

• Before you leave, however, call your charge-card issuer to determine the currency-conversion surcharge. American Express, Diners Club, First USA, MasterCard, and Visa all impose a charge on foreign purchases; rates run between 1 and 2 percent. (Visa generally has the best rates, but they can change.) Rates vary slightly from day to day, and card purchases made on the same day may not be processed at the same time, making after-the-fact comparisons difficult. However, even with these charges, plastic is still a cheaper option than getting or converting cash or using traveler's checks overseas.

Carry a little cash. A supply for a day or two only is prudent. If your cash is lost or stolen, chances of recovery are small (just as in the U.S.).

Use ATMs. If your ATM card works in the Cirrus or Plus network at home, you may be able to withdraw cash from foreign-bank ATMs belonging to the same network.

• Your withdrawal will be converted at the interbank exchange rate—the "wholesale" rate that banks use for large-scale financial transactions. (At banks, the rate may be 3 to 5 percent less favorable, plus many charge an additional fee of perhaps 2 to 5 percent.)

• ATMs outside North America may not accept a Personal Identification Number (PIN) longer than four digits. If your PIN is longer, ask your bank for a new number.

- You follow the same procedure as you would at a cash machine in the U.S. (Most ATMs affiliated with Cirrus or Plus provide an "in English" option.) As in this country, your bank may impose a fee for using an ATM elsewhere on the network.

- Keypads on many foreign ATMs have numbers only. If your PIN contains letters, use the telephone letter-number correspondences. Figure it out and remember it before your trip.

- Stock your checking account, since overseas ATMs may not let you choose which account you'll tap.

- Have backup money—you can't always find a participating ATM, and your card may not work in all locations. And sometimes you can get cash only by using a credit card (then paying interest on the "advance"). See if your charge card's issuing bank has a list of participating ATMs.

Traveler's checks. Widely accepted, traveler's checks are also "protected"—issuers typically provide worldwide refunds and emergency services in the event of loss or theft. They may not command as good an exchange rate as an ATM transaction, however.

- When you purchase your checks, you'll also receive a check record. Write down the number of each check you cash and keep the record separate—you may need backup if checks are lost or stolen.

- You can cash traveler's checks into foreign currency at exchange facilities, found in central business districts of cities; at airports and train stations; and at some banks (branches of large multinational institutions). Most facilities keep standard business hours, but some may be open later during peak vacation seasons. Rates are displayed, frequently in the window. However, you will have to pay a commission for each transaction.

- Hotels also cash traveler's checks, although they may charge a higher commission. Ask before you begin the transaction.

- You'll need to show ID each time you cash a traveler's check or use one in payment for a purchase. In the U.S., you can present a valid driver's license or credit card. (Even if you don't drive, the department of motor vehicles in certain states will issue a personal ID.) Overseas, you'll routinely be asked for your passport.

Another money option. The Visa TravelMoney card is a "plastic traveler's check." The card provides access to over 600,000 Visa ATMs in more than 130 countries worldwide. Here's how it works:

• You prepay whatever amount you choose plus a small service fee, then use the card like a debit card at Visa-network ATMs around the world. You'll also be provided with a hotline number if the card is lost or stolen.

• For information, call 877-762-3227. Or check *www.visa.com*.

Stay safe. Although security has been beefed up at many locations worldwide, and crowds may be thinner, you still must be vigilant about your money and personal safety.

• It's important to remain vigilant. Report suspicious behavior or packages to authorities.

• Avoid volunteering information to strangers about your trip, its duration, where you are staying, or your upcoming destinations. Do not discuss finances with those you don't know.

• Don't allow yourself to be distracted when sightseeing—scam artists often work in pairs or groups and use distractions to give them time to rip off tourists.

• Crowded tourist spots, such as museums, churches, or market-places, are prime locations, as are all mass-transit vehicles—subways, buses, and trains—along with transit terminals such as train stations and airports.

• In large cities, noisy (and intimidating) gangs of children and teens can surround you and, in the turmoil, make off with a purse, wallet, or other valuables.

• Some panhandlers on the street can be insistent, even following you. If you are harassed, go inside or find a policeman.

• Carry your cash and charge cards in a money belt, or a purse that fastens securely with a strap that crosses your body rather than just a shoulder strap or handle.

• Keep all valuables—cameras, binoculars, and wallets—out of sight. Avoid wearing jewelry that marks you as someone with cash.

• Don't push into crowds; try to go around them instead. When in a line or a throng of people, keep a distance from those around you; pickpockets can easily bump into you "accidentally," then grab a wallet or cash while you're distracted.

- Anyone watching you use an ATM or cashing a traveler's check may be sizing you up. Put money away safely and avoid the person, even if it means waiting inside until they've given up.

TAXES

Taxes can add considerably to your expenses. Confirm the tax rate for any travel service when booking.

Taxes in the U.S. A *Consumer Reports Travel Letter* survey revealed that taxes have risen the past several years.

- Airline travel levies two key taxes: a federal tax on every airline ticket sold in the U.S. (7.5 percent of the ticket price plus $2.25 per person for every flight segment) and a $3 passenger facilities charge (PFC) at almost every major airport, even if you're only connecting there.
- Lodging taxes average 12.7 percent of your room rate. (Chicago has the highest lodging tax, at 14.9 percent; Las Vegas the lowest, at 9 percent.) But even that lower rate transforms a $100 room to a $109 room, adding $45 for a week-long stay.
- Car rental taxes are the most confusing because of surcharges. You'll begin with sales tax on the rental rate. Some cities impose an additional airport concession fee; some may charge an off-airport fee. Most cities also add per-rental or per-day surcharges on top of the taxes.
- Comparing car-rental taxes at different locations can lead you to a better deal (or at least prepare you for your bill).
- Lodgings outside city limits may be not only more reasonably priced, but subject to a lower tax rate.

Taxes abroad. If you're booking a package, tour, or cruise, taxes will be included. (Although not strictly a "tax," a ticket surcharge ranging from $1.25 to $8 has also been added by some international airlines to pay for additional insurance and security.) Whenever you arrange any accommodation or rental car yourself, however, always ask if the price includes tax. The tax you may actually be able to ease abroad is the value added tax—the VAT.

- The VAT is actually a sales tax, which can run up to 20 percent (in Sweden), and as low as 7 percent (in Switzerland). You must pay it on goods purchased, then taken out of a store or shop.

- Any visitor to Europe may potentially get a VAT refund on merchandise (but not on travel services used while vacationing). The procedure is simple.

- Look for the Global Refund TAX FREE SHOPPING sign or sticker in a store's window. Whenever you make a purchase, ask for the tax-free shopping check for the amount of the refund.

- When leaving the country, declare your purchases to customs and have the agent validate your check(s). When shopping within the European Union, you will only need to declare your purchases on leaving the EU.

- You can then get your refund by cashing the checks at the Global Refund office after you have cleared passport control. Refunds are also available at any of their offices worldwide. You may also mail validated checks to them for a credit on your charge-card account.

- Those offering to help you with VAT refunds imply that you can save a bundle. However, in many countries you've got to spend a bundle first. Here's a rundown (limits may change): Austria, $66; Belgium, $110; Denmark, $36; Finland, $35; France, $154; Germany, $22; Greece, $106; Italy, $137; Luxembourg, $65; the Netherlands, $121; Norway, $34; Portugal, $51; Spain, $80; Sweden, $19; Switzerland, $302; the U.K., $43; Ireland has no minimum purchase.

- The minimum purchase you must make to qualify for a refund typically applies to all goods you buy at a single store during one shopping day.

- While the dollar is strong against the euro, goods bought abroad may carry attractive price tags. But if the dollar declines, those tempting goods may be cheaper in the U.S.

PHONING HOME

Long-distance company calling plans. Such plans can cut costs dramatically. The three big companies AT&T, MCI, and Sprint—offer discounted international calling plans for a monthly fee, allowing you to call the U.S. from abroad, as well as call overseas from the U.S. For a rate comparison, check the web site *http://abelltolls.com*.

• Although you can get a calling card linked to your home telephone account, these connections require operator assistance and calls are typically more expensive than those made with the plans.

• Even with a calling plan, avoid hotel switchboards, notorious for price-gouging. (Many charge even for local and toll-free calls.) Verify if you'll be billed for calls to the toll-free access number used with many plans. If so, call from a lobby telephone or a public pay phone.

Prepaid calling cards. Prepaid to a specific dollar amount or time allotment, cards are sold at retail outlets, on the web, and through print ads. But beware of glitches.

• Bad service is a common problem, such as nonworking access numbers and always-busy customer-service numbers. Or a company may just shut down, making the card worthless.

• Rate-shopping is tough; many cards are marketed only to specific regions. Pricing isn't standard, and you may discover hidden charges or bills for uncompleted calls. And some cards sold here won't work outside the U.S.

• You can buy a calling card abroad. They're typically sold at newsstands, tobacco shops, post offices, and cell-phone stores. Don't buy more time than you'll use, however; refunds are typically impossible.

Callback services. These reroute outgoing phone calls, turning them into incoming calls, thus getting lower U.S. phone rates.

• Sign up with a service provider, giving your number abroad. Once there, you dial a toll-free U.S. number, let it ring once or twice, then hang up. This (uncharged) call triggers the callback computer to phone you back with a U.S. line so you may make your calls.

• But most services require travelers to call from just one number—useful if you're renting property for a few months, but not when on a city-to-city tour. (Some companies let you instantly update your phone number on the web.)

• Callback systems generally can't navigate hotel switchboards. Some work with cell phones, but higher rates may apply.

Cruise-ship communications. All the major cruise lines now have satellite links allowing passengers to phone home, usually from their cabin. But charges are stiff for both outgoing and incoming calls. Passengers can save by using pay phones at ports of call. In addition, the biggest cruise lines are either already wired for e-mail—or will be soon.

The e-mail option. E-mail goes around the world—and you don't even have to take your own computer.

• The Internet Cafe Guide *(www.netcafeguide.com)* says it lists 3,000 cafes in 143 countries. The Cybercafe Search Engine *(www. cybercaptive.com)* says it has more than 7,100 listings in 167 countries. (Most cybercafes are in major cities.)

• Costs vary greatly from country to country, and from one cafe to another. Our quick price check in London, Paris, and Rome found costs ranging from almost $4 to about $7 per hour.

• Consider signing up for a free, web-based e-mail service (i.e., Yahoo.com or Hotmail.com). Your regular e-mail can also forward messages to your web e-mail. To stay secure, log out of web-based e-mail when finished, and never check bank accounts, make credit-card purchases, or access personal information from a public terminal.

How to complain effectively

Knowing what to say and to whom can bring relief and even compensation.

AIRLINES

Your rights depend on whether delays or other problems are caused by the airline or by outside circumstances.

Airline-induced events. These comprise any condition under the airline's control, including aircraft maintenance, crew problems, ticketing or boarding errors; along with late arrival of inbound airplanes because of these conditions.

• If you are flying on a major airline, the carrier will send you on the next available flight (one of its own or that of another airline), or will provide an upgrade at no cost if this upgraded seat is the next one available, or will grant a refund for the unused portion of the ticket.

• The exception is Southwest, which doesn't maintain interline agreements with other airlines. Instead, Southwest will either put you on another of its flights or offer a refund.

• Meals, ground transportation, and phone cards may be given in some cases. With certain restrictions, the major airlines will provide one night's lodging. (However, Southwest states that such decisions will be made by its staff.)

Force-majeure events. These include weather conditions; acts of God; riots; civil commotions; embargoes; wars; hostilities, disturbances or unsettled international conditions, whether actual, threatened, or reported; any strike, work stoppage, slowdown, lockout, or any other labor-related dispute involving or affecting service; any government regulation, demand, or requirement; any shortage of labor, fuel, or facilities; and any fact not reasonably foreseen, anticipated, or predicted.

• In these cases, the airline has no responsibility beyond giving you a refund for the unused portion of your ticket. The carrier will attempt to rebook you on the next available flight, when possible.

• Further amenities will be provided at the airline's discretion. (See Chapter 10 for more details.)

Forewarned is forearmed. Best case, you'll avoid delays and difficulties altogether. But if a problem arises, be prepared.

• Before your trip, download your airline's Customer Service Commitment—a list of promises to improve passenger treatment put forth in December 1999 under pressure by Congress and the DOT. (The Resource Guide has carrier web site listings.) Quoting from this statement may help. At the least, you will position yourself as an informed traveler.

• Or get a copy of the airline's Contract of Carriage. The DOT requires airlines to keep a copy at ticket offices and airport counters for any passenger to see. But if one is not available, a synopsis of the DOT's Rule 240, which outlines standards for passenger treatment (and is the basis of every carrier's contract), is posted at *www.mytravelrights.com.* (See "All travel companies," in this section, for details on this web site.)

• Query the airline (or check its web site) about interline agreements, which would allow you to switch to another carrier's flight. (Newer, smaller, and low-fare airlines may not have them.) It's tougher to get another airline to endorse an electronic ticket than a paper one, so go for a "traditional" ticket.

• Understand weather delays. That bad weather may not be at your origin or destination. It could be somewhere in between—or even in the place where your flight's aircraft originated. You can check weather forecasts at the FAA web site *(www.fly.faa.gov)*. Also remember that in really bad conditions, all flights will be grounded; your best strategy will be to work on other travel plans or start looking for accommodations.

Complaining constructively. When a delay or cancellation grounds you, be organized in your protest.

• Be polite. Why offend the very service representatives who have the power to help you? And, although all passengers should be treated equally, those dressed neatly may be more "equal."

• Take immediate action. Ask a passenger service agent for the cause of the problem, or call the airline's reservations center to determine who's at fault. Request perks, if the delay is long.

• For possibly better treatment, let the airline know if you are one of its frequent-flyers, have purchased a first- or business-class seat, or have bought a full-fare ticket.

• If you've booked through a travel agent, ask the agent to help rebook you on another flight and/or provide you with overnight accommodations.

Complaining some more. If an airline fails to provide you with reasonable help, you can pursue other channels later.

• Contact the airline in writing, explaining the situation. Even if this approach does not get you satisfaction, you'll have a written record of your problem and the response, a help if you take further action.

• You can file an air-travel-related complaint against a U.S. or foreign airline, travel agent, tour operator, or travel web site directly with the DOT. Call 202-366-2220 (automated menu only); or e-mail at *airconsumer@ost.dot.gov.*

• You can also be part of a DOT survey on poor airline service. Call 800-884-9190 or log on to *www.oig.dot.gov.*

CRUISE LINES

Nearly all cruise lines are based outside the U.S., which limits options for lodging complaints. But there are still means.

• Deal with complaints, especially those concerning cabin or service personnel, immediately by contacting the ship's hotel director or the purser. Even if you don't resolve the problem at sea, you'll be on record and can follow up after you disembark. Document your complaint with notes, including employee names.

• Types of complaints most likely to get a cruise-line response include changed itineraries, food poisoning, assaults, fire and smoke inhalation, and failure to deliver advertised services and facilities.

• When you return home, contact the cruise line about any unresolved complaints. Address a straightforward, nonemotional letter to the passenger-service or customer-service department, detailing the reason(s) for your complaint and the steps the cruise line should take to compensate you.

• Ask your travel agent to contact the cruise line on your behalf. Cruise specialists, usually affiliated with industry organizations such as the Cruise Lines International Association, often have additional clout because of their volume bookings.

• Federal authorities have little oversight of cruise lines based outside the U.S. But you can contact the Federal Maritime Commission's Office of Consumer Complaints (call 202-523 5807 or visit the web site, *www.fmc.gov*).

• Cruise lines rarely offer cash refunds; discounts for future cruises are the usual compensation. Even after September 11, cruise line responses to nervous passengers wishing to cancel or those unable to reach their cruise due a grounded flight ran the gamut from tight-fisted to generous. Many cruise lines were giving credits to clients for future cruises.

• To avoid losing your deposit (or the entire price of the cruise) in case you must cancel or the cruise line fails, purchase coverage—including that for supplier default—from a travel insurance company (See Chapter 4). Coverage through the cruise line is worthless if the line declares bankruptcy.

• Passengers only rarely recover damages via lawsuits, since cruise companies are protected from liability by maritime law, which often overrules state law. If you sue, however, act quickly. A passenger must file a claim of physical injuries within six months and commence a lawsuit within one year. Time limitations for non-physical injury can be much shorter. Before you file, read the details of a cruise line's liability (on the ticket and/or the brochure) for the—many—exclusions.

ALL TRAVEL COMPANIES

Always get reservations confirmations—a reservation number, a written copy, or, if booking via the web, a printed copy.

• In all cases your best protection against travel suppliers is to book by charge card. (However, policies of some issuing banks may not provide the same coverage as the major charge-card companies.) Whichever card you use, follow its procedures to stop a charge if service isn't delivered. With an overseas tour operator, don't book at all unless it accepts credit cards. Obtaining a refund will be too daunting otherwise.

• Again, pursue complaints in writing. Even if the problem was a minor inconvenience, the company is likely to offer you something—future discounts, an upgraded room or vehicle, or some other incentive to return.

• The Association of Retail Travel Agents has helped develop the non-profit Consumer Travel Rights Center (CRTC), designed to educate consumers about their rights when dealing with airlines, cruise lines, hotel chains, car-rental firms, tour operators, rail lines, and attractions. Annual membership is $12; members can use the CRTC to file complaints against travel suppliers. You can log on at *www.mytravelrights.com.*

• If you are a very frequent traveler, investigate travel insurance that covers all your travel for an extended period of time rather than for a single trip. Or weigh the cost of short-term insurance against a high-priced, one-time purchase, such as a cruise or extended tour.

COMPLAINTS

Access for disabled travelers

Conditions for disabled travelers have improved a lot. But shortfalls remain.

AIRLINES

In the 16 years since the Department of Transportation implemented the Air Carrier Access Act (ACAA), disabled air travelers in the U.S. have seen some progress in passenger ease and comfort. But advocacy groups report that much still needs to be done, and the airlines themselves acknowledge that even now, their employees sometimes have to be reminded of the law. Protect yourself with a knowledge of the law's provisions.

Main points. Here is a summary of the major stipulations.

• Airlines may not refuse passengers on the basis of disability. However, they may exclude a passenger if the safety of the flight would be compromised.

• Carriers may not require advance notice from a person with a disability. They may require up to 48 hours' notice for certain accommodations, such as a respirator hookup or transporting an electric wheelchair on an aircraft with fewer than 60 seats.

- Airlines may not limit the number of disabled persons on a flight, nor require a disabled person to travel with an attendant, except in certain limited circumstances.

- Newer aircraft with at least 30 seats must have movable aisle armrests on half the aisle seats. Compliance with onboard wheelchair requirements is mandatory (see below). Older planes being refurbished must add accessibility features.

- New twin aisle aircraft must have accessible lavatories.

- New aircraft with 100 or more seats must have priority cabin space for storing a passenger's folding wheelchair.

- All aircraft with more than 60 seats and an accessible lavatory must have an onboard wheelchair, regardless of the aircraft's age. (An onboard wheelchair, commonly called an "aisle chair," is a narrow, armless chair on wheels.)

- Airlines must provide assistance with boarding, deplaning, and making connections. Assistance within the cabin is also required; extensive personal services are not. Ramps or mechanical lifts were mandated by December 2000 for most aircraft with 19 through 30 seats at all U.S. airports with more than 10,000 annual enplanements.

- Carriers must accept battery-powered wheelchairs, packing the batteries in "hazardous materials" packages when necessary. The airline must provide the packaging, and must not charge for providing accommodations required by the rule, such as hazardous-materials packaging for batteries. But they may charge for optional services.

- Airlines must allow service animals to accompany passengers in the cabin, as long as they don't block the aisle or other emergency evacuation route.

- Airport terminals and airline reservations centers must have TDD telephone devices for persons with hearing or speech impairments.

- Passengers with vision or hearing impairments must have timely access to the same information given to other passengers at the airport or on the plane, such as gate assignments, delayed flights, safety, etc.

More information. Several areas on the DOT web site, plus an organization serving the disabled, offer details and advice.

- "Fly-Rights: A Consumer Guide to Air Travel," published by the DOT, has a section for passengers with disabilities *(www.dot.gov/airconsumer/flyrights.htm)*.

- More of the main points are summarized by the Aviation Consumer Protection Division at *www.dot.gov/airconsumer/disabled.htm*.

- Particulars on the regulations, plus guidance on such topics as airport accessibility, security screening, and boarding and deplaning, are available in an online booklet, "New Horizons: Information for the Air Traveler with a Disability," available at *www.gov/airconsumer/horizons.htm*.

- The Eastern Paralyzed Veterans Association (EPVA) has a free pocket card listing rights for disabled travelers (you may offer a donation, if you like). Call the publications department at 800-444-0120.

Uneven compliance. The latest report from the National Council on Disability (NCD), "Enforcing the Civil Rights of Air Travelers with Disabilities," concerning the effectiveness of the ACAA, was published in February 1999.

- At the time of the report, the conclusion was that "more accommodations are available for air travelers with disabilities than ever before, but the availability of accommodations is inconsistent, and discriminatory treatment continues."

- Complaints ranged from seating problems to lack of assistance to inaccessible airport facilities, such as elevators and restrooms.

- The largest number of complaints concerned delayed wheelchairs (which included the lack of onboard chairs), and inadequate assistance or misinformation from customer-service agents (including wheelchair assistance that was denied or challenged).

- Disabled passengers also reported that agents and flight personnel were unfamiliar with or untrained in assistance—for example, when a flight attendant must help move a passenger from a wheelchair to an airline-owned aisle chair.

- Another area of concern was unsafe conditions or injury during transfer or transport (when no jetbridge is available, as may be true overseas and at vacation destinations in the Caribbean, some travelers must be strapped into an aisle chair and carried on portable stairs by ground personnel).

Tips to remember. How to improve your safety and comfort.

• Even though airlines may not require advance notice from a disabled passenger, it's still a good idea to give—and get—as much advance information as possible.

• You may want to talk to your carrier about any special policies for security screening, or arrange for help with baggage if curbside check-in is not available at your airport.

• Take advantage of priority boarding to allow yourself extra time and to stow wheelchairs in onboard closets.

• If you have a complaint, airlines have complaint-resolution officials immediately available; ask to speak to one.

CRUISE SHIPS

In June 2000, a federal appeals court ruled that the Americans with Disabilities Act (ADA) applies to foreign-flagged cruise ships in U.S. ports. Although the cruise industry is still not required to build wheelchair accessibility into all new ships. Celebrity, Holland America, Princess, and Royal Caribbean lead.

Know what to expect. In general, the newer and larger the ship, the more maneuvering room for wheelchairs.

• Some ships have wheelchair lifts at embarkation and debarkation points; onboard ramps may feature grading comparable to that on dry land.

• Many older ships, however, are still poorly accessible to wheelchairs, with obstacles such as "lips" at the doors of cabins, bathrooms, and some public rooms.

• For a list of wheelchair-accessible features on various cruise ships, visit the Cruise Line International Association (CLIA) web site *(www.cruising.org;* click on Special Interest Guides to Cruising).

• Passengers with disabilities may require a physician's release form stating that they may travel. And it's wise to check the ship's offerings with the cruise line or your travel agent.

Check the facilities. You'll want the following:

- Be sure that passengers in standard wheelchairs or narrower travel chairs are accepted; specially-equipped, accessible cabins are available; travel chairs will be provided in certain cases; all public rooms have wide doorways and convenient access; ramps are provided throughout the ship; cabins have low or no sills; baths have safety rails; and elevators are large enough to accommodate wheelchairs.

- Passengers using motorized chairs and scooters should look for 30-inch-wide doors; wheel-in showers and fold-down seats; easily reachable water controls and shower heads; nonslip bath mats; sinks at wheelchair height; and raised toilet seats.

TRANSPORTATION

The Americans with Disabilities Act (ADA) contains provisions stipulating that public transportation—buses, and intercity and commuter rail systems—be accessible. In essence, operators must provide a level of service comparable to that they give to nondisabled passengers.

Train service. Rules cover commuter trains as well as intercity rail systems (Amtrak).

- The law states that at least one car per train must be accessible, that is, able to be entered from the platform by a passenger using a wheelchair.

- Such passenger coaches (and accessible food-service cars) shall also provide a wheelchair-accessible restroom.

- Stations must also be designed to accommodate the needs of disabled passengers, providing elevators if there is more than one floor, and accessible restrooms.

Buses. Those operated by public entities such as cities and towns must conform to the law—and so must those operated by any company "primarily engaged in the business of transporting people."

- A fixed-route system (a system on which vehicles operate along a prescribed route according to a fixed schedule) other than a commuter system must in addition provide paratransit and other special transportation services for the disabled.

- Demand-responsive systems (any system not operating on a

fixed schedule) are required to have accessible vehicles.

Advance information. Given the ADA requirements that paratransit trips be scheduled the day before (and the fact that private providers may also need advance notice), for your own comfort, you'll want to plot your route in advance.

• Preview what's available at your destination at *www.project action. org,* the web site run by Project Action of National Easter Seals. Select the city and state for a list of resources (with addresses and telephone numbers) of public transit operators, accessible van rental companies, private bus/tour companies, airport transportation, hotel/motel shuttles, some accessible taxis, and national toll-free numbers, including those for companies offering accessible car rentals.

• EPVA also offers "Accessible Transit Travel," which lists resources across the country (free, but you may offer a donation). Call 800-444-0120 for details.

• However, always contact any transportation provider directly and discuss what's offered, so you know exactly what to expect.

LODGING

The ADA mandates access to a multitude of facilities, from restaurants and stores to movie theaters and zoos. Also included are inns, hotels, and motels, with the permitted exclusion of a small (less than five-room) establishment if the proprietor lives on the premises.

Plan ahead. A small obstacle hardly noticeable to the average person can be a large block to a disabled traveler.

• When you book, discuss the facilities with the reservations person. You'll want to know about stairs and elevators, and get a solid description of the room, including the bathroom.

• Since agents at toll-free reservation lines may not be able to provide all the details you need, call the hotel directly. If you're unable to get the information you want, ask to speak to the manager.

• Consider posting a question at a guidebook or travel web site. Those who have been to your destination can give you a firsthand account of accessible facilities.

• The Society for the Advancement of Travelers with Handicaps

(SATH) posts travel advice on the organization's web site *(www.sath
.org)*, and has written information, too. You can also reach them by
phone (800-513-1126) and e-mail *(sathtravel@aol.com)*.

PARKS

U.S. citizens or permanent residents who have a permanent disability are eligible for the Golden Access Passport. The free lifetime pass
provides free entrance to most federal recreation areas plus a 50 percent discount on use fees, such as camping fees. It is available at
national parks or federal recreation areas.

OTHER RESOURCES

• The National Council on Disability *(www.ncd.gov)* is an independent federal agency that "promotes policies, programs, practices,
and procedures that guarantee equal opportunity for all individuals
with a disabilities." The agency is currently coordinating a multi-year
study on ADA implementation and enforcement.

• Self Help for Hard of Hearing People (SHHH) works to
increase communication access for people of all ages and degrees of
hearing loss. The web site *(www.shhh.org)* lists assistance and
resources.

• EPVA also has information available on its web site *(www.
epva.org)* on such topics as accessible architecture and sports and
recreation.

• Access-Able Travel Source *(www.access-able.com)* has a database of resources, covering such topics as which cities, states, and
countries have access guides; and which hotels are accessible. They
also offer extensive cruise ship information (including specific mea-
surements for all popular cruise lines), and a list of travel agents
geared toward special-needs travel.

Health tips
for travelers

Each year, millions of people travel, and up to 70 percent
report some health problems along the way.

Following are basic health guidelines for travelers, particularly those
going abroad. Every traveler, particularly those with special health
concerns (including pregnant or breast-feeding women, older persons, those with lowered immunity or chronic diseases, and anyone
traveling with an infant or young child), should consult a physician
or other health professional for specific advice or treatment.

BASIC PRECAUTIONS

Assess destination conditions. The health environment in larger
European cities compares to that of the U.S. But Asia, Africa, and
many parts of South and Central America may require special safeguards. And a journey of more than a month, particularly to a rural
area, may warrant added measures.

• The Centers for Disease Control and Prevention (CDC) has up-
to-date information for travelers at its web site *(www.cdc.gov/travel).*
Type in your destination for a conditions-and-advice summary. You
can also click to information on specific diseases, including locales

and risk; illness outbreak warnings; vaccination recommendations; guidance for special-needs travelers and those traveling with children; and, under "Reference Materials," the "Summary of Health Information for International Travel" (The Blue Sheet).

• You may also call the CDC's International Travelers' Hotline, 877-FYI-TRIP (877-394-8747). To receive information by fax, call 888-232-3299. Any material available by fax is also on the web site.

• Another valuable reference is "The International Travel Health Guide" (Travel Medicine, 12th edition, $19.95) by Stuart Rose, M.D. The 500-page compendium covers a multitude of topics, such as medical care abroad and diseases that plague travelers after they return home, as well as common complaints like motion sickness and jet lag. It also features the World Medical Guide, a country-by-country disease-risk summary. The guide is available in bookstores, online *(www.travmed.com)*, or by phone at 800-872-8633. Text and regular updates may also be downloaded from the web site.

Allow enough time for immunizations. See your physician at least six weeks before departure: Certain vaccines or vaccine-combinations may require careful spacing; possible reactions could require a week or more to subside.

• If you need no specific immunization, ask your physician for any precautions, based on the destination, time of year, trip duration, expected living arrangements, plus personal risk factors such as age, and current health and immunization status.

• Traveler or not, everyone needs routine immunizations protecting against such illnesses as measles and mumps. Adults without an adequate immunization history should consult a doctor for the safest strategy.

• Adult travelers should have had a tetanus-diphtheria shot or booster within the past 10 years. The CDC recommends a flu shot each year if you are 50 years of age or older, and a pneumonia shot if you are over 65 or have a chronic medical condition. Travelers born in or after 1957 should inquire about a second dose of measles vaccine.

Settle other health matters. If you are planning a long trip, have not had a physical in over a year, have a chronic disease, or have long-term medication needs, schedule an exam with your doctor. Other prudent steps: Have dental work done; get an eye exam; pack an extra pair of glasses or contact lenses plus a copy of your lens prescription.

IMMUNIZATIONS

Some countries require certain immunizations before you can enter. The CDC web site *(www.cdc.gov/travel)* and CDC Travelers' Hotline (877-394-8747) have information. Our overview lists possible immunizations; few if any travelers would need them all. Ask your doctor if you fall into a high-risk group (infants, pregnant women, those with lowered immunity); the risk from the vaccine may pose a greater health risk than the disease itself.

Health-wise traveling. Many diseases are spread by contaminated food or water or by insect bites. Immunization can never guarantee 100 percent protection. Even with the required shots, follow protective guidelines. (See "Water safety," "Food caution," and "Insect protection," later in this section.)

International Certificate of Vaccination. All immunizations may be recorded on this certificate—Form PHS-731—by a licensed physician. Each traveler needs a separate form; keep the completed certificate with your passport.

• Your physician or travel agent may provide the form. It is also available from your local health department, and from the Superintendent of Documents, U.S. Government Printing Office (stock #017-001-004405; $2 a copy).

• If your doctor advises you skip a required immunization for medical reasons, have the doctor note the omission on your certificate and attach a signed and dated statement on letterhead stationery specifying the reasons.

• Infants—and, sometimes, very young children—may be exempt from some countries' vaccination requirements. Check with the foreign embassy or consulate. See the State Department web site *(http://travel.state.gov/foreignentryreqs.html)* for embassy and consulate locations and phone numbers.

QUICK GUIDE TO DISEASES OF CONCERN

Listed in alphabetical order

Cholera. An acute intestinal infection spread by contaminated food and drink, cholera occurs in many developing countries of Africa and Asia, and in Latin America. Risk is very low, especially if you follow the usual tourist itineraries, stay in standard accommodations, and are careful about what you consume.

No cholera vaccination requirements exist for entry or exit in any country. The only licensed cholera vaccine in the U.S. has been discontinued, and has not been recommended because of brief and incomplete immunity. Two recently developed vaccines (Dukoral, Mutacol) are licensed and available in other countries, but neither is recommended for travelers.

Hepatitis A. This viral disease is transmitted by direct person-to-person contact; contaminated water, ice, or shellfish harvested from sewage-contaminated water; or fruits, vegetables, or other foods eaten uncooked and tainted during handling. Travelers to North America (except Mexico), Japan, Australia and New Zealand, and developed countries in Europe are at no greater risk than in the U.S. Risk of infection in developing countries increases with travel duration and is greatest to those traveling in rural or backcountry regions or eating/drinking in areas of poor sanitation.

Hepatitis A vaccine (Merck's VAQTA and Smith Kline Beecham's HAVRIX) is recommended if traveling to countries of intermediate or high rates of infection. (Check with the CDC and your doctor for specifics.)

Hepatitis B. Transmitted by contaminated blood or sexual contact with carriers of the virus (HBV), the disease is common in Africa, Southeast Asia, the Middle East except Israel, South and Western Pacific Islands, the interior Amazon Basin in South America, parts of the Caribbean (Haiti and the Dominican Republic), and possibly China and Korea. Risk to travelers is generally low. Besides the prevalence in the region, risk-assessment factors include the possibility of either sexual contact or direct contact with infected blood, and duration of travel.

Consider Hepatitis B vaccine if planning to reside for more than six months, especially in rural areas; anticipating sexual contact with the local population; or if you might need medical or dental care during your stay.

Vaccination (with Recombivax-HB or Energix-B) should ideally begin at least six months before travel to complete the full series. Some protection is provided by one or two doses.

Japanese encephalitis. This mosquito-borne viral infection is transmitted in the summer and autumn in temperate regions of mostly rural China, Japan, Korea, and eastern areas of Russia. Risk to short-term travelers and those in urban areas is slight.

Malaria. Caused by a mosquito-borne parasite, malaria is present in Central and South America, Haiti and the Dominican Republic, Africa, South and Southeast Asia, the Middle East, and Oceania (the South Pacific islands). Anyone traveling to infected regions is at risk. To prevent insect bites, travelers are advised to use DEET repellent on exposed skin and clothing, and flying-insect spray in the room where they'll sleep.

No vaccine against malaria is available, but there are antimalarial drugs to help prevent the disease. Visit your doctor at least four to six weeks before departure for antimalarial drugs. Those often recommended are chloroquine (Aralen), hydroxychloroquine sulfate (Plaquenil), mefloquine (Lariam), the combination drug atovaquone-proguanil (Malarone), and the antibiotic doxycycline. Note that all of these medications can cause unpleasant side effects, especially mefloquine (Lariam), which appears to cause more neuropsychiatric problems than the others. The type prescribed will depend on your destination and any medical conditions you may have. The antimalarial drug sulphadoxine-pyrimethamine (Fansidar) can be taken along as a backup should symptoms develop. But seek medical advice as soon as possible.

If you develop a high, spiking fever; chills; sweating; headache; and muscle aches (which may appear as early as a week after arrival or months after returning home), seek immediate medical help, even if you have taken antimalarial drugs.

Plague. Transmitted by rodent fleas, plague is a bacterial infection found in the western third of the U.S., and in Africa, Asia, and South America, primarily in rural mountainous or upland areas. Risk to travelers is very small. Vaccination is not required by any country as a condition for entry and is rarely indicated for travelers, particularly if visiting urban areas with modern accommodations. (The efficacy of plague vaccine in humans has not been demonstrated in a controlled trial.) Travelers who risk possible exposure should consider short-term antibiotics during their stay.

Polio. An acute viral infection, polio is acquired by water and food contaminated by the feces of human polio-virus carriers. Although it continues to occur in developing countries of Africa, Asia, the Middle East, and Eastern Europe, there is no infection risk in the Western Hemisphere. Adults traveling to polio-endemic areas and who have previously completed immunization may be given another dose of inactivated polio vaccine (IPV) or live oral poliovirus vaccine (OPV). However, the need for further supplementary doses has not been established. Pregnant women or immuno-compromised people should not receive the "live" vaccine.

Spinal meningitis. A bacterial infection transmitted by contaminated food and drink and by human carriers, meningitis is found in sub-Saharan Africa, particularly in the savannah area from Mali to Ethiopia. Other advisories are issued by the CDC. Check "Outbreaks" on the web site *(www.cdc.gov/travel)*.

Vaccination is not a requirement for entry into any country. But it is indicated for high-risk areas, especially if you go during the dry season (December to June) and/or you will be in close contact with the local populace.

Typhoid fever. Caused by bacteria and spread by contaminated food and water, typhoid is found in the Indian subcontinent, and in other developing countries in Asia, Africa, and Latin American. Risk is greatest for travelers to these areas who will have prolonged exposure to potentially-contaminated food and drink, particularly those visiting smaller cities, villages, and rural areas off usual tourist itineraries.

Both oral and injectable vaccines are available. All have been shown to offer 50 to 80 percent protection, meaning you must still carefully monitor food and drink.

Yellow fever. Transmitted by mosquitoes, this viral disease is found in certain jungle locations of South America and Africa. Yellow fever is a very rare cause of illness in travelers, but most countries have regulations and requirements for vaccination that must be met before entering. However, most will also accept a medical waiver for a legitimate contraindication to vaccination. The CDC recommends obtaining written waivers from consular or embassy officials before departure.

Both the yellow fever vaccine (good for 10 years) and the required Certificate of Vaccination must be obtained at an officially designated Yellow Fever Vaccination Center. Your own physician may also be licensed to administer the vaccine. Or contact your county or state health department for the location of the nearest vaccination center. (The CDC does not keep a list of registered vaccination sites.)

HEALTH DEFENSE

Be prepared for emergencies or illness.

Carry a medical history. This written record can provide emergency information. You can create a form with your doctor—or photocopy the sample at the end of this section. Staple on copies of current prescriptions and, if pertinent, your most recent EKG.

Have additional backup. For those with a life-threatening medical condition, the nonprofit Medic Alert Foundation International provides a necklace or bracelet engraved with your medical condition and a 24-hour toll-free telephone number for access to your medical history, and names of physician and close relatives (membership fee, $35; annual renewals, $20). Call 800-763-3428 for information.

Check insurance coverage. Your own health insurance may cover some medical care and emergency services during travel. Coverage is also available if you become ill or injured anywhere in the world. See Chapter 4 for specifics.

Pack a medical kit. Pharmaceutical safety standards abroad may

HEALTH

not meet those of the U.S. So take along your own medications, packing enough to outlast your trip. Refuse any unfamiliar remedies urged upon you by friends or pharmacies. Keep all drugs shielded from heat, light, moisture—and children. Have your doctor define prescription drugs by generic name (brand names vary). The drug's name and strength should be clearly readable on the pharmacy's original label. If any drug contains a narcotic (such as codeine), pack a copy of the prescription to satisfy customs. Keep over-the-counter drugs in their original containers. The following are suggestions.

Medications

- Prescription drugs
- Pain medication (aspirin or acetaminophen)
- Altitude-sickness medication
- Motion-sickness medication
- Antacid
- Multipurpose antibiotic
- Cold remedies
- Diarrhea remedy
- Hydrocortisone cream
- Laxative
- Nausea remedy
- Sedative
- Fungicidal preparation

Supplies

- Ace bandage
- Adhesive bandages and tape
- Rubbing alcohol
- Clinical thermometer
- Corn pads
- Scissors
- Tweezers and needle
- Facial tissues
- Moist towelettes
- Flashlight
- Condoms/contraceptives
- Menstrual pads/tampons
- Water heater/electric immersion
- Water purification solutions or tablets
- Paper coffee filters (for filtering of water)
- Insect repellent
- Snakebite kit
- Sunscreen

'ECONOMY-CLASS SYNDROME'

Long-haul airline and automobile travel may carry an increased risk of deep vein thrombosis (DVT)—blood clots in leg veins that can kill by traveling to the lungs. Travelers at increased risk include those with coronary artery disease, cancer, or certain blood diseases, and women who are pregnant or taking birth-control pills or hormone-replacement therapy. But everyone should follow precautions.

• On long drives, try to take a 15-minute break every two hours to get fresh air and help circulation.

• When booking a flight, request an aisle, emergency-row, or bulkhead seat with additional legroom so you can stretch and get up more easily. (Chapter 11 has seat-choice tips.)

• Exercise legs while seated in a plane or car, stretching lower legs in particular and flexing your feet. Massage or squeeze muscles to help promote blood flow.

• In flight, periodically walk around the cabin. Drink plenty of water or fruit juice; minimize caffeine and alcohol.

• Travelers with increased risk factors should consult a doctor on other preventions, such as taking aspirin or other blood thinners before flying, or wearing compression stockings.

• Swelling or pain in the legs immediately or even days after travel may indicate DVT (but some people report no symptoms). A sudden onset of coughing or chest pain could indicate that a piece of the clot has broken off and moved to the lungs, requiring immediate medical attention.

WATER SAFETY

Beyond being the agent in spreading many diseases, untreated water may also carry diarrhea-causing parasites.

Drinking water. Although often safe in large cities, drinking water may be contaminated in rural regions by bacteria, viruses, or parasites. If chlorinated tap water is not available, or if local conditions are questionable, stick to bottled water or other beverages or purify the water yourself. Be especially wary of cloudy water.

• Generally, only the following are safe to consume: boiled water, hot beverages made with boiled water, and canned or bottled carbonated beverages, beer, and wine. Avoid ice cubes, which may be made from unsafe water.

• Since glasses and cups may be contaminated, drink either from fresh disposable paper containers, or directly from the can or bottle —after carefully wiping it clean. In areas where water is contaminated, do not use tap water to brush your teeth.

Water purification. Boiling is the most reliable method. Bring water to a rolling boil for one minute—three minutes if above 6,500 feet; allow to cool. Of the chemical treatments, iodine is more efficient than chlorine, providing greater disinfection and efficacy in many more circumstances. Use tincture of iodine or tetraglycine hydroperiodide tablets (Globaline and Potable-Aqua, available at pharmacies and sporting-goods stores). If water is cloudy, strain through a clean cloth and double the number of disinfectant tablets. Allow cold water to warm or give tablets increased time to work.

• Don't necessarily trust very hot tap water; many disease-causing organisms can survive a hotel's hot water heater. The CDC makes no recommendation on portable water filters, due to lack of independently verified results.

Swimming. Whether you dive in or fall in (say, on a rafting trip), you risk swallowing contaminated water. Parasites and infectious agents can also enter the body through open cuts, however small, and even through healthy skin.

• Fresh water (especially warm, dirty water in the tropics) is the riskiest; avoid any fresh-water dips. Adequately chlorinated pools are usually safe, as is salt water. However, some beaches may be contaminated with sewage; inquire locally.

Schistosomiasis. Travelers to endemic areas of the Caribbean, South America, Africa, and Asia risk exposure. Acute infection may produce fever, abdominal pain, nausea, diarrhea—or be asymptomatic. Chronic infections can cause disease of the lung, liver, intestines, and bladder.

• Infected snails in freshwater streams, ponds, or lakes release large numbers of minute, free-swimming larvae (cercariae). Larvae can penetrate unbroken skin during even brief exposure.

• If bath water is untreated, heat it to 120°F (50°C) for five minutes, treat with iodine or chlorine as you would drinking water, or filter through coffee filters. Or allow it to stand for 72 hours, as cercariae rarely survive past 48 hours.

• In case of accidental exposure—falling from a boat or being splashed—remove clothes and vigorously towel-dry skin. Those who may have been exposed while traveling should undergo screening tests upon returning home.

FOOD CAUTION

Food in large European cities may present no problems, but in other areas, pay careful attention to your choices. The general guideline is "boil it, cook it, peel it, or forget it." And wherever you are, always wash your hands before eating.

- Any raw food may be contaminated, particularly in areas of poor sanitation. Of particular concern are salads, uncooked vegetables and unpeeled fruit, unpasteurized milk and milk products, raw meat and shell fish. Fruit you peel yourself is generally safe.

- Cooked foods that are improperly handled—touched by unclean hands or contaminated utensils, or spoiled by inadequate cooking, poor storage, or careless serving methods—may also cause problems. However, food that has been cooked and is still piping hot is generally safe.

- Some fish may be unsafe even after cooking due to toxins in the flesh: Tropical reef fish, red snapper, amber jack, grouper, and sea bass can be toxic at unpredictable times if caught on tropical reefs instead of in the open ocean. Avoid barracuda and puffer fish, often toxic. Islands of the West Indies, and the tropical and Pacific Oceans are highest-risk areas.

- Where sanitation, food handling, or refrigeration are a problem, avoid raw egg mixtures, cream and milk (even if pasteurized), and milk-containing foods such as cream sauces and many pastries, ice cream, frozen desserts, whipped cream, and any other dairy products. In risky regions, canned, evaporated, condensed, or powdered milk is safe only if used straight or reconstituted with boiled water.

- Cheese must either be made from pasteurized milk or aged for at 60 days. (Most European cheeses are cured at least that long.) Any cream-cheese-like cheese has not been cured; avoid unless you're sure it's made with pasteurized milk. Infants younger than six months should be breast-fed or given powdered commercial formula prepared with boiled water.

HEALTH

TRAVELER'S DIARRHEA

Diarrhea is the most common illness of travelers. Areas of high risk include developing countries of Africa, Asia, the Middle East, and Central America. Travelers diarrhea is caused by fecal-contaminated food and water. Carefully choose what you eat and drink.

• Typical symptoms are diarrhea, nausea, bloating, urgency, and malaise, usually lasting about three to seven days. Travelers diarrhea is rarely life-threatening to adults, but infants and young children risk potentially-dangerous dehydration. Consult a physician rather than depending on self-treatment, especially if diarrhea is severe, bloody, long-lasting, or accompanied by fever and chills, and the traveler is unable to maintain fluid intake.

• For severe dehydration, especially in infants and young children, the use of an oral rehydration solution is advised. Ask your doctor to recommend an antidiarrheal medicine. (The CDC does not recommend preventive antibiotics because they can cause additional problems.)

INSECT PROTECTION

Insects carry dangerous diseases, particularly in the tropics. Avoid insect territory from dusk until dawn. When going out, cover skin, including feet. Wear long-sleeve tops; tuck long pants into socks and/or boots. Avoid dark colors, which attract some insects. Don't use scented toiletries.

• Apply insect repellent to clothing and exposed skin (not on cuts or open wounds). The most effective contain DEET in a 30 to 35 percent strength for adults. CONSUMER REPORTS medical consultants advise against using DEET-based repellents on children under age two. Use them sparingly on children under six. On any child, use no more than a 10-percent concentration..

• Consider spraying your clothes with parmethrin (Repel Permanone).

• Sleep in an air-conditioned or well-screened bedroom, or under mosquito netting. Shower daily, and check for lice and ticks. Store food in insect-proof containers. Dispose of garbage immediately and properly.

HEAT AND SUN HAZARDS

Heat dangers. Overexertion in oppressive heat can lead to heat exhaustion or heat stroke.

• The warning signs of heat exhaustion are headache, weakness, dizziness, blurred vision, cramps, and, sometimes, nausea and vomiting. Get out of the sun, lie down with feet elevated, and sip cool water. If symptoms persist, seek professional medical help.

• Heatstroke, in addition to the above symptoms, is also marked by hot, dry, flushed skin; disorientation; racing pulse; mental confusion; rapid breathing; and high fever. The victim should lie down, indoors or in the shade. Bring body temperature down with cold, wet towels. Seek immediate medical care.

• Peak heat hours are generally 10 a.m. to 3 p.m. Avoid the hot sun, and schedule exercise for earlier in the morning or late afternoon and evening.

• Drink plenty of fluids, except those containing caffeine or alcohol, which promote dehydration. Shower at least once a day in water that's lukewarm—not very hot or cold.

• Wear a broad-brimmed hat and lightweight, light-colored, loose clothing made of cotton or linen rather than synthetics.

• Choose cotton socks and lightweight shoes or open sandals (unless in an insect-infested area).

Sun hazards. Sun is most dangerous in tropical zones and at high altitudes. Ultraviolet (UV) rays can also cause skin reactions in those taking certain drugs, including some antibiotics, diuretics, and antihypertension medication.

• Wear sunscreen. Each has a "sun protection factor" (SPF); choose an SPF of between 15 and 30, in a water-resistant formula. Apply to all exposed areas about an hour before you go out. Reapply after swimming, sweating profusely, and/or toweling or wiping your skin. Wear a broad-brimmed hat and UV-protective sunglasses at midday. No sunscreen protects completely; avoid overexposure.

• Sunlight reflected off snow can burn even more quickly than summer sun; pack sunscreen for winter vacations. Protect against snow blindness with UV-protective sunglasses or goggles.

HEALTH

• Treat mild sunburn with cool compresses or a cool bath. A hydrocortisone cream may help decrease inflammation; moisturizing lotion rehydrates skin. Within the first 24 hours, aspirin or ibuprofen can help calm the inflammations (take no more than one or two every four to six hours). If you experience fever, chills, or blistering, seek professional care.

COLD DANGERS

The risks are frostbite and hypothermia (abnormally low body temperature); older people are most vulnerable.

• Dress to preserve body heat: loose-fitting layers that trap insulating pockets of air; thin liners under fur-lined or down- or synthetic-filled mittens; wool socks over cotton socks with extra room in boots or shoes.

• Frostbite occurs at subfreezing temperatures; the colder the weather, the quicker and more severe. Frostbitten skin is painful, then numb, turns white or bluish, and becomes stiff. Gently wrap affected areas in a blanket, clothing, or newspaper; do not rub or thaw with intense heat. Get indoors—preferably to a hospital.

• If no medical facility is available, start treatment indoors. Immerse frostbitten areas in tepid (not warm, never hot) water for up to an hour. Feeling, function, and color should slowly return. If blisters appear, do not touch them. Acetaminophen, aspirin, or ibuprofen may be taken for pain. After initial thawing, cover affected skin with sterile gauze. Victim should then go to a hospital.

• Life-threatening hypothermia is caused by cold (particularly combined with wetness), but may occur above freezing. At the first signs—mental confusion, slurred speech, violent shivering, difficulty walking—the victim should seek shelter. The advanced symptoms of progressive disorientation or even unconsciousness require immediate medical help.

ALTITUDE RISKS

Until becoming used to high altitudes, you may experience mountain sickness—headache, nausea, shortness of breath, insomnia, fatigue, poor appetite, and mental confusion, especially if you ascend too rapidly.

- Acetazolamide (Diamox) may be prescribed to prevent the condition, unless you have an allergy to sulfa drugs.

- Anyone with heart or lung problems should consult a doctor before traveling to altitudes over 5,000 feet (1,515 meters), where oxygen levels become dangerously low.

MEDICAL CARE ABROAD

Well-trained physicians and modern hospitals can be found in most large cities worldwide. But in developing regions, substandard practices can have long-term health implications.

- The nonprofit International Association for Medical Assistance for Travelers (716-754-4883; *www.sentex.net/~iamat*) provides members with a worldwide directory of English-speaking physicians adhering to a set fee schedule, along with material on immunizations, climatic and sanitary conditions, and more.

- Most hotels keep a list of local English-speaking physicians. Other sources: an American military base or, in remote areas, Peace Corps volunteers.

- In developing countries, sterilization and blood-screening policies (for HIV and other diseases like hepatitis B) may be lax, so consider packing sterile medical items such as needles. Should you require a blood transfusion, ask if your spouse or traveling partner can donate, if feasible. If there's a language barrier, request an English interpreter.

WHEN YOU'RE BACK HOME

Delayed-onset symptoms, such as fever or intestinal problems, can be caused by malaria, schistosomiasis, typhoid fever, hepatitis, sexually transmitted diseases, and certain parasitic infections. Any symptoms occurring six months or even a year after your return could indicate a travel-related disease. Consult your doctor for a thorough evaluation.

HEALTH

Consumer Reports Ratings

For 65 years, CONSUMER REPORTS has bought products and tested them so consumers can make informed buying decisions. From methodical, scientific evaluations, it develops its Ratings, including the luggage Ratings that start on the following page.

To determine what to test, our engineers, market analysts, and editors attend trade shows, read trade publications, and look at what's in stores to spot the latest products and trends. Our market analysts query manufacturers about product lines and update in-house databases listing thousands of models. Eventually, staff shoppers visit dozens of stores or go online to buy the selected models. Next, a test plan is prepared to evaluate performance and other aspects of the product.

In the luggage Ratings, the Overall Score gives the big picture in performance. Notes on features and performance for individual models are listed under "Recommendations and Notes." Use the handy key numbers to locate the details on applicable models to connect them to the descriptive paragraphs. We verify availability for most products. Some tested models may no longer be available.

Another source for CONSUMER REPORTS Ratings is our Annual Questionnaire, where we ask millions of our readers for their experiences with a variety of products or services. The hotel Ratings in this book are based on responses to our 2000 Annual Questionnaire from about 41,000 readers. They reflect subscribers' experiences at lodging chains in the U.S. between 1999 and 2000.

Luggage

There are many very good choices in each of the various luggage categories including
many CR Best Buys. Base your selection on the size and shape of the bag and
the features you require. Mesh or plastic-lined pockets, expansion gussets,
and multiple handles are some of the many available options. Frequent travelers might consider one of the more durable bags regardless of price.
They're more likely to hold up well over time. Except for high-end bags like
Andiamo, Hartmann, and Tumi, you should never have to pay full retail price.
Discounts are widely available on the web. Department stores and mass merchan-
disers have frequent sales.

Overall Ratings

Excellent ⊖ Very good ⊖ Good ○ Fair ◐ Poor ●

KEY NO.	BRAND & MODEL	PRICE	OVERALL SCORE	DURA-BILITY	FEATURES	EASE OF USE
			0 · · · · 100 P F G VG E			
WHEELED CARRY-ONS						
1	**Atlantic** Professional 2520 33992-94F **A CR Best Buy**	$170		⊖	⊖	⊖
2	**Delsey** Horizon 61274 NO **A CR Best Buy**	170		⊖	⊖	⊖
3	**Victorinox** Travel Gear Medium Mobilizer 34011	335		⊖	⊖	⊖
4	**Tumi** Fold-a-Way 2222	450		⊖	○	⊖
5	**Protocol** (J.C. Penney) Business Gear II 047-5353 **A CR Best Buy**	125		⊖	⊖	⊖
6	**Hartmann** Intensity Mobile Traveller 5021 312	335		⊖	⊖	⊖
7	**Pathfinder** (Paragon) Avenger 6822	130		⊖	⊖	⊖
8	**U.S. Luggage** Logistix Rolling 1L21RS4	150		⊖	⊖	⊖
9	**Travelpro** Crew4 7122-01	200		○	⊖	⊖
10	**Andiamo** Tuxedo Journeyman TJ22SX	470		⊖	⊖	⊖
11	**h Studio** Primary Collection 600 3130	250		○	⊖	⊖
12	**Ricardo Beverly Hills** Big Sur Ballistic 8322	150		○	⊖	⊖
13	**Jaguar** (J.C. Penney) Centennial II Expandable 047-3803	50		○	○	⊖
14	**Samsonite** 700 Series Silhouette 7 281111101	180		◐	⊖	⊖
15	**LL Bean** Ballistics Collection OKW86	300		●	⊖	⊖

Overall Ratings, cont.

Ratings legend: Excellent ⊖ · Very good ⊖ · Good ○ · Fair ◐ · Poor ●

KEY NO.	BRAND & MODEL	PRICE	OVERALL SCORE (0–100)	DURABILITY	FEATURES	EASE OF USE
LARGE WHEELED UPRIGHTS						
16	**Travelpro** Platinum II 9926-01	$350		⊖	⊖	⊖
17	**Travelpro** Crew4 7126-01 **A CR Best Buy**	240		⊖	⊖	⊖
18	**Pathfinder** (Paragon) TX2 9826	340		⊖	⊖	⊖
19	**Delsey** Horizon 61277 NO	200		○	⊖	⊖
20	**Lands' End** Check-Thru 6134-3AJ9	250		⊖	⊖	⊖
21	**Pathfinder** (Paragon) Revolution 2527	210		○	⊖	⊖
22	**Skyway** Celebrity 4387ZC	140		○	⊖	⊖
23	**Samsonite** 700 Series Silhouette 7 Hybrid 281111202	250		○	⊖	⊖
24	**Atlantic** Infinity IV 4-Runner 37992-36F	190		●	⊖	⊖
25	**Briggs & Riley** Baseline Collection U-26X	420		●	⊖	⊖
26	**Samsonite** 700 Series Silhouette 7 281111102	200		●	⊖	⊖
27	**Victorinox** E-Motion 360 Mono Traveler 39452	300		◐	⊖	⊖
28	**Ricardo Beverly Hills** Big Sur Ballistic 8326	170		●	⊖	⊖
29	**Lark** Classic 937111102	280		●	⊖	⊖
30	**Protocol** (J.C. Penney) 047 636-3337 0299	100		●	⊖	○
31	**Rimowa** Salsa 811.70	285		●	○	⊖
WHEELED BACKPACKS						
32	**Eagle Creek** Switchback Expandable 20065	200		⊖	○	⊖
33	**JanSport** Adventure Travel Collection: Mesa 41814 **A CR Best Buy**	100		⊖	◐	⊖
34	**High Sierra** Adventure Travel Gear AT141 **A CR Best Buy**	85		⊖	◐	⊖
35	**Kipling** Alcatraz 2027D	180		⊖	◐	⊖
36	**Pierre Cardin** Sport Tech II 047 6121 15	100		●	◐	⊖

Overall Ratings, cont.

Excellent ⊖ Very good ⊖ Good ○ Fair ⊕ Poor ●

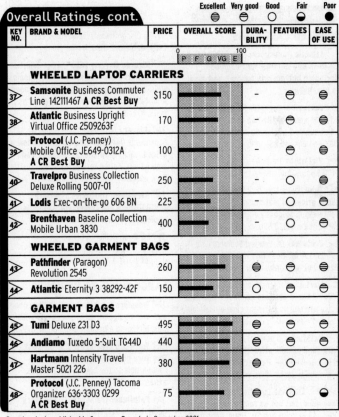

KEY NO.	BRAND & MODEL	PRICE	OVERALL SCORE	DURA-BILITY	FEATURES	EASE OF USE
			0 100 P F G VG E			
WHEELED LAPTOP CARRIERS						
37	**Samsonite** Business Commuter Line 142111467 **A CR Best Buy**	$150	▬▬▬	–	⊖	⊖
38	**Atlantic** Business Upright Virtual Office 2509263F	170	▬▬▬	–	⊖	⊖
39	**Protocol** (J.C. Penney) Mobile Office JE649-0312A **A CR Best Buy**	100	▬▬▬	–	⊖	⊖
40	**Travelpro** Business Collection Deluxe Rolling 5007-01	250	▬▬	–	○	⊖
41	**Lodis** Exec-on-the-go 606 BN	225	▬▬	–	○	⊖
42	**Brenthaven** Baseline Collection Mobile Urban 3830	400	▬▬	–	○	⊖
WHEELED GARMENT BAGS						
43	**Pathfinder** (Paragon) Revolution 2545	260	▬▬▬▬	⊖	⊖	⊖
44	**Atlantic** Eternity 3 38292-42F	150	▬▬▬	○	⊖	⊖
GARMENT BAGS						
45	**Tumi** Deluxe 231 D3	495	▬▬▬	⊖	⊖	⊖
46	**Andiamo** Tuxedo 5-Suit TG44D	440	▬▬▬	⊖	⊖	⊖
47	**Hartmann** Intensity Travel Master 5021 226	380	▬▬▬	⊖	○	○
48	**Protocol** (J.C. Penney) Tacoma Organizer 636-3303 0299 **A CR Best Buy**	75	▬▬▬	⊖	○	◗

Based on tests published in Consumer Reports in December 2001.

TESTS BEHIND THE RATINGS

Overall score is based primarily on durability, features, and ease of use. For **durability,** we packed each piece of luggage with the appropriate weight for its size and tumbled it in our luggage drum up to 1,000 times, checking periodically for damage. The best bags suffered only minor cosmetic damage. The worst had problems, such as irreparably broken zippers or pull handles. (Most bags have a limited lifetime warranty; exceptions are noted in the Recommendations & Notes.) The **features** score covers a bag's complement of expansion gussets, inside and outside pockets, carrying handles, and more. **Ease of use** takes into account ease of pulling and maneuverability. Price is the approximate retail.

RATINGS

Recommendations & notes

WHEELED CARRY-ONS

1▷ Atlantic Professional 2520 33992-94F **A CR Best Buy Durable, well-equipped (including bottom grip handle), and easy to use.** 11½ lb.

2▷ Delsey Horizon 61274 NO **A CR Best Buy The equal of the bag above.** Durable, well-equipped (including bottom grip handle), and easy to use. 11 lb.

3▷ Victorinox Travel Gear Medium Mobilizer 34011 **Roomy, but heavy.** Durable. 13 lb.

4▷ Tumi Fold-a-Way 2222 **Status brand name, priced to match.** Small but very light weight. Modestly equipped, with no garment carrier. 8½ lb.

5▷ Protocol (J.C. Penney) Business Gear II 047-5353 **A CR Best Buy Heavy for its size.** 10-yr. warranty. 12 lb.

6▷ Hartmann Intensity Mobile Traveller 5021 312 **There are less expensive choices.** Noisy wheels. No garment carrier. Main zipper was damaged in durability tests. 9¼ lb.

7▷ Pathfinder (Paragon) Avenger 6822 **Very good overall, attractively priced.** Long (43 in.) pull handle. Main zipper was damaged in durability tests. 10-yr. warranty. 11¼ lb.

8▷ U.S. Luggage Logistix Rolling 1L21RS4 **Very good, but not as roomy as some.** Long (43 in.) pull handle. Zipper tabs broke off and pull handle became stiff in durability tests. Polyester shell. 12 lb.

9▷ Travelpro Crew4 7122-01 **An OK choice.** Well-equipped, including a bottom grip handle. Pull handle became stiff in durability tests. 12¼ lb.

10▷ Andiamo Tuxedo Journeyman TJ22SX **Light, roomy, and expensive.** Bag hit panelists' heels while being pulled. Pull handle became stiff in durability test. 10½ lb.

11▷ h Studio Primary Collection 600 3130 **May not meet some airlines' carry-on criteria.** Pull handle broke in durability tests.

11¾ lb. Discontinued; replaced by 22" Expandable 602 3130.

12▷ Ricardo Beverly Hills Big Sur Ballistic 8322 **Not as sturdy as some.** Noisy wheels. Main zipper and pull handle were damaged in durability tests. Garment carrier holds 2 suits. 10¾ lb.

13▷ Jaguar (J.C. Penney) Centennial II Expandable 047-3803 **Bare-bones, but low-priced.** Lacks garment carrier, lining, and side handle. Fabric tore in durability tests. 5-yr. warranty. Ramie/polyester shell. 7¼ lb.

14▷ Samsonite 700 Series Silhouette 7 281111101 **There are better, more durable choices.** 10-yr. warranty. 10½ lb.

15▷ LL Bean Ballistics Collection OKW86 **Fragile.** Unconditional warranty. Short (37 in.) pull handle. 10¼ lb.

LARGE WHEELED UPRIGHTS

16▷ Travelpro Platinum II 9926-01 **Very good and well-equipped.** All the bells and whistles, including a bottom grip handle. 17¼ lb.

17▷ Travelpro Crew4 7126-01 **A CR Best Buy Very good and well-equipped.** Comparable to the bag above, but less expensive. 17¼ lb.

18▷ Pathfinder (Paragon) TX2 9826 **Very good, but heavy.** Main zipper was damaged in durability tests. Long (43 in.) pull handle. 18¾ lb.

19▷ Delsey Horizon 61277 NO **Very good and well-equipped.** Has bottom grip handle. Components broke off in durability tests. Long (43 in.) pull handle. 14 lb.

20▷ Lands' End Check-Thru 6134-3AJ9 **A very good basic bag.** Has no garment carrier. Main zipper was damaged in durability tests. Unconditional warranty. 15¼ lb.

21▷ Pathfinder (Paragon) Revolution 2527 **Very good.** Piping damaged in durability tests. Long (44 in.) pull handle. 16 lb.

22▷ Skyway Celebrity 4387ZC **Very good.** Minor components broke off in durability tests. 15-yr. warranty. 13½ lb.

23▷ Samsonite 700 Series Silhouette 7 Hybrid 281111202 **Very good.** Has bottom grip handle. Pull handle, piping, and minor parts damaged in durability tests. 10-yr. warranty. Short (39 in.) pull handle. Nylon/plastic shell. 13½ lb.

24▷ Atlantic Infinity IV 4-Runner 37992-36F **Good overall.** Unique (but hard to engage) feature pops out 2 extra wheels to help carry the load. Fragile. Pull-handle opening can let in rain. 16¼ lb.

25▷ Briggs & Riley Baseline Collection U-26X **Good, but fragile.** Garment carrier holds 1 suit. Long (43 in.) pull handle. 17 lb.

26▷ Samsonite 700 Series Silhouette 7 281111102 **Good, but fragile.** Not a good choice for frequent travelers. 13½ lb.

27▷ Victorinox E-Motion 360 Mono Traveler 39452 **Good.** Better for casual travel because it has no garment carrier. 5¾ lb.

28▷ Ricardo Beverly Hills Big Sur Ballistic 8326 **Good overall, but fragile.** Not a good choice for frequent travelers. 13¼ lb.

29▷ Lark Classic 937111102 **Fragile.** There are better choices. Garment carrier holds 1 suit. 10¼ lb.

30▷ Protocol (J.C. Penney) 047 636-3337 0299 **Fragile.** There are better choices. 10-yr. warranty. Shell material not stated. 12 lb.

31▷ Rimowa Salsa 811.70 **Fragile.** There are better choices. Has no garment carrier. 5-yr. warranty. Short (39 in.) pull handle. Plastic shell makes it look like hard-sided luggage. 7 lb.

WHEELED BACKPACKS

32▷ Eagle Creek Switchback Expandable 20065 **Very good, with good details, such as contoured shoulder straps, organizers.** Zippers have rain flaps, but pull-handle opening can let in rain. 7 lb.

33▷ JanSport Adventure Travel Collection: Mesa 41814 **A CR Best Buy All the features of the backpack above.** Pull handle is leak-resistant. 5½ lb.

34▷ High Sierra Adventure Travel Gear AT141 **A CR Best Buy Very good overall, but better as a bookbag.** Pull-handle opening can let in rain. Long (42 in.) pull handle. Polyester shell. 5½ lb.

35▷ Kipling Alcatraz 2027D **Very good.** Zippers and pull-handle opening can let in rain. 2-yr. warranty. 6¼ lb.

36▷ Pierre Cardin Sport Tech II 047 6121 15 **Stylish, but large, heavy, and fragile.** Bag hit panelists' heels while being pulled. 5-yr. warranty. Short (38 in.) and leak-resistant pull handle. Polyester shell. 7½ lb.

WHEELED LAPTOP CARRIERS

37▷ Samsonite Business Commuter Line 142111467 **A CR Best Buy Very good, but heavy.** Has room to pack personal gear for an overnight business trip. But accessing computer can be awkward. 3-yr. warranty. Long (41 in.) pull handle. 10¼ lb.

38▷ Atlantic Business Upright Virtual Office 2509263F **A very good choice.** Room to pack personal gear for an overnight business trip. Easier to access computer in a cramped coach seat. 8½ lb.

39▷ Protocol (J.C. Penney) Mobile Office JE649-0312A A CR Best Buy **A very good choice.** Room to pack personal gear for an overnight business trip. Easier to access computer in a cramped coach seat. Tips easily. 10-yr. warranty. 9¾ lb.

40▷ Travelpro Business Collection Deluxe Rolling 5007-01 **Good, but heavy.** Organizer section can be collapsed to pack clothing. Elastic sling affords good protection for a laptop. Pull-handle opening can let in rain. Long (41 in.) pull handle. 10¾ lb.

41▷ Lodis Exec-on-the-go 606 BN **Small and light, but holds little more than a laptop.** Shoulder strap is a convenience. Tips easily.

Pull-handle opening can let in rain. Bag hit panelists' heels while being pulled. Short (36 in.) pull handle. 6¼ lb.

42> **Brenthaven** Baseline Collection Mobile Urban 3830 **Good, but priced for the CEO.** Affords much protection for a laptop, including shock-absorbing wheels. Pull-handle opening can let in rain. 8½ lb.

WHEELED GARMENT BAGS

43> **Pathfinder** (Paragon) Revolution 2545 **First-rate.** Rain can get in through pull-handle opening. 14 lb.

44> **Atlantic** Eternity 3 38292-42F **A decent bag at a decent price.** Piping and fabric damaged in durability tests. Rain can get in through pull-handle opening. Polyester shell. 13 lb.

GARMENT BAGS

45> **Tumi** Deluxe 231 D3 **Excellent but very expensive.** Nicely made, with a contoured, padded shoulder strap. 7 lb.

46> **Andiamo** Tuxedo 5-Suit TG44D **Excellent but expensive.** The heaviest garment bag tested. Contoured, padded shoulder strap. 10¼ lb.

47> **Hartmann** Intensity Travel Master 5021 226 **Very good but expensive.** 7½ lb.

48> **Protocol** (J.C. Penney) Tacoma Organizer 636-3303 0299 **A CR Best Buy As durable as the others, but shoulder-strap pad is small and not contoured.** 10-yr. warranty. Ramie/polyester shell. 6 lb.

Hotels

First decide on the amenities you want—and how much you're willing to pay for them.

On either end of the spectrum, you get what you pay for—ultra luxury or basic, bare-bones accomodations. Many people can find a happy medium—and even some good deals within the upscale and moderate categories, especially in the current state of the travel and tourism industry.

Reader score summarizes overall satisfaction. A score of 100 would mean all respondents were completely satisfied; on average, 80 means they were very satisfied; 60, fairly well satisfied; 40, somewhat dissatisfied. Differences of five or more points are meaningful. **Value** is based on the percentage of readers judging the hotel an excellent value. **Problems** reflects readers' gripes about the experience. **Service** reflects readers' opinions of hotel clerks' efficiency at check-in and check-out. **Upkeep** reflects readers' views of the condition and cleanliness of the room, grounds, and public spaces. Scores for value, problems, service, and upkeep are relative: Hotels with the highest (or lowest) scores are far better (or worse) than average. Even the chains that scored lowest for value, problems, service, and upkeep were seen as OK by most readers. Properties/rooms lists the number of each chain's U.S. properties and its total rooms. Except as noted, hotels are located nationwide.

Overall Ratings

Legend: Excellent ⊜ Very good ⊖ Good ○ Fair ◑ Poor ●

HOTEL	READER SCORE	VALUE	PROBLEMS	SERVICE	UPKEEP	PROPERTIES/ ROOMS
LUXURY						
Four Seasons	90	⊜	⊜	⊜	⊜	22/7,111
Ritz-Carlton	87	⊖	⊖	⊖	⊖	23/7,998
Renaissance	82	⊖	⊖	○	⊖	47/19,475
Hyatt	78	◑	○	⊖	⊖	120/59,429
Westin	78	○	○	○	⊖	69/32,853
UPSCALE						
Harrah's	85	⊖	⊖	○	⊖	14/11,581
Embassy Suites	83	⊖	⊖	⊖	⊖	155/37,715
Walt Disney's Resorts	80	○	○	○	⊖	28/27,000 [1]
Marriott	80	○	⊖	⊖	○	270/110,690
Hilton	77	○	○	○	○	210/80,000
Crowne Plaza	77	○	○	○	○	74/22,289
Wyndham	75	○	○	○	○	107/30,135
Omni	75	○	○	○	○	37/14,265

Overall Ratings, cont.

Legend: Excellent ⊜ — Very good ⊖ — Good ○ — Fair ◔ — Poor ●

HOTEL	READER SCORE	VALUE	PROBLEMS	SERVICE	UPKEEP	PROPERTIES/ ROOMS
Omni	75	○	○	○	○	37/14,265
DoubleTree	75	○	○	○	○	159/43,000
Sheraton	74	◔	◔	○	○	184/64,085
Radisson	72	◔	◔	○	○	251/56,381
Adam's Mark	68	●	●	○	◔	24/13,298
MODERATE						
Homewood Suites	82	⊜	⊖	○	⊖	94/10,474
Residence Inn by Marriott	82	⊜	○	○	○	316/39,841
Country Inn & Suites by Carlson	81	⊖	⊜	○	○	189/13,941 [2]
Drury Inn/Suites	81	⊖	⊖	○	○	89/11,182 [3]
Hampton Inn	81	⊖	⊖	○	○	1,297/186,037
AmericInn	81	○	⊖	○	○	161/6,440 [3]
Courtyard by Marriott	80	○	⊖	○	○	433/63,997
AmeriSuites	79	⊖	○	○	○	134/17,100
Fairfield Inn	78	⊖	○	○	○	412/41,346
Hawthorn Suites	78	⊖	○	○	○	139/13,293
Baymont	77	⊖	⊖	○	○	178/17,514
La Quinta	77	○	○	○	○	306/39,136
Best Inns/Suites	75	○	○	○	○	106/8,252 [4]
Clarion	73	○	◔	○	◔	114/18,537
Holiday Inn	72	●	◔	○	◔	1,071/200,432
Best Western	72	◔	◔	◔	◔	2,109/187,542
Four Points Hotel	71	○	●	○	◔	138/26,000
Quality Inn	71	○	◔	◔	●	436/48,921
Ramada	63	●	●	●	●	973/120,117
Howard Johnson	62	●	●	●	●	425/42,373

rce guide

list of phone numbers and website addresses for
l providers. Some companies may have only a
a web address, but not both.

	PHONE	WEB SITE (WWW.)

LINES & TOUR OPERATORS

	PHONE	WEB SITE (WWW.)
....	800-999-9046	atusa.com
....	800-282-1202	airhitch.com
....	800-262-3701	
....	800-782-2424	der.com
....	800-645-2555 / 516-935-8500	fantasyholidays.com
....	800-332-5332	france-vacations.com.
....	800-558-3050	funjet.com.
....	800-225-5498	gwvtravel.com
....	800-223-5570	homerictours.com.
....	800-627-8462	martinair.com.
....	800-677-0720	newfrontiers.com.
....	800-242-9244	pleasantholidays.com
....	800-732-3588	travel@rebeltours.com
....	800-221-0924	sceptretours.com
Agency ...	800-246-8687, 415-454-4932	skytours.com
....	800-786-8747, 408-432-1101	suntrips.com

Overall Ratin[g]

HOTEL
BUDGET
Sleep Inn
Microtel
Super 8 Motel
Red Roof Inn
Motel 6
Days Inn
Econo Lodge
Travelodge
Knights Inn

Based on a survey publi[shed]
① *Calif. and Fla.* ②

THE SURVEY BEHIND
The Ratings are base[d]
41,000 readers, and t[he]
between 1999 and 20[00]
population at large. [With]
many as 7,500 for H[otel]
amenities, readers' pe[rceptions]
Comfort Inn, was
Questionnaire.

Resou[rce]

The following is[
a variety of tra[vel]
phone number [

CHARTER A[

Adventure Tours USA....
Airhitch.....................
Amber Travel.............
DER Travel Services ......
Fantasy Holiday...........

France Vacations ....
Funjet Vacations..........
GWV International........
Homeric Tours ....
Martinair ....
New Frontiers/Corsair ...
Pleasant Holidays ....
Rebel Tours.................
Sceptre Tours ....
Redwoood Skytours Trave[l]
SunTrips ....

NAME	PHONE	WEB SITE (WWW.)

DOMESTIC AIRLINES

Air Canada .... 888-247-2262 .... *aircanada.ca/home.html*

Air North .... 800-764-0407, 800-661-0407 (Can.) .... *airnorth.yk.net*

AirTran .... 800-825-8538 .... *airtran.com*

Alaska Airlines .... 800-252-7522 .... *alaska-air.com*

Aloha Airlines .... 800-367-5250 .... *alohaair.com*

American Airlines .... 800-433-7300 .... *aa.com*

American Trans Air (ATA) .... 800-225-2995 .... *ata.com*

America West Airlines .... 800-235-9292 .... *americawest.com*

Continental Airlines .... 800-525-0280 .... *flycontinental.com*

Delta Airlines .... 800-221-1212 .... *delta.com*

Frontier Airlines .... 800-432-1359 .... *frontierairlines.com*

Hawaiian Airlines .... 800-367-5320, 800-882-8811 (HI) .... *hawaiianair.com*

Horizon Air .... 800-547-9308 .... *horizonair.com*

LTU International Airways .... 800-888-0200 .... *ltu.com*

Midwest Express Airlines .... 800-452-2022 .... *midwestexpress.com*

Northwest/KLM .... 800-225-2525 .... *nwa.com*

Southwest .... 800-435-9792 .... *iflyswa.com*

Spirit Airlines .... 800-772-7117 .... *spiritair.com*

Sun Country .... 800-752-1218 .... *suncountry.com*

United Airlines .... 800-241-6522 .... *ual.com*

US Airways .... 800-428-4322 .... *usairways.com*

Vanguard Airlines .... 800-826-4827 .... *flyvanguard.com*

FOREIGN AIRLINES

ACES Airlines .... 800-846-2237 .... *acescolombia.com*

Aer Lingus .... 800-223-6537 .... *aerlingus.ie*

Aerolineas Argentinas .... 800-333-0276 .... *aerolineas.com.ar*

AeroMexico .... 800-237-6639 .... *aeromexico.com*

NAME	PHONE	WEB SITE (WWW.)
Aeropostal	888-912-8466	aeropostal.com
Air Caledonie/Solomon	800-677-4277	pacificislands.com/airlines/airlines.htm
Air-Do		airdo.co.jp (requires Japanese fonts)
Air France	800-237-2747, 800-667-2747 (Can.)	airfrance.com
Air Jamaica	800-523-5585	airjamaica.com
Air Lib	800-892-9136	airliberte.fr
Air Littoral	800-237-2747	airlittoral.com
Air New Zealand & Ansett Australia	800-262-1234, 800-663-5494 (Can.)	airnz.com
Air Niugini	949-752-5440	airniugini.com.pg/
Air Pacific	800-227-4446	airpacific.com
Alitalia Airlines	800-223-5730	alitalia.it
ANA – All Nippon Airways	800-235-9262	fly-ana.com
Asiana Airlines	800-227-4262	flyasiana.com
Austrian Airlines	800-843-0002	aua.com
Avianca	800-284-2622	avianca.com.co
Aviateca	800-327-9832	grupotaca.com
Braathens	800-548-5960	braathens.no
British Airways	800-247-9297	british-airways.com
British Midland	800-788-0555	flybmi.com
buzz		buzzaway.com
Cathay Pacific Airways	800-233-2742	cathay-usa.com
China Airlines (Taiwan)	800-227-5118	china-airlines.com
Condor German Airlines	800-524-6975	condor.de
Copa	800-359-2672	copaair.com
CSA – Czech Airlines		csa.cz
Easy Jet		easyjet.com
El Al Israel Airlines	800-223-6700	elal.co.il
Emirates	800-777-3999	ekgroup.com
EVA Airways	800-695-1188	evaair.com.tw
Finnair	800-950-5000	finnair.fi
Freedom Air International		freedomair.com

NAME	PHONE	WEB SITE (WWW.)
Garuda Indonesia	800-342-7832	garuda-indonesia.com
Go		go-fly.com
Gulfstream International	800-992-8532	gulfstreamair.com
Gulf Air	800-553-2824	gulfairco.com
Iberia Airlines of Spain	800-772-4642	iberia.com
Icelandair	800-223-5500	icelandair.is
Japan Airlines (JAL)	800-525-3663	jal.co.jp
KLM	800-225-2525	nwa.com
Korean Air	800-438-5000	koreanair.com
Kuwait Airways		travelfirst.com/sub/kuwaitair.html
Lacsa Airlines	800-225-2272	lacsa.com
LanChile	800-735-5526	lanchile.com
LAPA		lapa.com.ar
Lloyd Aereo Boliviano		labairlines.com
LOT Polish Airlines	800-223-0593	lot.com
Lufthansa	800-645-3880, 800-563-5954 (Can.)	lufthansa.com
Malaysia Airlines	800-552-9264	malaysiaairlines.com
Mexicana Airlines	800-531-7921	mexicana.com.mx
Nica	800-831-6422	grupotaca.com
Olympic Airways	800-223-1226	olympic-airways.gr
Pakistan International Airlines		piac.com.pk
Philippine Airlines	800-435-9725	philippineair.com
Polynesian Airlines	800-264-0823	polynesianairlines.co.nz
Qantas Airways	800-227-4500	qantas.com.au
Ryanair		ryanair.com
Royal Jordanian Airline	800-223-0470	rja.com.jo
SAS	800-221-2350	sas.se
Saudi Arabian Airlines	800-472-8342	saudiairlines.com
SilkAir	800-742-3333	singaporeair.com
Singapore Airlines	800-742-3333	singaporeair.com
Skymark		skymark.co.jp

NAME	PHONE	WEB SITE (WWW.)
South African Airways	800-722-9675	flysaa.com
Swissair	800221-4750, 800-267-9477 (Can.)	swissair.com
Taca	800-535-8780	grupotaca.com
TAP Air Portugal	800-221-7370	tap-airportugal.de
Thai Airways	800-426-5204, 800-668-8103 (Can.)	thaiair.com
TransBrasil Airlines		transbrasil.com.br
Turkish Airlines	800-874-8875	turkishairlines.com
Varig Brazilian Airlines	800-468-2744	varig.com.br
Vasp		vasp.com.br
Virgin Atlantic Airways	800-862-8621	fly.virgin.com
Virgin Express	800-862-8621	virgin-atlantic.com

CRUISE LINES

American Canadian Caribbean Line	800-556-7450	accl-smallships.com
Carnival Cruise Lines	800-327-9501	carnival.com
Celebrity Cruises	800-437-3111	celebritycruises.com
Clipper Cruise Line	800-325-0010, 314-727-2929 (MO)	clippercruise.com
Costa Cruises	800-462-6782	costacruises.com
Crystal Cruises	800-446-6620	crystalcruises.com
Cunard Line	800-528-6273	cunardline.com
Delta Queen Steamboat Co.	800-458-6789	deltaqueen.com
Discovery Cruises	800-866-8687	www.discoverycruiseline.com
Fantasy Cruises & Tours	800-798-7722	fantasycruises.com
Holland America	800-426-0327	hollandamerica.com
Maris Freighter Cruises	800-996-2747	freightercruises.com
Norwegian Cruise Line	800-327-7030	ncl.com
Princess Cruises	800-421-0522	princesscruises.com
Radisson Seven Seas Cruises	800-477-7500	rssc.com
Royal Caribbean International	800-327-6700	rccl.com
Royal Olympic Cruises	800-221-2470	epirotiki.com
Seabourn Cruise Line	800-929-9595	seabourn.com

NAME	PHONE	WEB SITE (WWW.)
Windjammer Barefoot	800-327-2601	windjammer.com
Windstar Cruises	800-258-7245	windstarcruises.com
World Explorer Cruises	800-854-3835	wecruise.com

HOTELS AND MOTELS

1-800-USA-HOTELS (broker)	800-872-4683	1800usahotels.com
Accommodations Express (broker)	800-906-4685	accommodationsexpress.com
Adam's Mark	800-444-2326	adamsmark.com
Admiral Benbow Inns	800-451-1986	admiralbenbow.com
AmericInn	800-634-3444	americinn.com
AmeriSuites	800-833-1516	amerisuites.com
Aston Hotels	800-922-7866	aston-hotels.com
Baymont	800-428-3438	baymontinns.com
Best Inns & Suites	800-237-8466	bestinn.com
Best Western	800-528-1234	bestwestern.com
Bradford Homesuites	888-486-7829	bradfordsuites.com
BridgeStreet Accommodations	800-278-7338	bridgestreet.com
Budget Host Inns	800-283-4678	budgethost.com
Candlewood Suites	800-946-6200	candlewoodsuites.com
Choice Hotels	800-221-2222	choicehotels.com
Circus Circus	800-634-3450	circuscircus.com
Clarion	800-424-6423	clarioninns.com
ClubHouse Inn & Suites	800-258-2466	clubhouseinn.com
Club Med	800-258-2633	clubmed.com
Coast and WestCoast	800-663-1144	coasthotels.com
Colony	800-777-1700	
Comfort Inns & Suites	800-424-6423	comfortinns.com
Concorde Hotels	800-888-4747	concorde-hotels.com
Country Hearth Inns	888-443-2784	countryhearth.com
Country Inns & Suites	800-456-4000	countryinns.com
Courtyard by Marriott	800-321-2211	courtyard.com

NAME	PHONE	WEB SITE (WWW.)
Cross Country Inn	800-621-1429	crosscountryinns.com
Crossland Economy Studios	800-398-7829	crosslandstudios.com
Crowne Plaza Hotel	800-227-6963	crowneplaza.com
Days Inns	800-329-7466	daysinn.com
Delta Hotels & Resorts	800-877-1133	deltahotels.com
DoubleTree	800-222-8733	doubletree.com
Downtowner	800-251-1962	reservahost.com
Drury Inn	800-325-8300	druryinn.com
Econo Lodge	800-424-6423	econolodge.com
Embassy Suites	800-362-2779	embassysuites.com
Exel Inns of America	800-356-8013	exelinns.com
Extended Stay America	800-398-7829	extstay.com
Fairfield Inn by Marriott	800-228-2800	fairfieldinn.com
Fairmont Hotels	800-441-1414	fairmont.com
Family Inns	800-362-1188	familyinnsofamerica.com
Fiesta Americana	800-343-7821	fiestaamericana.com
Forever Resorts	800-255-5561	foreverresorts.com
Four Points	800-325-3535	fourpoints.com
Four Seasons	800-332-3442	fshr.com
Golden Tulip	800-344-1212	goldentulip.com
Grand Heritage Hotels	800-437-4824	grandheritage.com
Hampton Inns & Suites	800-426-7866	hamptoninn.com
Harrah's	800-427-7247	harrahs.com
Hawaiian Hotels & Resorts	800-222-5642	hawaiihotels.com
Hawthorn Suites	800-527-1133	hawthorn.com
Heartland Inn	800-334-3277	heartlandinns.com
Helmsley	800-283-3824	helmsleyhotels.com
Hilton	800-445-8667	hilton.com
Holiday Inn	800-465-4329	holiday-inn.com
Homewood Suites	800-225-5466	homewood-suites.com
Hotel Discounts (broker)	800-715-7666	hoteldiscounts.com

NAME	PHONE	WEB SITE (WWW.)
Howard Johnson/HoJo Inn	800-446-4656	hojo.com
Hyatt Hotels and Resorts	800-233-1234	hyatt.com
Innkeeper	800-466-5337	lexres.com
Inns of America	800-826-0778	innsamerica.com
InnSuites	800-842-4242	innsuites.com
Inter-Continental Hotels & Resorts	800-327-0200	interconti.com
Jameson Inns	800-526-3766	jamesoninns.com
Keddy's	800-561-7666	keddys.ca
Kimpton	800-546-7866	
Knights Inns/Arborgate Inn	800-843-5644	knightsinn.com
La Quinta	800-531-5900	laquinta.com
Leading Hotels of the World	800-223-6800	lhw.com
Le Meridien Hotels & Resorts	800-543-4300	flemeridien-hotels.com
Lexington Suites	800-537-8483	lexhotels.com
Loews Hotels	800-235-6397	loewshotels.com
MainStay Suites	800-660-6246	mainstaysuites.com
Manhattan East Suite Hotels	800-637-8483	mesuite.com
Marc Resorts	800-535-0085	marcresorts.com
Marriott	800-228-9290	marriott.com
Masters Economy Inns	800-633-3434	mastersinns.com
Master Hosts Inn	800-251-1962	reservahost.com
Microtel Inn & Suites	888-771-7171	microtelinn.com
Milner Hotel	800-521-0592	milner-hotels.com
Moat House Hotels	800-641-0300	moathouse.com
Motel 6	800-466-8356	motel6.com
National 9 Inns	800-524-9999	
Nendels Inns	800-547-0106	
Nikko Hotels International	800-645-5687	nikkohotels.com
Oakwood Corporate Housing	800-888-0808	oakwood.com
Omni Hotels	800-843-6664	omnihotels.com
Outrigger Hotels & Resorts	800-688-7444	

NAME	PHONE	WEB SITE (WWW.)
Pan Pacific Hotels & Resorts	800-327-8585	panpac.com
Park Inn and Plaza	800-437-7275	parkhtls.com
Passport Inn	800-251-1962	reservahost.com
Preferred Hotels	800-323-7500	preferredhotels.com
Prince Hotels	800-542-8686	princehotelsjapan.com
Quality Inns Hotels & Suites	800-424-6423	qualityinns.com
Radisson	800-333-3333	radisson.com
Ramada	800-272-6232	ramada.com
Red Carpet Inn	800-251-1962	reservahost.com
Red Roof Inns	800-843-7663	redroof.com
Regal Hotels International	800-222-8888	regal-hotels.com
Renaissance Hotels & Resorts	800-468-3571	renaissancehotels.com
Residence Inn by Marriot	800-331-3131	residenceinn.com
Ritz-Carlton	800-241-3333	ritzcarlton.com
Rodeway Inn	800-424-6423	rodeway.com
Scottish Inns	800-251-1962	reservahost.com
Sheraton	800-325-3535	sheraton.com
Shilo Inns & Resorts	800-222-2244	shiloinns.com
Shoney's Inn	800-552-4667	shoneysinn.com
Sierra Suites Hotels	800-474-3772	sierra-orlando.com
Signature Inns	800-822-5252	signature-inns.com
Sleep Inn	800-424-6423	sleepinns.com
Small Luxury Hotels of the World	800-525-4800	slh.com
Staybridge Suites by Holiday Inn	800-238-8000	staybridge.com
Sofitel, Hotel	800-763-4835	sofitel.com
Sonesta	800-766-3782	sonesta.com
Studio PLUS	800-646-8000	studioplus.com
Suburban Lodges	800-951-7829	suburbanlodge.com
Summerfield Suites Hotels	800-833-4353	summerfieldsuites.com
Super 8	800-800-8000	super8.com
Susse Chalet	800-524-2538	